D1460391

DISCOVER
ENGLAND & WALES

THE BIG TRAVEL BOOK

Discover England & Wales

Foreword

While it is still an insider tip for many, England offers an abundance of cultural and natural experiences. Together with Wales, it makes up the lion's share of Great Britain. The past and the future have lived side by side here since time immemorial. The cradle of modern democracy, its citizens hold on to the monarchy to this day. No other country in Europe boasts quite so many powerful castles, palaces and cathedrals. The Beatles and William Shakespeare, Agatha Christie and William Turner – English culture is known and appreciated all over the world. Nature also has plenty of delights to offer, from gently rolling hills to mysterious moors, from spectacular cliffs to dreamy park landscapes.

Contents

Top: the Snowdonia National Park
in Wales at sunrise
Previous pages:
pages 2-3: Durdle Door in Dorset
pages 4-5: sunrise at Belstone Tor
in the Dartmoor National Park
pages 6-7: Millennium Bridge and
St Paul's Cathedral in London

SCOTLAND

NORTHERN IRELAND

BELFAST

IRELAND

DUBLIN

Point of Ayre
Isle of Man
Ramsey
Peel
Douglas
Calf of Man
Spanish
Head

Irish
Sea

St.Bees Head

Solway
Firth

Scafell Pike
978 ▲
1
Lake District
National Park

Cross Fell
▲893

Northumberlan
National Park

The Cheviot Hil

815

S.Tyne
Eden
Swale
Ure
Yorkshire Dales
National Park

Walney Island
Morecambe
Bay

Blackpool

Preston

Blackburn
Bradford

Harewood ★
Leeds

Carmel Head
Holyhead
Holy Island
Anglesey
Bangor
4
Caernarfon
Caernarfon
Castle
1085
Snowdon
Gt.Ormes
Head
Llandudno
Abergele
Birkenhead
Liverpool
Warrington
2
Oldham
Manschester

Wakefield

Doncas

Liverpool Bay

Llanelli

Rotherham
Sheffield ★ Chatsworth
House

Caernarfon
Bay

Lleyn

Bardsey Island

Tremadog
Bay
3
Snowdonia
National Park
Cadair Idris
892

Erddig

Peak District
National Park

Stoke-on-Trent

Derby
Nottingha

Cardigan
Bay

Aberystwyth

Plynlimon
752 ▲

Cambrian Mts.
Powis
Castle

Midlands

Wolverhampton
Dudley
Walsall

Leiceste

St.George's Channel

Pembrokeshire Coast
National Park
St.David's Head
St.Bride's Bay
536

Teifi

WALES

Carmarthen

Radnor Forest
660

Birmingham
5
Rugby

Shakespeare's
Birthplace
Warwick
Castle

Northampto

Milford Haven
Pembroke
St.Govan's
Head

886

811 Black
Mtns.

Tywi

Brecon Beacons
National Park

Wye

ENGLA

Swansea
Port
Talbot
Abergavenny
Monnow
Bridge
Tintern
Abbey
Severn

Cotswold Hills

7
Oxford 260
Woburn
Abbey

Chiltern Hills

Bridgend
Newport

Bristol Channel

CARDIFF

Bristol
9
Bath
Swindon

Reading

Windsor

Lundy Island

Barnstaple
Bay

Hartland Point

Exmoor 519
Exe
National Park

Longleat
House ★

Salisbury Plain

Stourhead

Celtic Sea

Isles of Scilly

St. Mary's

St.Michael's
Mount

Land's End

Mount's
Bay

Lizard
Point

10

Tamar

Cornwall

eden project

Plymouth

621
Dartmoor
National Park

Start Point

Jurassic Coast
(East Devon Coast)

Durdle Door

Bill of
Portland

Lyme
Bay

Jurassic Coast
(Dorset Coast)

Poole

Bournemouth

The
Needles

Isle of Wight

New Forest
National Park

Southampton

Portsmouth

South Downs
National Do

Selsey
Bill

Brighto

English

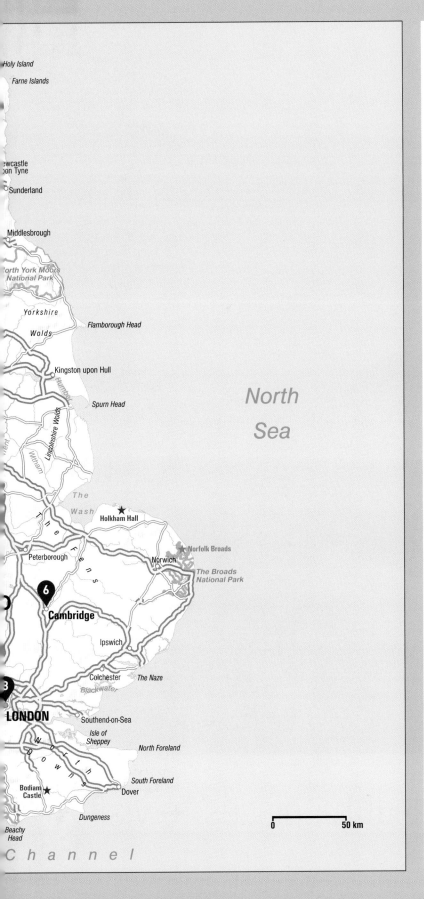

❶ Lake District National Park
The scenic Lake District has always inspired poets and painters, and the picturesque villages in this dreamy landscape invite you to linger.

❷ Manchester
The cradle of industrialization, today the north of England boasts a flourishing artistic and cultural scene.

❸ Snowdonia National Park
Majestic mountain chains traverse this Welsh national park, a paradise for walkers and fans of the outdoor life.

❹ Caernarfon Castle
In the 13th and 14th centuries, King Edward I had numerous castles built. One of the most outstanding examples stands in Caernarfon in Gwynedd, Wales.

❺ Warwick Castle
The archetypal castle, with towers, ramparts, dungeons, huge halls of armour and sumptuous chambers, Warwick Castle transports you back to the Middle Ages.

❻ Cambridge
In addition to its venerable colleges such as King's, Queen's and Trinity, the university town attracts visitors with punting trips on the River Cam.

❼ Oxford
The world-famous university city has numerous architectural highlights and many exciting museums to offer.

❽ London
The whole world in one city: the British capital combines the traditional with the ultra-modern, monarchy and finance, history and the future.

❾ Bath
This Roman town allows you to relax in a spa, feast on high tea and Sally Lunn buns and enjoy world-class dinners.

❿ Cornwall
England's south coast with its steep cliffs, picturesque seaside villages and attractive beaches is the island's most popular holiday region for good reason.

The most beautiful places to visit

Magnificent landscapes, Gothic cathedrals, the ancient sites of England and traditional folklore in Wales – the British Isles offer a great diversity of travel experiences. England and Wales are made up of counties. Originally these were jurisdictions under the sovereignty of a lord or other aristocrat, but today they have evolved into purely administrative regions. The following chapters takes us to the most interesting places to visit in each county.

South East England

The coastline of South East England, in the counties of Sussex and Kent, alternates between white chalk cliffs and pebble beaches at its famous seaside resorts such as Brighton and Eastbourne. Further inland, the scenery shifts to enchanting green hills and idyllic gardens and parklands. History enthusiasts will enjoy visiting moated Leeds Castle, picturesque towns such as Canterbury with its famous cathedral, and the cradle of Anglo-Saxon culture in Winchester.

Discovering Kent

The famous White Cliffs of Dover and fine sandy beaches characterize the coast of Kent, while inland the county known as the 'Garden of England' is traversed by gently rolling hills and dotted with blooming orchards and hop fields. The extremely varied natural landscape between the English Channel and the Thames estuary is peppered with impressive testimonies of the past.

INFO

ENGLAND

Area: 130,395 sq km
Coastline: 4,422 km
Highest mountain: Scafell Pike 978 m
Largest lake: Windermere 14.7 sq km
Longest river: Thames 346 km
Population: 54.3 million
Population density: 417 inhabitants/sq km
Capital: London 8.5 million inhabitants
Currency: Pound Sterling (£)

INFO

KENT
County town:
Maidstone
Area:
3,544 sq km
Population:
1.57 million
Population density:
443 inhabitants/sq km

The gateway to England opens at Dover (above) and its famous chalk cliffs (top).

*** Broadstairs Quaint old cottages built of dark stone, colourful Victorian spa architecture and Kingsgate Castle, sitting majestically on top of the cliffs – that is Broadstairs on the north-eastern tip of Kent. It is above all the seven beautiful bays with their golden-yellow sand, partly framed by white chalk cliffs, which make this former fishing village a popular seaside resort. The most famous guest was Charles Dickens, who spent his summers here between 1837 and 1859. In Bleak House, a former coastal station with a wonderful view, he wrote, among other things, *David Copperfield*. A Dickens festival is held in Broadstairs in the writer's honour every June, when the whole town dons Victorian costumes and embarks on seaside fun with beach festivities, tea parties and picnics – just like 150 years ago. And, of course, drama performances of the great writer's work always form the main attraction.

** Dover In prehistoric times, the coastal strip in the far southeast of England was connected to the continent of Europe. Today, however, the

only land connection is the Channel Tunnel, through which high-speed trains zoom their way from Folkestone near Dover to Calais in France under the sea bed. When the sun shines, the chalk cliffs on either side of the port city of Dover gleam a radiant white, welcoming visitors who have cruised in from mainland Europe via ferries across the English Channel. Soaring up on the western side is Shakespeare Cliff. The bard was a frequent visitor here, and the cliff features in a scene of his tragedy *King Lear*. The mighty Dover Castle, meanwhile, towers in the east. The limestone under the Norman fortress has been hewn into a maze of passageways dating back to the 13th century and Napoleonic times. Named Fan Bay Deep Shelter, these also doubled as Churchill's war rooms during the Battle of Britain in 1940.

Although both Dover and Broadstairs are on the coast, they were able to retain their separate characters. Dover Castle (top) was once the 'Key to England' because of its strategic location. Construction of the castle, perched atop a banked-up hill, began in 1168. The fishing village of Broadstairs (below), meanwhile, features picturesque beaches and is also overlooked by a castle.

Charles Dickens

In 1837, the literary magazine *Bentley's Miscellany* began to print a new serial novel entitled *Oliver Twist, or, The Parish Boy's Progress*. The readers were appalled to learn about the mire of misery, injustice and malice which the hero had to endure. Yet they were also fascinated by the exciting story, the secret of Oliver's origins and the witty literary tone of the writing. What no one knew at the time is that the author of the novel, 25-year-old Charles Dickens, had himself also been forced to labour in a blacking factory as a child and that his father had ended up in the debtors' prison. He also lived near a workhouse on a couple of occasions. During his life, Dickens wrote 15 novels and many short stories, of which *Oliver Twist*, *David Copperfield*, *A Christmas Carol* and *A Tale of Two Cities* are just some of the most famous.

** Kent Downs If you set off from Dover with its white chalk cliffs towards London, you should take some time to appreciate the extraordinarily beautiful landscape characterized by rolling hills. The Downs extend in a wide arc past Canterbury and Rochester to the edge of the British capital. Everything that is considered so typical of rural England can be found here – meadows and fields, rivers and lakes, hedges and woodlands, romantic surroundings and picturesque villages. The Kent Downs are home to a multitude of rare plants and birds and offer almost limitless opportunities to relax. The best way to explore nature is on one of the countless footpaths or hiking trails, by bike, or perhaps on a leisurely canoe tour through the Medway Valley. You should also make sure that you do not miss some of the many fascinating local museums, stunning mansions and gloriously English gardens that invite you to visit.

Canterbury Cathedral combines Romanesque and Gothic elements.

View into the 75-m-high crossing dome.

Thomas Becket

In 1162 King Henry II appointed his Lord Chancellor Thomas Becket as Archbishop of Canterbury and thus as Primate of all England. Initially perceived as clever, the move turned out to be a fatal mistake because Becket, previously his king's most dedicated followers, now became the loyal servant of God. Until then, the power struggles between the king and the Church in England had been minor, but that all changed with Becket. The fronts hardened over the question of whether a secular or an ecclesiastical court was responsible for clerics who had committed criminal offences. The conflict between king and archbishop dragged on for years, until four royalist knights murdered Thomas Becket. As the man who had stood up to the king, he was quickly pronounced a martyr and a saint.

*** Canterbury At the heart of English church history right from the outset, two World Heritage-listed religious sites in Canterbury attest to this early era. St Martin's Church, outside the city centre, is the oldest church in England still in use, dating back to the 4th century (possibly even to the time of the Roman occupation). The second site are the ruins of the Benedictine abbey founded in 597 by St Augustine, who converted the Britons to Christianity. The abbey became the focal point of the newly created Bishopric of Canterbury. It was in Canterbury Cathedral, whose initial construction in Norman style began in 1070, that Archbishop Thomas Becket was murdered by royalist knights in 1170. His grave there subsequently became a popular pilgrimage destination. Following a fire in 1174, the cathedral was rebuilt, bringing Gothic architecture to England for the first time.

The rolling hills of Kent gave the county the name 'Garden of England'.

The Canterbury Tales

Not long after his death, the murdered Thomas Becket was venerated as a saint. Canterbury soon started to welcome large numbers of pilgrims. *The Canterbury Tales* tell of such a pilgrim group, comprising 30 very different people. They agree that each of them should tell a story on the way there and another on the way back to keep the others entertained. These stories turn out to be as different as the characters, sometimes

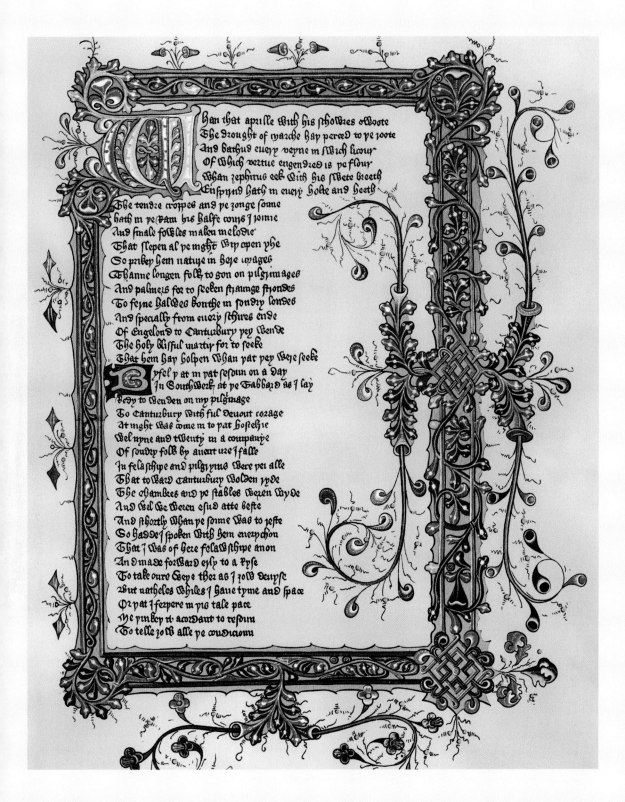

Han that aprille with his sholres owoote
The drought of marche hay perced to ye roote
And bathud euery veyne in swich licour
Of which vertue engendred is ye flour
whan zephirus eek with his swete breeth
Enspyred hath in euery holte and heeth
The tendre croppes and ye zonge sonne
hath in ye ram his halfe cours y ronne
And smale fowles maken melodie
That slepen al ye nyght with open yhe
So priketh hem nature in here corages
Thanne longen folk to gon on pilgrimages
And palmers for to seken straunge strondes
To ferne halwes konthe in sondry londes
And specially from euery shires ende
Of Engelond to Canturbury pey wende
The holy blisful martir for to seeke
That hem hay holpen whan pat pey were seeke

Byfel p at in pat sesoun on a day
In Southwerk at ye Tabbard as y lay
Redy to wenden on my pilgrimage
To Canturbury with ful deuout corage
At nyght was come in to pat hostelrie
Wel nyne and twenty in a companye
Of sondry folk by auenture y falle
In felaschipe and pilgryms were pei alle
That toward Canturbury wolden ryde
The chambres and ye stables weren wyde
And wel we weren esud atte beste
And shortly whan ye sonne was to reste
So hadde y spoken with hem euerychon
That y was of here felaweschipe anon
And made forward erly to aryse
To take oure wey e ther as y yow deuyse
But natheles whiles y haue tyme and space
Or pat y ferpere in pis tale pace
Me pinkey it acordaunt to resoun
To telle yow alle ye condicioun

---

moody, sometimes very serious and moralizing, but also heavily romantic. Some stories were told in verse, others in prose. Despite this diversity, they were all written by one and the same man – Geoffrey Chaucer, an official at the court of King Edward III and King Richard II. In fact, he only penned 24 stories in the end, not 120 as he had originally planned. *The Canterbury Tales,* which Chaucer wrote around 1397, are his last work.

He began his literary career long before with the translation of the popular French *Le roman de la rose* (The Romance of the Rose). It was an unusual undertaking at the time, since the nobility and the educated classes in Norman England usually spoke French. *The Canterbury Tales* were also written in English, and so Chaucer initiated a cultural revolution. He is today considered the founder of English literature.

For more than 900 years, the somewhat mystical and very English-looking Leeds Castle has stood in Kent, surrounded by its moat.

** High Weald

It is easy to understand that the High Weald, an open wooded landscape between the English Channel and the Thames, was once home to the largest and densest forests in England. They still make up a quarter of the area today, something that is hardly found anywhere else on an island of this size. A large part of it was laid out before 1600 and is now under protection. Together with the heathland and the farmland, whose traditional, small-scale structure has survived, a fairy-tale cultural landscape developed. More than 2,000 kilometres of hiking trails traverse the High Weald, where rare plants and animals have been preserved due to the restricted use. Bewl Water also offers its visitors a wide range of opportunities for water sports.

** Leeds Castle

Inland in the county of Kent, almost 6 km (4 miles) southeast of Maidstone, the moated Leeds Castle rises in the middle of a spacious park on two islands in the River Len. Leeds Castle, first mentioned in 857, is for many the epitome of a medieval stone castle, although it owes its present appearance mostly to the Tudors. At least the gatehouse has been preserved, however, as a testimony from the 13th century, when King Edward I had the former manor house expanded into a royal palace. Leeds Castle was made famous especially by its female residents. Because many queens and royal widows made it their residence which earned it the nickname 'Lady's Castle'. The

grandiose interior often formed the backdrop for film productions such as the 1949 British black comedy *Kind Hearts and Coronets*.

** **Rochester** The city owes its importance to its strategic bridge over the Medway River, just before it flows into the North Sea. The military and shipbuilding have played a key role here ever since Roman times. But Rochester is also the island's second oldest diocese after Canterbury. It was shaped by the Norman conquest of England in the 11th century, and indeed has the first Norman bishop, Gundulf, to thank for its impressive cathedral, which has managed to maintain its essential appearance despite numerous demolitions, reconstructions and extensions. Rochester Castle, one of the best preserved fortified tower complexes anywhere, is another typical example of Norman architecture, while many buildings in the old town, such as the Guildhall, were erected in 1667 following a raid by the Dutch.

Rochester Cathedral fuses Norman, Gothic and Romanesque architecture.

The town of Rochester awakening to a spectacular dawn, with the cathedral and castle reflected in the Medway River.

The organ is a particularly imposing sight, colourfully ornate much like the side walls.

Little paradises: England's gardens

If you don't know why the British are considered the most passionate gardeners, you should plan a visit to Sissinghurst Castle in Kent. The garden of Vita Sackville-West and her husband, who lived here from 1930, offers plenty of space to breathe deeply and be amazed, from meticulously pruned hedges to enchanted corners that look like biotopes. The whole estate is divided into a total of ten different 'garden rooms'. Some visitors

are particularly enchanted by the White Garden, in which only white and silver-flowering plants grow, others by the spice garden, where the scents of saffron and thyme tickle the nose at different times of year. Also in Kent, the park of the gardens at Hever Castle Hever Castle welcomes its visitors with artfully maintained hedges, lush flower beds, a historic English yew maze as well as a splashing Water Maze. Here, too, one recognizes the principle of English garden culture since the 18th century: a beautiful garden must always remain close to nature and not be laid out too symmetrically. 'Nature abhors a straight line', postulated the English horticultural architect William Kent. In the gardens at Hever Castle, a near-natural lake and seemingly wildly overgrown paths therefore create the necessary contrast to the garden geometry and precisely cut English lawn.

Discovering East Sussex

Along the picturesque East Sussex coast, in between cosmopolitan Brighton and the historic town of Rye, you will encounter magnificent mansions, stately castles, beautifully landscaped gardens and charming medieval villages.

EAST SUSSEX
County town:
Lewes
Area:
1,709 sq km
Population:
555,000
Population density:
325 inhabitants/sq km

INFO ✳

life as a picturesque ruin, immortalized in numerous paintings and since then repeatedly restored for this very purpose. Today, Bodiam represents an 'ideal' medieval castle, attracting large numbers of visitors as if indeed by magic.

** Hastings Around 100 kilometres southeast of London is the Hastings battlefield, where the legendary battle between the Norman William the Conqueror and King Harold of England took place in October 1066. The Duke of Normandy was crowned king after his victory in Westminster and had Battle Abbey built as one of the first new structures. Located near the village of Battle, to which the battlefield belongs, is today's seaside resort of Hastings, where William the Conqueror first set foot on English soil. Most famous here is the Hastings Pier on the 5 kilometre-long beach promenade, which was opened in 1872 and has again been accessible to the public since 2016 after lengthy repairs and renovation.

** Eastbourne An 8 kilometre-long pebble beach and its sheltered location make the seaside town of Eastbourne one of the top resorts on the Channel coast, not least because of the good transport connections to London. In the 19th century, the landowners purposefully turned the small town into a seaside resort for ladies and gentlemen. Three terraced prome-

*** Bodiam Castle When the legendary British surreal comedy troupe Monty Python satirized the Arthurian Legend and the English people's penchant for the Middle Ages in *Monty Python and the Holy Grail* (1975), it was here at Bodiam that the 'knights' fought against the seemingly impenetrable walls. The moated castle, with its mighty towers, was built in the late 14th century, and was not designed to be defended. From a military perspective, the merlons of the battlements are much too low, and even the pretty lake could be drained in a day. After its destruction during the English Civil War (1642–1651), the building soon began a new

nades line the beach, overlooked by Victorian-style hotels and guesthouses. The pier, which opened in 1870, is also famous for its shops, cafés and superb views of the English Channel. The huge structure extends 304 metres by 20 metres into the open sea. The town itself

has grown enormously after the devastation of World War II, but it suffers from the fact that the British people generally prefer to spend their holidays abroad. Eastbourne also attracts many visitors who wish to improve their English in the local language schools.

In addition to centuries-old fortresses such as the 14th-century Bodiam Castle (opposite top) and Hastings Castle dating from 1066 (opposite below), East Sussex has other architectural masterpieces worth visiting such as Eastbourne Pier (above).

Rye

The town of Rye presents itself as an enchanted fishing village, just like in the old days. Mermaid Street is particularly famous for its steep slopes and cobbled streets and the Mermaid Inn, where in the 18th century smugglers met and built secret hiding places and passages. Many legends abound, particularly around the Hawkhurst Gang. But there is more to Rye than smugglers' hideouts. Antique shops and art galleries line the streets in the old town, with attractive restaurants in between. In the course of the last century, the pottery trade gained in importance, and many souvenir shops still sell beautiful ceramics today. The port, one of the historic Cinque Ports, also continues to play an important role, not only for trade but also for yacht owners.

Re-enactment of the Battle of Hastings.

*** South Downs National Park

White is a colour nature reserves for the most special moments – the ephemerality of sea spray, the transitoriness of snow or the elixir that is salt. Only very rarely does it lend its pure hue to stone, making the impression all the more overwhelming when it does end up doing the full reveal on a grand scale. Mother Nature opens her heart the widest on the famous white chalk cliffs of southern England, whose most spectacular section is found in the South Downs of Sussex and Hampshire. The cliffs rose out of a tropical sea aeons ago, and consist of millions of compressed coral and crab skeletons, their flawlessness making them picture-perfect for eternity. Unfortunately, their beauty is fleeting. The rock is so soft that it cannot put up any resistance to strong wind or heavy rain, and slowly the gleaming white chalk will crumble and sink back into the sea.

** Beachy Head

The captivating landscape of the Seven Sisters Country Park, named after the seven gleaming white chalk cliffs, begins just beyond Eastbourne. Following the coastline is the South Downs Way footpath, which runs along the top of the striking cliffs. The 163-metre-high Beachy Head, the tallest chalk cliff in Great Britain, provides a breathtaking vista over the English Channel and the famous 100-year-old Beachy Head Lighthouse in the sea. You can only appreciate the picture-postcard view of the Seven Sisters, however, from the next cliff along, known as South Hill. This chalk cliff formation is located between the towns of Eastbourne and Seaford in the county of Sussex. The Seven Sisters are considered to be the most imposing chalk cliffs in the entire South Downs coastal region.

The most striking formation in the South Downs between Eastbourne and Seaford (both pictures), the Seven Sisters will return to the sea one day for the chalk is crumbling.

The Beachy Head Lighthouse has acted as a signpost for ships since 1902.

The sun rises out of the sea at the Cuckmere estuary, hidden behind the clouds.

The Seven Sisters line the stormy coastline between Eastbourne and Seaford.

** **Lewes** In the 13th century, the Second Barons' War, in which a number of nobles rebelled against the king's forces, raged near Lewes. A monument still bears witness to the battle today, but the streets of the town centre no longer evoke the drama of the place. Lewes Castle towers above everything; its ruins can be visited. The residence of William de Warenne, 1st Earl of Surrey, it remained in the family's possession until the 14th century. Lewes is also known for the house of Anne of Cleves, the fourth wife of Henry VIII. She received the building from him after their divorce, but never actually lived in it. Today you can find a museum in it, in which the history of Lewes is detailed.

The evening sunset bathes Lewes and the castle in a soft reddish hue.

** **Brighton** In the mid-18th century, the physician Dr Richard Russell extolled the positive effect of seawater, particularly in Brighton, on certain illnesses, resulting in the fishing town enjoying an unexpected surge in popularity. In 1786, the Prince Regent (later George IV) ordered the construction of the Royal Pavilion

Romantic Lewes – a warmly lit scene with cobblestones and a bench.

Lewes Bonfire Night

The 5th of November 1605 went down in English history as the day of the Gunpowder Plot. Dissatisfied with the Protestant King James, Robert Gatesby and other Catholic conspirators planned an assassination in Westminster Palace, in which not only the entire royal family, but also all parliamentarians were to be killed. To facilitate the plot, Guy Fawkes brought 36 barrels of gunpowder to the palace's cellars, but the conspiracy was exposed and Fawkes was caught red-handed. The whole of England still commemorates this failed attack on 5th November with Bonfire Night, when 'the Guy' is burned and fireworks light up the sky. The world's largest event of its kind takes place in Lewes every year. The spectacle includes several parades, attracting thousands of visitors.

in Indian Mughal style featuring minarets, columns and a lavish interior. It all but ennobled the town, adding a mystical, oriental touch and prompting more and more people to flock here. Today, Brighton continues to be a popular destination, in part due to its proximity to London. The city was once famous for its West Pier. It was built in 1899, but closed in 1975 and destroyed by fire and storms in 2003. Brighton Palace Pier, formerly known as Palace Pier or Brighton Pier, hosts an amusement arcade, various rides and roller-coasters and a famous fish and chips restaurant. Further along the seafront, the i360 observation tower is a gigantic and therefore undisputed new attraction.

A wide variety of architectural styles meet in Brighton: the historic Brighton Pier bears testimony to the Victorian style (opposite top left), the Royal Pavilion exudes an air of oriental mysticism (opposite below), while Brunswick Square is dominated by Neoclassical Regency terraces (top).

Lewes Downs

The Lewes Downs, a south-facing slope of the South Downs, are characterized by rolling hills and brightly coloured pastures. Many hiking trails traverse this nature reserve. The Downs are particularly worth seeing because of the extraordinary variety of plants growing here. You will find early-spider, burnt-tip and pyramid orchids, among others. Wild roses and herbs such as marjoram also abound.

Discovering West Sussex

Located between the counties of East Sussex, Hampshire and Surrey, West Sussex features a multitude of landscapes, ranging from Wealden and downland to coastal, dotted with historical mansions, Victorian villas, enchanting castles and legendary palaces.

*** Arundel Castle This early-medieval castle, erected as a classic fortress on a mound of earth in the 11th century, is the stuff of fairy tales. It has been home to numerous noble families, and has been extended and modified countless times over the centuries. Most impressive are its traditional towers, battlements and drawbridges, as well as its magnificent gardens, which provide the perfect setting for the cultural festival held here at the end of August, featuring a Shakespeare play, jousting tournament and historical re-enactments. The small town of Arundel is just as charming, welcoming its visitors with cobbled streets and meticulously restored buildings, adorned with climbing roses and ivy. The attractive cafés, meanwhile, are great places to recharge your batteries.

** Chichester The Chichester Cross, dating from the late 15th century, stands in the middle

INFO ✳

WEST SUSSEX
County town:
Chichester
Area:
1,991 sq km
Population:
859,000
Population density:
431 inhabitants/sq km

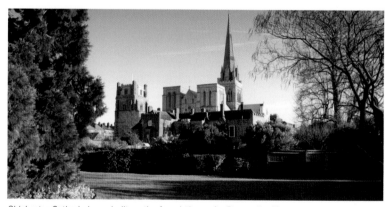
Chichester Cathedral was built on the foundations of a Roman basilica.

Fountains, lush greenery and stone structures provide a perfect setting for strolls through the gardens of Arundel Castle.

Goodwood Festival of Speed

Every year in the summer, Chichester becomes a meeting place for motorsport fans from around the world when the Goodwood Festival of Speed takes place in the grounds of the historic Goodwood House. This is the time to see many cars and motorcycles whiz through the estate and back up the hill. And it's not just about speed and noisy engines – the festival presents vehicles from throughout the entire history of motorsport, from the latest sports cars to models such as the Lancia Stratos HF and the Mercer Raceabout 35R of 1912. Visitors, cars and drivers come very close here, because all the paddocks are open and freely accessible. And if you still haven't seen enough of the historic vehicles, you simply have to come again in the autumn, for the Goodwood Revival.

of the city and once served as a market hall, where the poor could sell their wares. The highlight of the small town, however, is undoubtedly its huge cathedral, whose choir is one of the most beautiful and impressive examples of the Early English style, a British variant of the Early Gothic. The church is also the only one in England that still has a free-standing bell tower as well as double aisles. In addition to a visit of the cathedral, which was constructed in the 11th century, a stroll through the town originally built by the Romans is also worthwhile. Different architectural styles from the Gothic archway to Georgian townhouses and traditional cottages are found in close proximity to one another and this gives the town its very special charm. The Chichester Festival Theatre, which hosts the festival of the same name over summer months, has been the meeting place for the country's best playwrights, directors and actors since 1962 and transformed Chichester into the avant-garde's preferred theatre town.

Discovering the Isle of Wight

Located in the English Channel, the Isle of Wight is popular not only because of its mild climate, the large number of hours of sunshine and the resulting splendour of its flowers, but also because of its quiet, unspoiled villages with their characteristic thatched cottages.

*** **Isle of Wight** A strait known as the Solent separates the Isle of Wight from the English mainland. The diamond-shaped island off the coast of Southampton is part of southern England's chalk cliff formations. And nowhere is this more apparent than at the southern tip, where the Needles continue the trail of chalk stacks rising up in the island's interior. The Isle of Wight is considered a mecca for water sports fans. Every August, sailing enthusiasts meet here in Cowes for the Commodores' Cup, before embarking on a one-week regatta. Every second year, the island also hosts the

The Osborne House estate features beautiful parkland, walled gardens and a woodland walk.

ISLE OF WIGHT
County town:
Newport
Area:
380 sq km
Population:
142,000
Population density:
372 inhabitants/sq km

Alum Bay attracts with its sandy cliffs, created by erosion and glowing in many different hues.

renowned Admiral's Cup race, which first set off from here in 1851. Eleven years earlier, the Isle of Wight secured what is widely considered its most famous resident in Queen Victoria, who, in search of a quiet, private retreat with her husband Prince Albert, had Osborne House built here in Italianate style.

** Alum Bay Alum Bay not only attracts geologists, but also a large number of visitors thanks to its famed sand rocks – caused by erosion, they glow in a large range of different colours. A popular souvenir from here are glass jars filled with layers of the multicoloured sand. A cable car takes visitors to the top of the sandstone cliffs in just a few minutes, and there are also a number of footpaths.

** Blackgang Chine Smugglers are said to have used the natural hiding spots on the Blackgang Chine coast. Today the name stands for 'The Land of Imagination', England's oldest theme park. The smugglers have not completely disappeared – at the entrance to the amusement park an oversized statue of a smuggler greets visitors. Families with children come to the park today. The attractions are diverse, including pirate ships and hedge mazes as well as dinosaur skeletons and a replica Wild West village. The skeleton of a whale that was once washed up on the coast can also be admired. In addition, fairies, giant bugs and many other fantasy creatures are omnipresent.

The gardens of the Italianate Osborne House (top) have been lovingly planned and planted, allowing you to admire a colourful variety of flowers all year round.

Isle of Wight Festival

The Isle of Wight Festival had its historical beginnings in the years 1968–70. Well-known musicians such as Miles Davis, Joni Mitchell, The Who and Joe Cocker performed here in front of a large number of fans, and in 1970 the number of visitors even earned the festival an entry in the *Guinness Book of Records*. Around 30 years later, in 2002, the Newport event was finally revived and has since taken place annually, albeit at a different site. The bands and musicians of today are no less famous than those of the 1960s. Fleetwood Mac performed here as did the Rolling Stones, Boy George, Amy Winehouse, R.E.M. and Coldplay. The 'love and peace' atmosphere of the hippie era can still be felt. Photos from the historical festivals are on display at Dimbola Lodge.

Cowes Week

When hundreds of racing yachts cavort around the Isle of Wight in August, one of the most traditional sailing events is celebrated. It all began on 10th August 1826, when seven members of the Royal Yacht Club met in Cowes for a race from the Isle of Wight – the strait is considered to be one of the best, but also most difficult sailing areas in England because of its currents. During the reign of King George IV, who was a great sailing

enthusiast, the event became a permanent fixture, which took place every year, with the exception of the world wars and the pandemic in 2020. In the 1890s, the German Emperor Wilhelm II, who was obsessively competitive, regularly joined the race with his yacht *Meteor* – and just as regularly lost against his uncle, the future king of the United Kingdom and Ireland, Edward VII. That would certainly have put an additional strain on the already difficult British-German relations. Meanwhile, Cowes Week has grown from an exclusive delight for the upper classes to one of the biggest events in the world. Every year around 8,000 participants take part on 1,000 sailing boats. ON land, around 100,000 spectators a year follow the races while frequenting the many bars and restaurants, and enjoying the extensive programme of concerts and cocktail parties.

Cricket

Men, and sometimes women, dressed in white or colourful clothes stand on an elliptical field and take turns hitting a ball with strangely shaped clubs, sometimes for days. In between the game is interrupted for tea breaks. What may look strange to non-British eyes inspires nevertheless half the world – at least the countries belonging to the British Commonwealth. Cricket is the name of this team sport, its tradition stretching back

to the 17th century. And cricketers look a little contemptuously down on the newfangled American version of the game known as baseball. In essence, the sport is a duel between the bowler, the batsman and the wicket-keeper. The bowler tries to hit the wicket, a small structure standing behind the batsman, with his ball. The batsman defends the wicket by hitting the ball away thus scoring runs. If he hits the ball a particular distance, he has time to sprint across the ground to a second wicket. If he succeeds in doing this before the opposing team can retrieve the ball and destroy the wicket, his runs contribute to his team's points total or innings. If, however, his wicket is damaged, he has to cede his position to a teammate. Once all eleven players have had a go at being batsmen, the opposing team provides its own eleven batsmen and tries to score.

Discovering Hampshire

Hampshire is blessed with a perfect blend of coastal areas and features urban and rural life as well as plenty of culture. While the port cities of Portsmouth and Southampton revel in their maritime atmospheres, historic Winchester boasts a medieval flair.

* Portsmouth The city's port has long been the main base and the home of the Royal Navy, with the old fortresses attesting to its tremendous importance. Henry VII had Europe's first dry dock built here in the late 15th century, and in 1805 it was from Portsmouth that Admiral Nelson embarked for the legendary Battle of Trafalgar. His flagship, the HMS Victory, can today be visited by the public. Wharves and heavy industry later came to define the city, making it an important target for German bombers during World War II. Portsmouth was also the departure point for the Allied troops bound for the D-Day landings in Normandy in June 1944. It took a long time for the city to recover from the war and subsequent structural changes. While only small sections of the old

INFO *

HAMPSHIRE
County town:
Winchester
Area:
3,769 sq km (sq miles)
Population:
1,38 million
Population density:
366 inhabitants/sq km

Bramble Bank Cricket Match in Solent

Not for those who shy away from the water: every year a cricket match takes place in the Solent - on a sandbank! At low tide, Bramble Bank is hardly or not at all covered by water and is used as the venue for the match. The game is always played between the teams of the Royal Southern Yacht Club and the Cowes Island Sailing Club, and the winner is determined in advance. It's not seriously about winning – rather, it's about the fun of standing in the sand or ankle-deep water with your trousers rolled up and honouring the sport. And in the event that a swing turns out to be particularly wide and the ball lands in the sea, boats and swimmers are ready and waiting to retrieve it.

Portsmouth Port – modern and historic. The 170-metre-high Spinnaker Tower, designed by British architects Scott Wilson Group and featuring a viewing platform, serves as a reminder of the city's maritime history.

town were rebuilt, Portsmouth boasts a new, imposing landmark and attraction in the form of the 170-metre-high Spinnaker Tower, which was erected in 2005.

** **Spitbank Fort** In the middle of the sea, in the magnificent sailing area off Portsmouth, rises the striking Spitbank Fort, an artificial artillery fortress built to protect the important ports on the Solent, the arm of the sea that separates the Isle of Wight from the English mainland. Built from 1862 to 1878, the circular fort was intended to fight enemy ships that were able to break through between the Horse Sand and No Man's Land forts, which were also built in the sea. Huge amounts of steel and concrete were used to withstand even the most powerful guns – although the emphasis soon changed to combatting light naval forces. After decommissioning and standing empty, several private owners tried to revive and redesign the fort. For some years now, anyone who wants to and can afford it has been able to check in and stay as a hotel guest within the mighty walls.

Portsmouth offers fascinating glimpses of the past by day and by night.

Jane Austen

In the end, everyone in Jane Austen's novels gets married. The confident Elizabeth Bennet gets the wealthy Mr Darcy; the over-indulged Emma Woodhouse marries the level-headed Mr Knightley; the sensible Elinor Dashwood ties the knot with her sister-in-law's brother Edward Ferrars; the withdrawn Anne Elliot weds her childhood sweetheart Captain Wentworth; the romantic Catherine Morland walks down the aisle with

her cheeky young Henry Tillney; and the shy Fanny Price ends up with her cousin Edmund. Yet, unlike other, now forgotten female authors of her time, the reverend's daughter from Hampshire took a highly sarcastic, clear-sighted look at the conventions, constraints and quirks of the landed gentry, the 'better society' of upper middle classes and lower aristocracy, before reaching her happy endings. The focus was on the need for women to find a good match. Her heroines resist this, despite considerable pressure. The mix of love story and social criticism was well received even during Austen's lifetime. Her sharp observations and elegant style garnered praise from none other than Sir Walter Scott, the undisputed best-selling author of the time. Jane Austen herself never married – she was fortunate to have come from a large, well-read and tight-knit family.

** Southampton The history of the city of Southampton as the most important port on the English Channel goes back to Roman times. In 1620 the Pilgrim Fathers set off on the *Mayflower* for the New World from here, and many ships started from Southampton on their way to discover what became the British Empire. At the beginning of the last century, the city developed into a port for shipping lines across the Atlantic, especially to New York. The *Titanic* also departed from here in 1912. To this day, the port is the point of embarcation for many cruise ships. It still wows with its great atmosphere, although large parts of the city were destroyed in World War II. The picturesque remains of the medieval city wall can be seen from the esplanade. In addition, new buildings from a range of different epochs tell of the changing times.

** New Forest National Park England likes to hold fast to its traditions come what may. Historical continuities exist in this country that would be unthinkable elsewhere. The New Forest in Hampshire, for example, regardless of its name, is not a new forest, but an ancient one. William I of England, better known as William the Conqueror, had the area declared a royal hunting ground as early as 1079. The residents were evicted and strict laws were passed to protect game. The stags of the New Forest in particular ended up as a delicacy on the royal table and their antlers were usually hung in the monarch's castle. To this day, 90 percent of the New Forest is the property of the Crown – almost as if nothing has changed since the time

The Bargate...

... marks the entrance to the medieval city of Southampton.

of William the Conqueror. Only nature itself has changed – in the 18th century many trees were felled for use by the Royal Navy and today the park is covered almost entirely in heathland.

** **Winchester** Built from 1079 to 1093, Winchester Cathedral attests to the construction boom to which England owes a number of new churches following the Norman Conquest (1066), and named after the English variety of the Romanesque style: Norman architecture. The crypt and northern transept have been preserved from this time. The Triforium Gallery, arcades and clerestories in the nave – the longest in Europe, measuring 168 metres – and the retrochoir are all characteristic of English church-building. The retrochoir, indeed, marked the start of the cathedral's conversion to the late Gothic style, which gave preference to slender design elements. Fan vaulting was added to the central nave in the 14th century, during which the west façade, with its tracery and large window, was also created. Winchester Cathedral is famous for its artistically crafted chantry chapels.

Cattle roam the heathland of the New Forest National Park (top) as the sun sets.

The main nave and choir of Winchester Cathedral date back to the 14th century.

The fate of the RMS Titanic

Disaster nearly happened as soon as it left the port: when the almost 270-metre-long *Titanic* set out on its maiden voyage at 12 noon on Wednesday, 10th April 1912, the port of Southampton was completely overcrowded due to a coal strike. In the pull generated by the huge ship, the tether lines of another steamer broke, and a collision was only avoided by a hair's breadth. It would probably have prevented the later, much

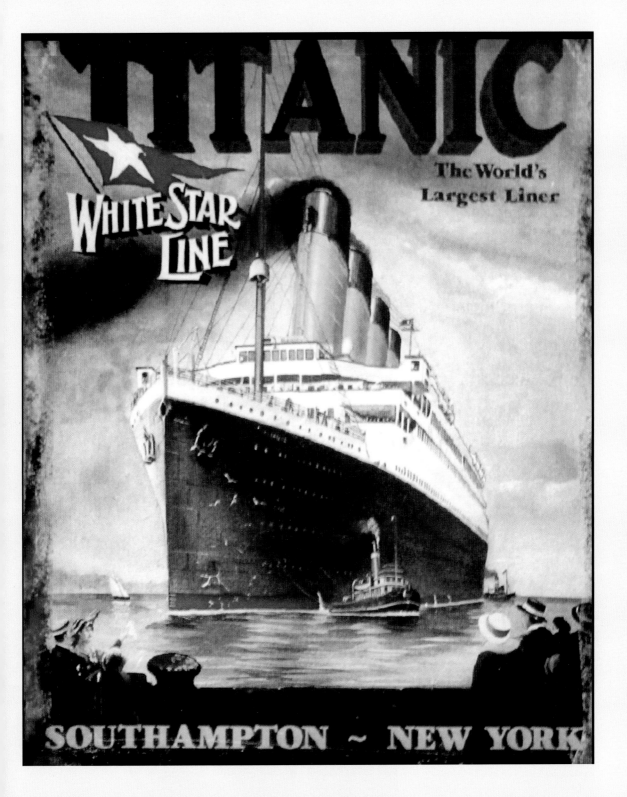

greater misfortune, because on Sunday, 14th April, shortly before midnight, the *Titanic* collided off the tip of Newfoundland with an iceberg that had been discovered too late in the haze. Although the ship was considered 'practically unsinkable' due to its 16 separate sections that could be sealed off from one another, no one had expected that six of these sections could be cut open at the same time. The steel colossus stayed afloat for two hours and 40 minutes. But as there were only a few lifeboats available, and these were not used optimally by the largely inexperienced crew, a shocking 1,514 of its 2,200 passengers perished. Although there have been more serious ship accidents since, the sinking of the luxury liner moves people's hearts to this day, as it was considered a symbol of the almost infinite possibilities of modern technology.

Discovering Surrey

Although Surrey is only a stone's throw from the metropolis of London, the affluent county is actually very rural. The most densely forested region of England impresses with both its proximity to the capital and an impression of typical English country life.

INFO *

SURREY
County town:
Kingston upon Thames
Area:
1,663 sq km
Population:
1,19 million
Population density:
716 inhabitants/sq km

*** Guildford Guildford succeeds in setting itself apart from the formidable metropolis of London, although many commuters live in Surrey's capital. The university town is considered modern and open-minded, which may also have been a reason for Lewis Carroll (1832–1898), the creator of *Alice's Adventures in Wonderland*, to spend a lot of time here. Today you can experience high culture at the Yvonne Arnaud Theatre, which presents opera, ballet

and – at Christmas – pantomimes. Of course there are also traces of the Normans in Guildford, above all Guildford Castle, which dates back to the time of William the Conqueror and whose ruins have been preserved today. Guildford Cathedral dates back to the 1930s and towers over the city on Stag Hill.

While the High Street (above) is busy with shoppers, Guildford Castle and the Wey and Arun Canal attract visitors with their idyllic natural surroundings (right from the top).

Discovering Berkshire

With the construction of Windsor Castle in the 12th century, Berkshire became the home of the royal family, something that can still be witnessed today, at Ascot for example.

** Sandhurst A degree from the Royal Military Academy Sandhurst (RMAS) certifies that the owner has graduated from one of the best and most prestigious officer training courses in the world. The young men of the English royal family all have to attend courses at Sandhurst, and the sons of many other ruling houses, especially those of smaller states such as Luxembourg, Jordan and the Gulf States, are also often sent to the academy located on the border between Berkshire and Surrey. The original military college had become too small by the beginning of the 19th century, and so in 1812 the facilities moved to Sandhurst, into the purpose-built Old College building. The magnificent New College building was not added until around 100 years later. In recent years, the academy has also increasingly accepted the generous donations from Arab countries for extensions and restorations.

Idyllic tranquillity reigns supreme at Horseshoe Lake (top right), away from the comparatively grey town of Sandhurst (below, the Old College).

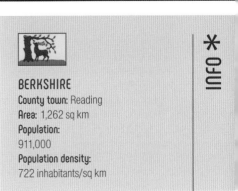

BERKSHIRE
County town: Reading
Area: 1,262 sq km
Population:
911,000
Population density:
722 inhabitants/sq km

* INFO

Ascot

Since 1807 the Ascot Gold Cup has been the central horse race at the Royal Ascot Meeting, which takes place every year in mid-June in the small town of Ascot, south of Windsor. Riders and horses fight for victory on the two-mile-and-four-furlongs-long, triangular racetrack – but the main competition takes place away from the course, for Gold Cup Day is also Ladies' Day at Ascot, and every year the ladies of British high society com-

pete to see who can don the most striking headgear. The towering fascinators, filigree plumes and extensive flower bowls demand one thing above all of the wearer: an upright posture. But the dress code for the gentlemen is equally strict – morning dress is not complete without a top hat and the traditional cutaway morning coat. Last but not least, Ascot is also a royal entertainment, because every day of racing is crowned by the arrival of the royal family. However, if you want to get right up close to the royals, you will need to have excellent connections, because only if a long-term visitor to Ascot vouches for you can you gain access to the inner circle, the delimited area of VIPs and the Royal Enclosure. Up until the 1950s, the obstacles were even greater – if you were divorced you had to stay outside, no matter how extravagant your hat.

*** Windsor Castle

Windsor Castle, from which the British Royal Family takes its name, is not only Great Britain's largest castle, it is also the longest continuously inhabited one. A castle has stood on this site to the west of London for almost 1,000 years, first erected as a fort by William the Conqueror around 1070, and extended, modified, rebuilt and inhabited by English royalty ever since. It has been used as a fort, prison and garrison. The modern-day complex essentially dates back to the 14th century, when Edward III added the State Apartments, Round Tower and Norman Gate. The last major redesign occurred in the early 19th century under George IV. The castle today continues to be one of the four official royal residences along with Holyroodhouse in Edinburgh, Hillsborough Castle in Northern Ireland and Buckingham Palace in London, and is the preferred home of Queen Elizabeth II.

*** St George's Chapel

St George's Chapel in the imposing Windsor Castle complex is a masterpiece of English Late Gothic, its size and decor rendering it more akin to a cathedral than a mere castle chapel. It was able to escape dissolution and retain its magnificence during the

The Long Walk connects the Great Park to the castle, and in late summer makes for an idyllic sight.

A wonderful detail in the nave's ceiling.

The Waterloo Chamber was built to celebrate victory at the Battle of Waterloo.

Reformation primarily thanks to being directly subordinate to the monarch and the College of St George, which is dedicated to the English patron saint. It is also the mother church of the Order of the Garter, one of Great Britain's most exclusive orders, whose members include the respective monarch, the heir to the throne and no more than 24 knights. The Order was founded in the 14th century, and was intended to be evocative of King Arthur's Round Table. Many kings and their families are buried in the chapel, from Edward IV (1493) and Henry VIII (1547) to the much-loved Queen Elizabeth (2002), the mother of Queen Elizabeth II.

Opposite: Queen Victoria's youngest son and one of her grandsons were buried in the Albert Memorial Chapel.

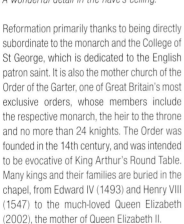

Windsor Castle has been in the possession of the royal family for more than 900 years.

Discovering Buckinghamshire

It often comes as a surprise that Aylesbury – and not Buckingham – is the capital of Buckinghamshire, and that this often underrated county has numerous recreational and leisure possibilities on offer.

*** Chiltern Hills To the northwest of the suburbs of the city of London, in the area of the Thames and its headwaters, rise the Chilterns, a tranquil landscape of chalk hills featuring extensive areas of ancient open woodland. Although the origin of the chalk formations is not obvious to the naked eye, they owe their formation to the last Ice Age, when glaciers stretched all the way to this point. The Chiltern Open Air Museum in Chalfont St Peter tells us about the settlement history of the area since the Iron Age. The best way to explore the beautiful region between Oxford, Reading and Luton, however, is on foot. A great number of hiking trails and footpaths lead to the most striking elevations such as Haddington Hill, the highest hill in the area, Ivinghoe Beacon or the steeply sloping Dunstable Downs in the far east of the

BUCKINGHAMSHIRE
County town:
Aylesbury
Area:
1,565 sq km
Population:
540,000
Population density:
345 inhabitants/sq km

* INFO

Chilterns. Primordial beech forests, on the other hand, characterize the gentle slopes in the southwest of the area.

Pubs – public living rooms

Pubs, or public houses, have a permanent place in the social life of the British people. They resemble a public living room – mostly furnished in a traditional way, featuring plenty of wood and carpets, and often decorated with fan merchandise from the local football team. This is where people meet after work to play snooker or darts, to watch football together, to discuss daily politics and, of course, to drink beer. There are snacks to nibble and often crisps and peanuts that make you thirsty and eager to order the next pint. But while the closing times have now been relaxed and you can drink until late at night and even later in the large cities, at some point the innkeeper will inevitably ring the bell and shout: 'Last orders, please!'

** Eton Anyone who crosses the Thames Bridge in Windsor comes to the quiet little village of Eton, home to what is probably the most famous college in the world. The King's College of Our Lady of Eton was founded in 1440 by Henry VI as a charitable act and is now considered the island's elite training ground, and not just for the British upper classes. However, the traditional boarding school is reserved exclusively for boys aged 13 and over. Not only the Princes William and Harry, but 19 future prime ministers as well as other greats such as John Maynard Keynes, George Orwell and Ian Fleming swotted in its venerable buildings. The areas where pupils are supposed to develop their sportsmanship – in their very own team disciplines – are extensive. The college estate also includes Dorney Lake, an artificial lake on which the rowing and canoeing competitions of the Olympic Games were held in 2012.

The Chiltern Hills are especially romantic when the day's last rays of sunshine fight their way through the haze (top).

Discovering Oxfordshire

The city of Oxford is rightly famous for its venerable university, but Oxfordshire also features the gently rolling landscape of the Cotswolds, home to many small picturesque villages. All in all, this is a concentrated experience of history, nature and culture.

INFO ✳

OXFORDSHIRE
County town:
Oxford
Area:
2,605 sq km
Population:
688,000
Population density:
264 inhabitants/sq km

*** Oxford Students dominate the townscape of Oxford, the home of Great Britain's oldest university, whose origins date back to the 12th century. The venerable colleges, the libraries with their precious stock – such as the Bodleian Library with its 4.5 million volumes, considered one of the world's most distinguished libraries – and the prospect of good jobs are all motivating factors for students to take their lectures here. Oxford's towers, particularly Christ Church Cathedral's Tom Tower, and Magdalen Tower, are visible from afar. It is worth paying a visit to the cathedral and the Christ Church Picture Gallery, which houses masterpieces from the Renaissance and baroque eras. You can also enjoy the view of the Radcliffe Camera building over a coffee and book at Blackwell's attractive bookshop.

** Blenheim Palace In 1704, the people of England gifted John Churchill, the first Duke of Marlborough, this magnificent residence in Oxfordshire as thanks for his successful crusade against French and Bavarian troops in the Battle of Blenheim (Blindheim on the Danube). Blenheim Palace was built between 1705 and 1722 under the supervision of one of England's most renowned architects, Sir John Vanbrugh

(1664–1726). The three wings of the two-level baroque palace, with its towers and columned halls, were set around a large courtyard, and the sprawling gardens. The park created by Henry Wise, and modelled on Versailles, was renaturalized by landscape gardener Capability Brown in 1764, and transformed into a romantic setting comprising waterfalls and a lake to meet the demands and the taste of the time.

Oxford is dominated by its 39 colleges and their venerable libraries and chapels (opposite and top). Blenheim Palace (below).

Blenheim Palace's Red Drawing Room, with its numerous portraits of the aristocracy.

Iohn Churchill
Duke of Marlborough

Glory: the 1st Duke of Marlborough

In the War of the Spanish Succession at the beginning of the 18th century, England fought alongside the Habsburgs against France and its allies. The Habsburg and English troops won an important victory on the Danube in 1704, in the Battle of Blindheim, named after the small town of Blindheim near Höchstädt, which is known in England as the Battle of Blenheim. The name Blenheim was also given to the magnificent palace

which Anne, Queen of England, had built for her glorious general John Churchill (1650–1722). The queen made him the first Duke of Marlborough immediately after her coronation in 1702. Churchill was in the queen's favour thanks to her close friendship with his wife Sarah. The latter – obviously a strong-willed woman with high standards – pushed through a number of costly changes when building Blenheim Palace. The consequence was a temporary break in the construction work as her husband could no longer afford to pay, and the queen no longer wanted to – the former friends had fallen out. Nevertheless, Blenheim Palace became the most magnificent and largest private mansion in England, and the family's most famous offspring, the eminent statesman Sir Winston Churchill, was born here in 1874.

** Kelmscott Manor In the Cotswolds Hills near the upper reaches of the Thames stands this fascinating property, which was built from local limestone around 1570, with an additional wing being added in the late 17th century. The limestone manor house became famous as the country retreat of William Morris, the famous Arts and Crafts artist, textile designer and poet, who lived here with his wife Jane and their two daughters from 1871 to 1896. Morris designed the house together with his friend, the painter Dante Gabriel Rossetti, who was the defining figure among the Pre-Raphaelites and was hosted here by Morris until 1874. Today, Kelmscott Manor continues to impress visitors with its exceptional craftsmanship and the superb furnishings created by Morris and his friends. Everything fits naturally into its rural surroundings, and visitors are inspired by the harmony, the flowers and trees.

Kelmscott Manor, a typical Cotswold house.

The amazing Uffington White Horse is surrounded by myths.

William Morris

Perhaps it was not only thanks to the considerable family fortune, but just as much to his – for the time – very liberal upbringing that William Morris (1834–1896) was able to develop his many different talents. As a poet, architect, painter, entrepreneur and, not least of all, social reformer, he was a colourful contemporary who opposed the style mix of historicism and the 'soulless' industrial products of his day. He was one of the founders of the Arts and Crafts movement. Morris himself excelled as a modern designer of carpets, wallpaper and furniture. In order to manufacture his own designs, Morris also ran a number of factories together with partners. Last, but not least, his political beliefs also made Morris a pioneer of the socialist movement in Great Britain.

*** White Horse Hill Southwest of Oxford, what is probably England's oldest chalk figure blends spectacularly into the landscape. The stylized outlines of a horse were dug out of the top soil so that the underlying chalk could be seen from afar. The contours, which are up to 3 metres wide and 60 to 90 centimetres deep, extend over a total length of 110 metres. In the Middle Ages, the White Horse was known as one of the 'wonders of England', around which many myths grew – such as that about the legendary Germanic invaders Hengist and Horsa in the 5th century and the victory of Alfred the Great against the Danes in 878. However, recent research dates the Uffington White Horse to the late Bronze or Iron Age, and its references to images of horses in Celtic art are unmistakable, so today it is assumed that the horse is a representation of the goddess Epona, the protector of horses.

You cannot properly make out the contours of the White Horse from the ground, but close up it is even more impressive.

South West England

Nowhere is England more diverse than in its south-west. Stone circles at Stonehenge, Celtic heritage, medieval churches, bustling ports and seaside resorts make this region one of the most popular. Its natural landscapes range from the lovely Severn and Avon river banks and a Mediterranean ambience on the south coast, to barren and haunted scenes on Dartmoor and Exmoor and spectacular cliffs on the wild Atlantic coast, which stretch as far as Land's End.

Discovering Gloucestershire

The fact that fierce battles once took place in this area is hard to imagine when you see the River Severn, which winds like a pretty ribbon through the fertile farmland. The romantic Cotswolds villages awaken nostalgic feelings in many visitors.

*** Cotswolds The rolling green hills of the Cotswolds stretch across several counties from the south-west to the north-east. Affectionately known as the 'Heart of England', they were designated an Area of Outstanding Natural Beauty in 1966. This status is equivalent to a national park, and requires special landscape protection measures. The small towns of the Cotswolds are typified by their construction materials – many buildings were made of the local golden limestone and have

since become covered in dark green moss. The beautiful 'wool churches' date back to the time when the wool industry brought prosperity to the region. Today, its affluence comes from the fact that wealthy Londoners and many celebrities have set up their second homes in the lush Cotswolds.

** Bourton-on-the-Water The Romans settled in Bourton-on-the-Water, but most of the houses date from the 17th century, and are

built with typical Cotswolds stone and featuring charming gables and similar ornaments. But it is the River Windrush, a tributary of the Thames, above all that gives the place its special appeal. Tree-lined and barely knee-deep, it meanders through Bourton-on-the-Water. Several small stone bridges without railings, built from the 17th century onwards, take visitors from one side of the tranquil river to the other, earning the village the nickname 'Venice of the Cotswolds'.

GLOUCESTERSHIRE
County town:
Gloucester
Area:
2,653 sq km
Inhabitants:
634,000
Population density:
239 inhabitants/sq km

Lower Slaughter is a typically quaint Cotswolds village.

Looking at the characteristic stone buildings, you might think that you have woken up in a Rosamunde Pilcher film (below). Right: the Curfew Tower in Moreton-in-Marsh.

** Stow-on-the-Wold The village of Stow-on-the-Wold played a crucial role not only in the English Civil War, but also through its status as a market town. Located at the crossroads of major roads in the region and dating from Roman times, the wool trade flourished here in the past. Fairs have traditionally been held here, and the marketplace is still in frequent use today. While sheep are no longer traded, the farmers from the surrounding area sell their home-grown fruit and vegetables here every month.

** Moreton-in-Marsh One of the main market towns in the northern Cotswolds, Moreton-in-Marsh also owes its size and importance to trade in the 13th century. Centuries later, the Redesdale Market Hall was built to accommodate these traders, and it is still an attraction for visitors today, as is the weekly market every Tuesday. Another landmark in the village is the Curfew Tower. It is the oldest surviving building in Moreton-in-Marsh and served as a lock-up for local drunks and minor criminals as there was no other place of confinement in town. Until 1860, its bells rang every night.

Authentic Cotswolds architecture in Bibury.

Cotswolds: Stow-on-the-Wold

You almost think you have been transported into a fairy tale or at least a fantasy film. Yet although Stow-on-the-Wold is certainly enchanting, it is also a busy community. This door, flanked by majestic trees, belongs to St Edward's Church, which was damaged in the English Civil War. The church was probably built from the 12th century, and several renovations and extensions followed later.

Once a Benedictine monastery, Tewkesbury Abbey is now a place of wonder.

** Tewkesbury Abbey

A fine example of Norman church architecture can be found in Tewkesbury, a small town not far from the confluence of the Severn and Avon. The Benedictine Abbey was built by Robert Fitzhamon, a cousin of William the Conqueror. As can be seen from the two choirs and the magnificent vaults, Tewkesbury Abbey became one of the richest abbeys in England in the High Middle Ages. It was the scene of a massacre in the Wars of the Roses in 1471 after the defeated soldiers of the House of Lancastertook refuge here. When the monasteries were dissolved under Henry VIII, extensive destruction could be prevented if the citizens claimed the church as their parish church and purchased it themselves. So it is thanks to them that one of the most beautiful churches in England can still be visited today.

*** Gloucester

The Roman settlement established on the banks of the River Severn owed much of its development to the port and the last bridge before the river mouth. The city was easily accessible from both the sea and the river, and later also via a canal that was independent of the tides. St Peter's Abbey was founded as early as 679, and underwent substantial extensions during the Norman period. Edward II, an unpopular king during his lifetime, is buried here. The monks were skilfully able to market his grave site as a pilgrimage destination, and the plentiful income resulting from this publicity was used to redesign the abbey with superb stained-glass windows – including the oldest depiction of the game of golf as a sport – and delicate fan struts. The Late Gothic Perpendicular style remained the standard in English church-building for more than 100 years. And if the ornate cloisters look somewhat familiar, it's because scenes from three Harry Potter movies were filmed here.

Norman architectural style meets Gothic at St Peter's Cathedral in Gloucester. The large stained-glass windows in the chancel (large picture) and cloister (above left) are particularly attractive, while the painted pipes on the organ are also an unusual feature. In Gloucester's city centre, Victorian warehouses line the docks (above right).

Discovering Wiltshire

Saxons, Normans, Romans and even Stone Age humans have left their mark on the landscapes and settlements of Wiltshire – and today it is a county where you can discover countless wonders, traditions, myths and legends.

** **Avebury** The remains of three stone circles are located in an area of about 15 hectares in and near the village of Avebury in the county of Wiltshire, near the city of Bath. According to scientists, the construction is said to date from 2600 to 2500 BC. The complex, which is said to once have consisted of 154 megaliths, remains a mystery. Mathematicians are particularly enthusiastic about the distance to nearby Stonehenge and the location of its central point, because the numbers show parallels to

the circumference of the earth. Although today there are only 36 of these huge stones left, it is difficult for the visitor to escape the mysticism of this place. Like Stonehenge, the approximately 4,500-year-old stone circle complex shows an orientation towards the sunrise. The significance of the Neolithic monuments at Stonehenge and neighbouring Avebury remains unclear to this day. It is believed that, in addition to their religious function, they also served to observe the stars.

*** **Stonehenge** The most famous prehistoric site in the British Isles and perhaps the world, Stonehenge and Avebury have together been listed by UNESCO as a place of World Cultural Heritage. Stonehenge is said to have been built by Beaker people in four stages between the years 3100 and 1500 BC. They transported 82 gigantic bluestones here from the Welsh mountains, presumably by river and over land. The incredible structural feats achieved by this Neolithic people continue to

INFO *

WILTSHIRE
County town:
Trowbridge
Area:
3,485 sq km
Inhabitants:
689,000
Population density:
198 inhabitants/sq km

The Avebury Stone Circles (above) and Stonehenge (top right).

inspire awe to this day. At the start of the Bronze Age, the bluestones were replaced with 7-metre-high sandstone blocks. The site has been modified on numerous occasions. Today, two concentric circles of stones sit at its heart, while 17 trilithons and two upright monoliths with a transverse stone form the outer circle, spanning a diameter of 30 metres. Visitors are not allowed to touch the stones. Stonehenge has attracted New Age believers, and in particular Druids, for the summer and winter solstice celebrations, when access is free.

Salisbury

No matter the direction from which you approach the city, the mighty spire of the Gothic cathedral is visible from afar. At 123 metres, it is the tallest in the country, offering spectacular views of Wiltshire's farming landscapes. The old town, with its historic inns and half-timbered houses, also attracts many visitors. Yet Salisbury is a planned remake. By the 13th century, the fortified town of Old Sarum, which was located 3 kilometres to the north and had been inhabited since Antiquity, had became too small. This prompted local bishop Richard Poore to build a new cathedral on the River Avon, a step which ultimately resulted in the entire city being relocated. It's worth making a quick detour to the picturesque Old Sarum hill, with the foundations of the fort and old cathedral.

Few people in England have not heard of Stonehenge – and hardly any visitor is left unmoved by the mystical and wondrous atmosphere that prevails there despite the large number of visiting tourists.

Discovering Bristol

Magnificent buildings and Bristol's picturesque location amid green hills and near the sea attract musicians and artists in particular to the dynamic and friendly city, which, among others, produced the world-famous street artist Banksy.

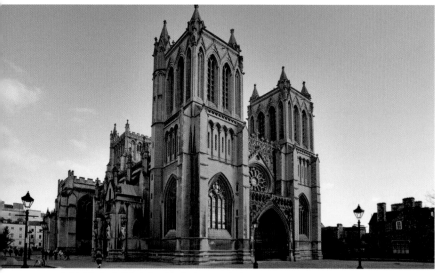

Bristol Cathedral is defined by its tracery windows.

The venerable Central Library of 1906..

*** Bristol The largest city in south-west England lies at the mouth of the River Avon, and shines resplendent in the vibrant charm exuded by its port and universities. It has been a place

Amphitheatre and Waterfront Square.

✳ BRISTOL
INFO

County town:
Bristol
Area:
110 sq km
Population:
463,000
Population density:
4,213 inhabitants/sq km

of trade since early times – with Ireland and later also North America – generating sizeable sums through the slave trade. Daniel Defoe found inspiration here for his novel *Robinson Crusoe* after talking with sailor Alexander Selkirk. The wealthy Knights Templar have also left their mark on Bristol. The historic centre was destroyed on numerous occasions, most recently in World War II, as evidenced by a park filled with ruins, including those of the Temple Church. Many buildings have been meticulously reconstructed. And for the last few years, one of the most popular characters of our time has been turning his fellow residents' lives upside down at Aardman Studios – he is none other than Shaun the Sheep.

❶ ** Bristol Temple Meads Bristol Temple Meads is not only considered to be the largest railway station in Bristol, but also the world's oldest surviving central railway station. Designed by the railway engineer Isambard Kingdom Brunel, it is particularly impressive from the outside, and its turrets are a typical example of Victorian architecture.

❷ ** The Floating Harbour When you came to Bristol by ship in the 18th century, you had to keep a close eye on the time, as the harbour was dependent on the tides and the river depth changed by up to 12 metres at low tide.

In the end, more and more ships were calling at other ports, such as Liverpool, which is why a tide-independent port was built. The grand opening took place in 1809.

❸ ** Central Library Located on the south side of College Green, the Bristol Central Library building was constructed in 1906 by Charles Holden. Built in the Edwardian style, it replaced the old library building on King Street, which is still standing today. The interior of the Central Library, on the other hand, is characterized by Neoclassical architecture.

❹ ** Foster's Almshouses Gables, turrets, wood-framed balconies and red brick give the Foster's Almshouses their special aspect. Built in the 15th century by John Foster, these poorhouses were used for charitable purposes until 2007. Today they are still attractive structures.

❺ *** Cathedral Church of the Holy und Undivided Trinity In Bristol Cathedral, as it is often called for short, you will encounter a wide variety of architectural styles – built on Romanesque foundations, the eastern hall church was created in Gothic style, and the high pointed arches and the portal also bear witness to the English Gothic style. The rose window, on the other hand, is reminiscent of the Gothic style found in France and Spain.

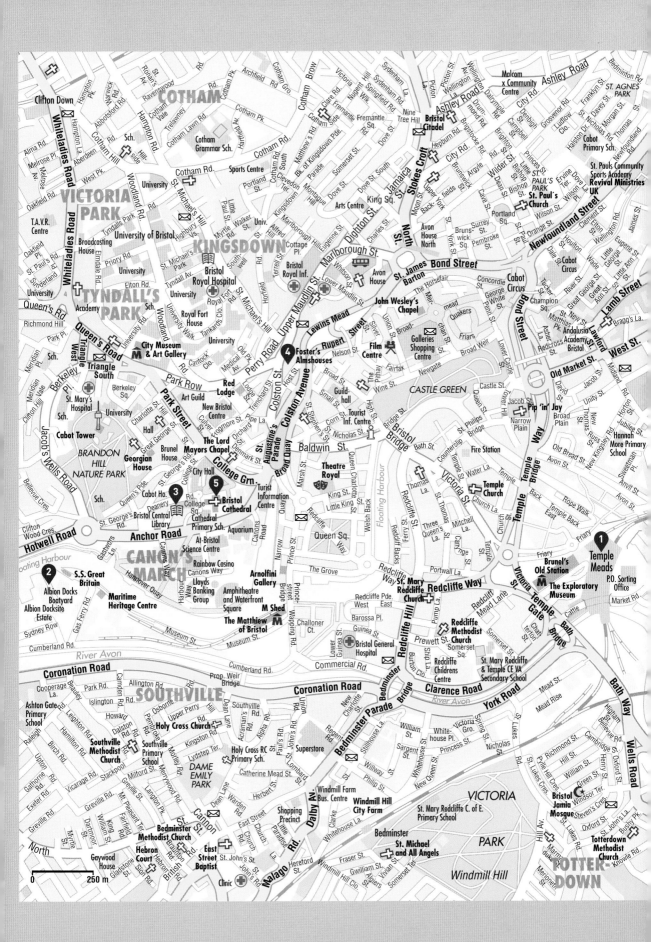

Discovering Somerset

Somerset impresses young and old alike with its unique cultural offerings. While the legendary music festival in Glastonbury tends to be a little boisterous, the Roman baths in Bath provide tranquillity and relaxation, plus an immersion into culture.

*** Bath The city of Bath is located in the county of Somerset, not far from Bristol. The Romans established spa facilities and baths here near the hot thermal springs. The city was known as Aquae Sulis at the time, and remains of a temple and bathing complex today continue to attest to its tradition as a place of recreation and recovery. Having been a bishop's see and centre of the medieval cloth trade since the 10th century, Bath became England's most popular bathing town and the most prominent social centre outside London in the 17th century. It was primarily thanks to the monumental construction projects in the late 18th century that the city acquired its compact Georgian townscape. Residential streets lead to Neoclassical masterpieces like the Roman Baths, the Royal Crescent and the Pulteney Bridge, crossing the Rver Avon and designed in 1770.

*** Thermae Bath Spa After an exhausting day of sightseeing, you will find the ideal place to unwind in the city centre, right next to Bath Abbey. In the Thermae Bath Spa you don't even have to take your eyes off the city, because from the open-air rooftop pool you can enjoy a beautiful view of the city that surrounds you. The spa also offers relaxing massages. The thermal bath complex, which was reopened in 2006, includes several baths

INFO

SOMERSET
County town:
Taunton
Area:
3,451 sq km
Population:
559,000
Population density:
162 inhabitants/sq km

Pulteney Bridge is one of only four bridges in the world lined with shops.

filled with natural thermal waters and a restaurant. However, in view of the modern construction by renowned architects von Grimshaw, with lots of glass and clean lines, it should not be forgotten that the Romans liked to bathe in the nearby Roman baths as early as 40 BC. And the Celts also made use of the hot springs. The remarkably well preserved Roman Baths still flow with natural spring water and are open to visitors as a museum.

Clifton Suspension Bridge

One of England's finest technical monuments is situated in Clifton, on the outskirts of Bristol. The wrought-iron suspension bridge has crossed the Avon Gorge since 1864. With its mighty towers and a span length of 214 metres, it was the longest in its day, devised and designed by engineer Isambard Kingdom Brunel. The high regard in which this technical pioneer – particularly of shipbuilding and railway construction – continues to be held to this day is evidenced by the fact that Brunel was ranked second behind Winston Churchill in a 2002 BBC poll of the top 100 greatest Britons. The spectacular views from his bridge are easily explored on foot, though the bridge itself is a toll road. Four members of Oxford University's Dangerous Sports Club had something entirely different in mind in 1979, when they organized the world's first-ever bungee jump here.

Bath is an example of the shift away from strictly geometrical Renaissance cities. The city demonstrates how architecture can be connected with the surrounding landscape.

** Cheddar Gorge Not only has the small town of Cheddar in Somerset given its name to England's favourite cheese, but it is also home to one of Britain's seven natural wonders. A wild gorge with walls up to 113 metres high and striking limestone formations extends for almost 5 kilometres. It was formed after the last Ice Age, when subterranean rivers created countless caves here. The almost 9,000-year-old Cheddar Man, the oldest fully preserved skeleton in Britain, was discovered here in 1903 in Gough's Cave, which had been inhabited for millennia. Studies of even older bones indicate the early dwellers were cannibals. The vibrant hues of the stalactite caves are a particularly popular attraction. Those interested can be whisked away into a fantasy world of lighting effects and video projections in Cox's Cave.

** Wells Wells owes its status as a cathedral city to its Early Gothic cathedral (built around 1180–1338). While the low side towers on the western façade make the building seem wider than its actual 49-metres, the some 300 stone statues give it a highly decorative overall appearance. The nave and chancel, both with three aisles and around 110 metres in length, are each crossed by a transept. The chancel

Believed to be the oldest residential street in England, Vicars' Close, is located in Wells.

Cox's Cave

Cheddar Gorge is home to several caves, including Cox's Cave, which was discovered by accident in 1837. The very next year, the person who discovered it turned it into a tourist attraction, even though not all of the subterranean chambers and passageways had been explored at the time. Even then, first attempts were made to impressively showcase the underground world with special lighting. In the meantime the candles have given way to electric lights. Light shows and magical sounds fascinate young and old as well as animating special adventurer events.

(built from around 1290 to 1340) is a master-piece of the English High Gothic Decorated style. It was extended by a retroquire and the octagonal Lady Chapel in the 14th century. The cloister, two-level chapter house and crossing tower also date from this time. The master builders came up with an ingenious way of supporting the crossing tower: they connected the crossing columns with pairs of mighty tapering scissor arches.

Whether at dusk or dawn – the soft light of the sun gives both the Cheddar Gorge and the west façade of Wells Cathedral (top) a glow and a very special aura.

** Glastonbury The A39 coastal road heads inland at Bridgwater and continues onto Glastonbury, a place of myths and legends attracting countless mystics. There are several reasons for this high concentration of all things paranormal here: the remains of King Arthur – and perhaps even his Holy Grail – are said to lie under the ruins of Glastonbury Abbey, with its curious, solitary tower; and Glastonbury is also believed to be the legendary island of Avalon. Historic documents attest to the founding of the first minster in the 7th century, construction of England's largest abbey church around 1000, and the dissolution of the monastery in 1539. The town is also known for its annual rock festival held here every June for midsummer, where mystics, rock fans and hippies pitch their tents – undeterred by the often rainy weather.

*** Exmoor National Park There are grim tales to be told in Exmoor; tales like that of the executioner who was himself hanged: a hapless sheep thief who, high atop a cliff, flung a rope around his neck to seize his prey – and subsequently strangled himself. Those who travel to this plateau in the counties of Devon and Somerset will immediately understand why such tales exist; it is a harsh landscape of treeless moorland and plunging valleys through which the wind cuts with the sharpness of a thousand swords. The seclusion and desolate vastness perhaps also play a role in the mini horror stories that emerge from this region. One thing that most certainly does not contribute, however, is the Exmoor pony, the oldest pony breed in Britain, which can occasionally be seen roaming the area, and which is more reminiscent of something from a young child's fantasy than a ghost story.

Glastonbury Festival

Mud and music – that's what the Glastonbury Festival is all about. It began during the hippy era, the first one being held on farmland in 1970. Visitor numbers have grown exponentially, and the festival has become internationally renowned. The programme ranges from rock to alternative to jazz, and there are also dance, theatre and circus performances as well as art installations. Some of the best-known artists and bands, such as Johnny Cash, David Bowie, Beyoncé, Bob Dylan, Paul McCartney, Foo Fighters and Coldplay, have all performed here. And even if rivers of rainwater run down the field and the field itself turns into a mudbath in the torrential rain – a true fan will not budge.

Pale blue water, pink heather in bloom and dark green grass make Exmoor National Park more vibrant than its bleak legends suggest (top). The lights of Glastonbury and the starry sky outdo themselves in the twinkling stakes at Glastonbury Tor (right).

Discovering Dorset

Apart from its more than 140-kilometre-long coastline, known for its stunning rock formations as well as for its fossil finds, Dorset especially attracts literature fans. Thomas Hardy and T. E. Lawrence, for example, both lived and died here.

Wareham Quay, featuring a typically English pub and the Lady St Mary Church.

Bournemouth Pier juts out into the sea in the middle of a seemingly endless sandy beach.

INFO

DORSET
County town:
Dorchester
Area:
2,653 sq km
Population:
750,000
Population density:
283 inhabitants/sq km

** **Bournemouth** The popular beaches at Poole Bay, the warmest and sunniest bay in England, stretch for 12 kilometres, from Sandbanks at the mouth of Poole Harbour in the west to Hengistbury Head in the east. Nowhere else in Britain does it rain as little as here. Bournemouth's 200-year development from a small village to today's vibrant town is almost entirely due to its being one of the top holiday destinations in Britain. Two piers jut out into the sea: Bournemouth Pier, home to a theatre and great entertainment facilities, and the architecturally attractive Boscombe Pier. In addition to the promenades, the well-tended and attrac-

tively planted gardens and parks that run along the River Bourne through the urban area are another attraction. The shopping opportunities are almost unlimited, and the variety of entertainment ranges from the Oceanarium to fascinating museums and great concerts to a number of festivals. There are, of course, also plenty of play, sport and amusement parks for children, especially in summer.

** **Corfe Castle** The beautiful ruins in the middle of the Isle of Purbeck are the stuff of storytelling. Located on a steep hill, access to the sea could be easily controlled from here. A fortification existed in Anglo-Saxon times, and legend has it that King Edward the Martyr was murdered here in 978. An enormous number of miracles were later ascribed to him. William the Conqueror also recognized the strategic importance of the castle. He had one of the first

Isle of Purbeck

Things are quiet on the Isle of Purbeck, which in fact is not an island but just a peninsula that shields Poole Harbour and the sandy beaches of Bournemouth from the open sea. It is famous for its great variety of wildflowers and boasts some pretty little villages. Probably the most beautiful hike is along the steep coast, which stretches from here around the south-western tip of England to Somerset, following the 1,014-kilometre South West Coast Path. The paths were once laid out for a different purpose. Here the men of the coastguard patrolled and tried to monitor the many bays and settlements, whose inhabitants lived for centuries from smuggling.

stone fortresses in England built here, which was expanded into a mighty complex in the 12th and 13th centuries. Corfe Castle was sold or given away several times and also under siege, however, it could never be captured. The Roundhead troops (the Parliamentarians) were initially repulsed during the English Civil War, but succeeded in a second siege in 1646 - but only through betrayal. As a result, the castle was blown up by the victors, which is why only a ruin can be seen today.

The immense force of the sea has carved sheer cliffs into the coast of the Isle of Purbeck. The horseshoe-shaped bay of Chapman's Pool is an extraordinary and also a very tranquil place, mainly because hardly a soul will find their way to the bay as it is such a long hike to get here.

** Jurassic Coast The Jurassic Coast, the name given to the spectacular coastal strip between Dorset and East Devon, sees deposits from the Triassic, Jurassic and Cretaceous periods on display like an open sandwich. The rocks are stony evidence of evolution, of the appearance and disappearance of flora and fauna, and not least of the dinosaurs. A species of dinosaur which only existed in this very location was discovered in 2000. Geologists were first alerted to it in the early 19th century through an accidental discovery by a little girl who said she saw a dragon on the coast. This was in fact the first complete set of prints of an ichthyosaurus. To this day, local hikers continue to find traces of prehistoric times here, with erosion constantly exposing new fossils, particularly after violent storms.

*** Maiden Castle The green rampart hills rise mysteriously into the Dorset sky. Why the residents began building such hill forts at the beginning of the Iron Age is not fully explained – it was probably not just about protection against attacks. The first fortification featuring two gates was built before 650 BC. By incorporating the neighbouring hill, the largest hill fort in Britain and quite likely in Europe was erected from around 450 BC, covering an area of 19 hectares. The fortification was complemented by three concentric ramparts with ditches. With a height of up to 25 metres, they still impress visitors today. Until the Roman conquest, the Celtic tribe of the Durotriges lived on Mai Dun, which means 'great hill' in the Celtic language. The foundations of a Roman temple from the 4th century have been preserved. The facility must have been vacated soon afterwards. Today you can follow a circular tour through the complex with helpful information boards.

The 500-metre-long pebble beach in Ladram Bay is surrounded by high cliffs.

Sherborne Abbey

In Anglo-Saxon times, a diocese was founded in Sherborne by St Aldhelm. After the Norman conquest, the bishop's see was transferred to Old Sarum. The Benedictines were allowed to stay, and so the cathedral became an abbey church, which Roger of Salisbury rebuilt in the Norman style. Unfortunately, only a few Anglo-Saxon elements have survived on the west gate. In the 15th century, the abbey was redesigned with a High Gothic choir and fan vaults in the Perpendicular style. The relationship between the monks and the population, however, grew worse and worse. In the course of the forced dissolution of the monasteries in 1539, Sir John Horsey saved the church and later sold it to the citizens of Sherborne as a parish church.

Fascinating scenery in Dorset: Durdle Door on the Jurassic Coast (above) and the ramparts of Maiden Castle (both below).

Discovering Devon

It is perhaps the stark contrasts between enchanting coastal towns such as Clovelly, with its Mediterranean feel, and mysterious moorlands, such as those found in the national parks of Dartmoor and Exmoor, that make Devon so special.

INFO ✳

DEVON

County town:
Exeter
Area:
6,564 sq km
Population:
795,000
Population density:
121 inhabitants/sq km

** **Exeter** There's no room for understatement when it comes to describing the magnificent Cathedral Church of Saint Peter in Exeter, built on the foundations of a Norman predecessor church in the 13th century. The western façade is ornate enough in itself, but once you step inside, you almost have to catch your breath. The more than 90-metre-long vaulted ceiling of the nave, the longest of its kind anywhere in the world, resembles a boulevard turned to stone. The cathedral is lavishly decorated, most notably with an astronomical clock that displays the time and position of the sun, as well as the phases of the moon with a silver ball. Equally impressive is the 18-metre-high, elaborately carved wooden bishop's throne, which was made without the use of a single nail, and is instead held together by mortice and tenon joints.

*** **Sidmouth** Sidmouth, like most places on the Jurassic Coast, began as a fishing village. And also like many others, the locals wanted to increase its importance and so initial plans to build a port were made. But despite numerous attempts, Sidmouth has remained without a port to this day, probably because the bay did not offer enough protection to build a larger port facility. Nevertheless, more and more visitors were attracted to the town and today it is particularly popular with retired people. In addition to the red rocks of the Jurassic Coast and the stone parish church, Sidmouth has hosted Sidmouth Folk Week every year since 1955. This festival transforms the town's squares and pubs into a large stage for dancing and music alike.

*** **Torquay** About 40 kilometres south of Exeter, on the so-called 'English Riviera', is the town of Torquay. The 30-kilometre-long coastal strip, with its numerous idyllic bays and palm-fringed beaches, owes this nickname to the mild climate and the laidback atmosphere. Three small towns – Torquay, Paignton and Brixham – have grown together to form the administrative unit of Torbay, but they have all retained their separate former identities. Elegant hotels, Victorian villas, and countless bars and restaurants around the small harbour create a holiday-like atmosphere. Thanks to the many opportunities for water sports, it is never boring in Torquay. The town's most prominent daughter is Dame Agatha Mary Clarissa

Christie, Lady Mallowan, who was born here in 1890 and became world-famous as a writer of detective novels as Agatha Christie.

** **Dartmouth** The picturesque harbour town at the mouth of the River Dart is popular with sailors today, especially at the end of August for the Royal Regatta. For many centuries, however, Dartmouth was a strategically important seaport and base for the English navy. It is home to the Britannia Royal Naval College, the Royal Navy's officer training college. It is also from here that the English participants in the second and third Crusades set out. The narrow estuary made it possible to cordon off the harbour with an iron chain between Dartmouth Castle and Kingswear Castle on the other bank. Narrow lanes and stone stairs, lined with a large number of historical buildings, many dating from the late Middle Ages or Elizabethan times, add to the town's charms The Butterwalk is the most impressive street, featuring a cantilevered upper floor resting on granite columns, which now houses the Dartmouth Museum.

The region, known as the 'English Riviera' thanks to its mild weather, is a popular sailing area. Right, from above: Sidmouth, Torquay, Dartmouth. Above: the world's longest vaulted ceiling in a church is found in Exeter Cathedral.

Agatha Christie

The grand old lady of the sophisticated English crime novel, Agatha Christie is considered the most successful crime writer of all time. It is estimated that over two billion copies of her 66 novels have been sold worldwide to date. Agatha Christie was born in Torquay, Devon, in 1890. In 1914 she married Colonel Archibald Christie, an aviator in the Royal Air Force. The marriage was unhappy and the couple divorced in 1928.

Her writing career began in 1921 with her first Hercule Poirot novel. The old spinster Miss Marple was added to the cast in 1930. Agatha Christie also wrote plays, including *The Mousetrap* (1947). This murder-mystery play has been performed continuously – with a pandemic-enforced break in 2020 and 2021 – at St Martin's Theatre in London since its premiere in 1952, making it the longest running play in the history of British the-

atre. Christie was also interested in archaeology and supported her second husband, the archaeologist Sir Max Mallowan, on his excavations in the Middle East. Their journeys also inspired some of her writing. In 1971, the writer was made a Dame Commander in the Order of the British Empire by Queen Elizabeth II. Christie died of a stroke on 12th January 1976.

*** Dartmoor National Park

The National Park, covering an area of 945 sqare kilometres, is a largely untouched woodland and moorland region on the south-west coast of England. It is situated almost 500 metres above sea level, and is one of Europe's largest national parks. Dartmoor is not a primordial landscape; it has been cultivated for millennia. Numerous archaeological sites – remains of Stone Age villages, stone avenues and circles, monuments and burial sites – all attest to its long history of settlement. An approximately 800-kilometre-long network of footpaths and hiking trails crisscrosses the landscape, where, in some parts, solid granite outcrops, known as 'tors', soar out of the ground. Russet fronds, heather and windblown saplings typify vast areas of the national park's scenery, particularly in the barren west. The shaggy Dartmoor ponies are particularly hardy, able to survive harsh winters and to cope with the poor vegetation.

** Lynton and Lynmouth

Located to the north of Exmoor National Park are the twin fishing villages of Lynton and Lynmouth. They have been connected by the Lynton and Lynmouth Cliff Railway since 1890. It took three years to build this funicular railway, and today it is primarily a tourist attraction. The special thing about the railway, which has to overcome a height difference of 150 metres, is that it has no motor – it is water-powered. The two cars, which can transport 40 people each, sit on parallel rails and are connected by a steel cable. River water is piped from the West Lyn River into the tank of the upper car, while the water is drained from the tank of the lower car until the upper car is heavier and,

This panoramic view of Lynmouth reveals the tranquility of the small coastal town.

Lundy

The 4.25 square kilometre island in the Bristol Channel has caused quite a stir throughout history. As early as the 12th century, there was a dispute between the von Marisco family and the Knights Templar about who the island belonged to. Over the course of centuries, pirates and privateers alternately claimed the island until William Hudson Heaven bought Lundy in 1834 and later settled there with his family. After the death of the head of the family, the island was resold several times and ultimately fell into the hands of Martin Coles Harman, who called himself King of Lundy and introduced his own postal and currency system. Today the island is the property of the National Trust and managed by the Landmark Trust. The *MS Oldenburg*, Lundy's own ship, brings visitors to the island five times a week if the weather permits.

thanks to gravity, begins its way down. The other car moves up with the aid of the steel cable. The speed of the trains is controlled by the drivers who communicate via hand signals. The upper and lower waiting rooms have Grade II listed status.

Dartmoor offers ever-changing views. Stone circles alternate with heather and granite rocks. The Nine Maidens (top left) is a notable stone circle, the Great Staple Tor (top) a popular collection of granite stacks.

Dartmoor: Longwool sheep

Devon and Cornwall Longwool sheep have been farmed in the South West for centuries, but they are considered to be a rare breed today. Large and sturdy sheep, they have short legs, making them look incredible cute. These sheep have so much wool that they can be sheared even when they're still lambs. The fleece is used to make carpets, dolls' hair and home furnishings

** Plymouth The town, with its beautiful natural harbour and sheltered bays, markets itself as the home of the great seafarers. Sir Francis Drake set out from here for his circumnavigation of the world in 1578, Humphrey Gilbert conquered Newfoundland from here in 1583 and James Cook explored the Pacific from Plymouth in 1768 aboard the HMS *Endeavour*. Trade and transport have always played an important role and ensure a cosmopolitan ambience. England's largest naval base has been located here for 500 years., and the British fleet is serviced in the Royal Navy Dockyards. This role, however, also led to considerable destruction by the German Air Force in Plymouth during World War II. To the north of the old harbour the Barbican, one of the oldest and most beautiful districts, has been preserved. Today it is home to many shops, restaurants and pubs.

.

** The Hoe The spot from which Francis Drake launched his attack on the *Armada* in 1588, the Hoe Park is located on a limestone plateau. From there you can enjoy breathtaking views of the Plymouth Sound, but the view from Smeaton's Tower is even better.

The Royal William Yard by Victorian architect Sir John Rennie is considered one of the most important military buildings in Great Britain.

Sir Francis Drake

On 19th July 1588, 55 English ships left the port of Plymouth to face the Spanish Armada, which had more than twice as many ships. On board as Vice Admiral was Francis Drake. The farm boy from Devon, who went to sea at the age of 13 because of a lack of alternatives, had already made a name for himself as a daring privateer, and he is still regarded as a daring gentleman pirate today. Drake first smuggled African slaves to America with his cousin John Hawkins, later he switched to capturing the Spanish silver ships that transported the precious metal from the New World to Europe. In between he also circumnavigated the whole world in a single expedition. His victory against the Armada was the glamorous climax of his career. Queen Elizabeth I awarded Drake a knighthood in 1581. In 1596 he died of dysentery on the Panamanian coast.

Once it stood as a lighthouse off the coast of Devon; in 1882 it was moved to Plymouth as a viewing tower. Francis Drake is honoured in The Hoe with a statue that measures no less than 3 metres in height. Perhaps equally well-known is the Tinside Lido, an Art Deco swimming pool which is fed by seawater.

*** The Barbican There is always something going on in the old, well-preserved harbour district. Early risers may stroll along the promenade at sunrise and look for a welcoming place to have breakfast. A boat or two also pull by and the cobblestones fill with more and more people who come to enjoy the local specialties in the many restaurants at lunchtime. In the evening people meet up in one of the pubs to party or under the romantic street lights for an evening stroll with a seaside amtosphere.

Visitors come to Plymouth's old harbour district not only to enjoy the local culinary delights, but also for the unique atmosphere.

Discovering Cornwall

Where the warmth of the Gulf Stream brushes against the English coast, you will encounter one postcard motif after another, featuring wild and romantic coastlines, picturesque cottages, quaint fishing villages and magnificent mansions. Once you've arrived on this romantic peninsula, you'll believe yourself in a Rosamunde Pilcher idyll.

CORNWALL
County town:
Truro
Area:
3,546 sq km
Population:
566,000
Population density:
160 inhabitants/sq km

** Looe A stone bridge has connected the two villages of West and East Looe on the opposing banks of the River Looe, which flows into the sea here, since the Middle Ages. It was not until 1898, however, that the two parts were united into one town, and only amid much protest. In addition to fishing, copper and tin ores were shipped from the hinterland via the ports until the railway took over this role. Thanks to the Victorian ideal of holidaying by the seaside, Looe also developed more and more into a tourist town with many hotels, bed and breakfast guesthouses and plenty of leisure activities on offer. The beach at Tailland Bay – not far away – is considered a 'playground' for the inhbaitants of Plymouth. In addition to hiking, sailing and diving, boat excursions to the open sea are a major attraction – and nowhere else on the coast are the chances of catching a real shark on the end of your rod this good.

** Eden Project You can spot the huge geodesic domes from afar: the spectacular Eden Project near Bodelva was realized here on a 14-hectare site in a disused kaolin pit. In its two gigantic greenhouses, gardeners recreated two climate zones: a tropical rainforest environment and a Mediterranean environment. The greenhouses are densely planted with numerous plants from both these regions, so that a natural ecosystem was able to develop. In a further, uncovered area, a botanical garden is home to a cool, temperate climate zone in which native British and some more exotic plants thrive in the mild Cornish climate. At 15,000 square metres in area and 50 metres in height, the larger of the two greenhouses is unique.

Trelissick

The gardens at Trelissick extends over an area of 60 hectares and is a true plant paradise all year round. Here you can find camellias, azaleas and rhododendrons, as well as a variety of palm trees, flowering cherries and apple trees. You can marvel at flora from all over the world on long hikes or even just a short walk. Trelissick house stands in the middle of the large park, enjoying views of the River Fal. Although it is not open to visitors, the mansion's exterior architecture alone is worth a closer look. The imposing building may look familiar to some – a large number of Rosamunde Pilcher films were filmed here and in the Trelissick gardens.

The futurist domes of the Eden Project.

*** The Lizard

The beautiful Lizard peninsula is the southernmost tip of England and has so far been spared from mass tourism. To experience the harsh landscape with its cliffs surrounded by the raging sea, narrow bays and small settlements up close, it's best to go for a walk along the South West Coast Path to Lizard Point. With its two octagonal lighthouses, it represents the northern entrance to the English Channel, which has been the undoing of many ships. In addition, the Lizard was also the first glimpse of country that people saw on ships returning from the Atlantic. Those interested in geology can discover on their tours that the oceanic crust has been pushed to the surface here. Nowhere else on the island have the colourful sedimentary rocks – such as the dark green serpentinite with its white and red veins – been as well preserved as here.

Sunrise on the beautiful coast of the Lizard peninsula.

A one-eyed seal, whom the people had named Nelson, loved Looe so much that he lived off the town's coast for 25 years, entertaining its visitors every day. After his death, the residents of Looe insisted on erecting a life-size bronze monument to the extraordinary seal, which can still be seen on a rock (top) at the entrance to the town.

*** Tintagel

Shrouded in legend, the ruins on Tintagel Head are considered to be the birthplace of King Arthur. Beyond the small village of Tintagel, a path and a new footbridge takes visitors over the 58-metre drop between two cliffs to a lush hilltop in the Atlantic, surrounded by crumbling walls. Excavations have found that, in the 5th century, the medieval ruins were the site of a Celtic monastery, home to a library, chapel, guesthouse, refectory and bathhouses. The castle, whose ruins can still be seen, dates back to the 13th century, making the speculation about this being the birthplace of the mythical British king questionable. But if you stand high atop the cliffs on a misty day and look down at the wind-whipped waves and the gaping cavern of Merlin's Cave, you may indeed feel you have been transported back to the times of King Arthur.

A place for storytelling. Whether or not the legends about King Arthur are true, the ruins of Tintagel Castle towering right by the sea are always impressive.

St Materiana's Church

Not far from Tintagel's ruins stands St Materiana's Church, serving as a place of prayer and worship just as it did in bygone times. It is presumed to have been built in the 11th or early 12th century, replacing an older church on the same site. Inside, the church dedicated to the Welsh Saint Materiana or Mertherian, is particularly impressive thanks to its wooden ceiling and the colourful stained-glass window behind the altar. A little more haunting, however, is the cemetery next to St Materiana's Church with its old graves, crosses and stones. The oldest tombstone still standing in its original place is a memorial to Mary Baron, dated 1689. The parish church of Tintagel, services are still held every Sunday in the historic church.

** Bedruthan Steps In a bay between Newquay and Padstow, five mighty boulders lie picturesquely scattered on the beach, as if thrown there by unearthly forces. From early times, they have fired travellers' imaginations; ultimately it was decided that they were the stepping stones for a shortcut used by the mythical giant Bedruthan. Yet, in fact, their formation is based solely on the erosion of the softer rock layers, including hematite, an iron ore that was mined in the area as early as the 19th century. If you dare, you may want to descend the breathtaking stairs at low tide and view the rocks and surf up close. For everyone else, it is a good thing that the National Trust not only looks after the land-scaped park above the cliffs, but also runs a café here. This way, the elemental forces of the sea can also be experienced from a safe distance during storms and high tides.

** Newquay The fishing village once specialized in sardines, which were exported to the Mediterranean region. Then, in the 19th century, it became the most important port on

Right in the heart of Newquay is the pleasant Towan Beach.

the north-west coast of Cornwall – mainly for coal and china clay, known as kaolin. With the development of the railway connection, tourists soon began to arrive, and this has made

the town one of the most important centres in the region for more than 100 years. A whole series of smaller beaches, protected by mighty rocky outcrops, invite young and old

visitors to swim. With its huge waves, Fistral Beach in particular is a mecca for surfers who meet here for their annual international competitions such as the Famous Night Surf and the National Surf Championships. The magnificent Trenance Gardens in the valley of the same name are famed for their tropical flora and are also home to the small but attractive Newquay Zoo.

In the evening, the boats bob quietly in the picturesque harbour at Newquay.

In the light of the setting sun, the pink beach carnations compete in their vibrancy with the colours of the evening sky, the deep blue sea and the black granite rocks of the Bedruthan Steps.

The Mines of Cornwall and West Devon

In the 19th century, two-thirds of the world's mined copper came from south-west England. From 1700 to 1914, Cornwall's economy, along with its landscape and social structure, was crucially impacted by mining. In 2006 UNESCO recognized this region and its history by including it on its list of World Heritage sites. The sale of copper, just like that of tin and arsenic which were also mined here, required a good infrastruc-

ture, and trams, canals, railways and ports all attest to the early industrialization of Devon and Cornwall. In addition to machinery and structural relics of the mines, manor houses and working-class towns with beautiful gardens have also been preserved. Several companies were involved in copper mining, and the quality of the copper deposits differed depending on the location. With the establishment of the mines came the building of of small towns, home to smelting plants and terraced houses. The World Heritage site today covers ten different mining areas: St Just, St Agnes, Tregonning and Gwinear, Camborne and Redruth, Wendron, Gwennap with Kennall Vale and Devoran and Perran Foundry, Luxulyan Valley with Charlestown, Caradon, Tamar Valley with Tavistock, and the Port of Hayle.

A blue and white painted rowing boat in the small harbour of Mousehole.

St Mary's Church dominates the harbour at Penzance.

*** St Michael's Mount Perched proudly atop a granite island just outside Penzance in St Michael's Bay is the old castle of St Michael's Mount. Legend has it that the Archangel Michael appeared before fishermen on the cliffs above the sea in 495. From then on, the rugged little island in western Cornwall was named St Michael's Mount, and a church was built on it. The former Benedictine monastery was taken into the possession of the throne in 1535 and converted into a fortress. Historians date the monastery's founding as occurring in the 8th century. At that time, Celtic monks erected a monastery on Mont Saint-Michel in France, which looks astonishingly similar to its counterpart in Cornwall. At low tide, the bay can be crossed on foot; boats operate the rest of the time. The 70-metre-high rocky outcrop rewards climbers with a magnificent view of the Penwith Peninsula.

** Penzance The largest town in Cornwall is Penzance, with a population of just 21,000. It is an excellent starting point for a wonderful 35-kilometre drive across the Penwith Peninsula to Land's End. The area is also known as the 'Cornish Riviera' because of its mild climate. Penzance was already an important tin

trading centre for the Roman Empire and medieval Europe. The centre of the town is the old quarter between Chapel Street and Market Jew Street, where the long-gone seafaring days can still be felt. Worth seeing are the former Barbican warehouse and the Egyptian House, which was richly decorated with Egyptian decorative elements in 1836. At the Penlee House, paintings are exhibited by the artists of the Newlyn School, a 19th century artists' colony in the nearby town of Newlyn.

Jubilee Pool

In 1935, an impressive outdoor swimming pool built in the Art Deco style was opened in Penzance. In the shape of a triangle, guests could bathe in the sea water without being troubled by the tides and protected from waves and currents. It was a hugely popular attraction for many years. After renovations in 1994, a violent storm hit the Cornish coast in February 2014 and the Jubilee Pool was not spared. The badly damaged facility had to be shut down. The extensive renovation of the pool took two years and cost around three million pounds, and it has drawn many visitors back to Penzance since it reopened in May 2016. The Art Deco style has been preserved and so the pool is much more than just an ordinary salt water pool.

** Mousehole Every village has its own legends. In Mousehole, the most famous one revolves around the brave fisherman Tom Bawcock. During a winter in the 16th century, a storm that lasted for several days is said to have prevented the Mousehole fishermen from going to sea, and the village, whose main source of food came from the Atlantic, was on the brink of starvation. But happily, on 23rd December, Tom Bawcock ventured out into the troubled waters and caught sufficient fish to feed the entire village. The event is celebrated every year. The village has retained its picturesque charm to this day, so that visitors will find an original ensemble of quaint houses and picturesque alleyways.

Picturesque views of the monastery at sunset from St Michael's Bay (top). The small island off the coast of Penzance, was most likely named after its original French counterpart, Mont Saint-Michel.

Pasties, Pies and Buns

The British are quite rightly proud of their pastries. These can be made from shortcrust, puff pastry or choux pastry, and can have sweet or savoury fillings. The Cornish pasty has become famous throughout the United Kingdom and beyond; it now has Protected Geographical Indication (PGI) status. A half-moon-shaped flaky pastry pocket filled with beef, potatoes, onions and swede, it was originally a simple take-

away meal given to miners. Today, stalls sell pasties with all kinds of unusual fillings, including chicken tikka and full English breakfast. Stargazy pies are another Cornish speciality, albeit a slightly curious one, as they have the heads of baked pilchards peeping out from under the crusty top. The most common savoury pie fillings are steak and kidney, chicken and mushroom or chicken and leek. Even in sweet pies,

the dough is usually left unsweetened as it is very rich. This base is then topped with fruit, such as apples or pears, blueberries, cherries or rhubarb, and then baked. Lemon meringue pie, with its set lemon filling and light meringue topping, is a popular treat, while mince pies, filled with mincemeat (a mixture of dried fruit and spices) are usually only eaten at Christmas.

Together, Porthmeor and Porthminster Beaches create the largest stretch of beach in St Ives.

*** St Ives Cornwall is today primarily associated with beaches and seaside holidays – and tourism is also the main source of income for the artists' town of St Ives, where the Romantic painter J. M. W. Turner praised the unique light. Grey granite houses characterize this former fishing village, which is home to one of Cornwall's finest beaches. Fascinated by the light and landscape, numerous painters and sculptors have been attracted to St Ives since the 19th century. The Tate Gallery has now opened a museum high above Porthmeor Beach in the north, the Tate St Ives, showcasing the work of local artists, including Patrick Heron and Ben Nicholson, who lived here with his wife, the artist Barbara Hepworth. The work of the latter can also be admired in her own museum, the Barbara Hepworth Museum and Sculpture Garden. Ornithologists, meanwhile, scour the region for rare visitors like chiffchaffs, warblers and vireos, who have lost their way and have been carried here by the westerly wind from America.

Rosamunde Pilcher

Love, passion, intrigue and the romantic English landscape – Rosamunde Pilcher brings all of this together in her successful books. They are usually romantic stories with a happy ending and yet they have cast a spell over a large number of people, probably precisely because of the romanticized world in which all will be fine in the end. Even the most complex intrigue can be resolved, families and friendships can be found again, and there is always someone there to comfort the heartbroken. The writer was born in Lelant in 1924 and began writing at the tender age of 15. Her first book was published in by Mills & Boon in 1949, under a pseudonym – Jane Fraser. She achieved her breakthrough in 1987 with *The Shell Seekers*, which was adapted for television.

*** Land's End The south-westernmost point in England is characterized by an open landscape of heaths and moors packed with archaeological sites: tombs from the Ice and Bronze Ages, stone circles, Celtic crosses, and entire villages from the time before Christ all attest to a settlement history spanning millennia. The waves of the Atlantic break unswervingly against the vast rocks which the Romans named Belerion or 'place of storms'. The tip of the British mainland is today dominated by a popular theme park covering Cornwall's history. Those preferring to get off the beaten track can instead explore the surrounding cliff and moor landscape on foot. The coast here boasts some spectacular scenery, with buffeted cliffs soaring up to 50 metres out of the water.

Land's End can be reached from Sennen Cove via a delightful 30-minute hike along the Coast Path. In theory, you can see all the way to the United States from here.

** **Isles of Scilly** The 140 Scilly Isles, accessed by ferry from Penzance, are located 40 kilometres off the south-west coast. The islands' approximately 2,000 local residents, who live predominantly off tourism and flower exports, are spread over five inhabited islands. While fishing used to be the main industry here, now it is tourism. With their rugged granite cliffs, white sandy beaches and turquoise bays, the islands are best explored on foot or by bike. Palms and exotic plants thrive in the mild climate, and a collection of typical Scilly flora can be found in the Tresco Abbey Garden. The English Atlantis, the lost kingdom of Lyonesse mentioned in the Arthurian Legend, is said to lie halfway between Land's End and these islands, although it is yet to be found. There is, however, a series of wrecks to admire.

The figurehead of a steamship, which sank off the Isles of Scilly in 1841, today adorns Neptune's Staircase in Tresco Abbey Garden.

Numerous subtropical plant species thrive in Tresco's only public park.

Hugh Town on St Mary's Island is the largest town in the Scilly Islands.

The Shell House does full justice to its name, featuring an interior lined entirely with shells.

Discovering the Channel Islands

When you arrive here, you will quickly notice that the Channel Islands exist exactly halfway between France and Great Britain. Culture, architecture and cuisine create an inspiring mix and combine the best of both countries.

INFO

JERSEY

Area: 120 sq km
Population: 102,700
Population density: 859 inhab./sq km
Capital: Saint Helier (33,500 inhab.)
Currency: Jersey Pound
Government: British Crown Dependency

INFO

GUERNSEY

Ares: 78 sq km
Associated islands: Guernsey, Alderney, Sark, Herm, Jethou, Brecqhou, Burhou, Lihou and smaller islands
Population: 62,000
Population density: 980 inhab./sq km
Capital: St. Peter Port (18,800 inhab.)
Currency: Guernsey Pound
Government: British Crown Dependency

*** Jersey The five inhabited Channel Islands – Jersey, Guernsey, Sark, Alderney and Herm – combine the best of two nations: French *savoir vivre* paired with British elegance and horticultural know-how. The five islands are only a stone's throw away from France, but they belong to the British crown. Anyone who has ever been to Jersey never wants to leave – no wonder the government strictly regulates immigration. The largest and most populous Channel Island, at 118 square kilometres and around 100,000 inhabitants, it offers everything your heart desires: deserted beaches, dramatic cliff formations, a mild climate thanks to the Gulf Stream and big city vibrancy in the island's capital St Helier, which nevertheless is small enough to be explored on foot. The tides regularly change the face of the island – sandbanks emerge from the floods only to sink back down into them just a few hours later. St Aubin, a small dreamy fishing village, is worth a detour.

Fishing villages and old forts such as Jersey's Mont Orgueil Castle mark the Channel Islands.

*** Guernsey Covering some 65 square kilometres, Guernsey is the second largest of the Channel Islands and a real gem. The cliffs in the south are rough, dramatic and exciting; large waves crash onto the jagged rocks here and cover them with a veil of white spray. A good 45 kilometres of cliff paths run along the cliff tops and offer panoramic views of the sea. The north and west are considerably softer and captivate with powder-fine sandy beaches, pale pink rocks and dune grass swaying in the wind. The turquoise sea forms a perfect contrast. Thanks to the Gulf Stream, the climate is very mild and banana trees, palms and other tropical plants thrive in front of traditional English cottages, and Guernsey was also always known as the tomato island.

*** Sark The island of Sark is enthroned on a rock plateau 100 metres high. The island covers just 5.5 square kilometres, but it offers quiet and secluded bays for sailors to anchor their boats. Cars are forbidden, and so visitors and residents move across the island in horse-drawn carriages. This ancient means of transport is very fitting here, because Sark is Europe's last feudal state – the Seigneur of Sark is in charge and the feudal system is alive and well here – even if democracy has been discovered in recent years. Like all the other Channel Islands, Sark is a British crown dependency, but it is not part of the United Kingdom. There is no income tax to pay nor social benefits to claim by its the approximately 500 inhabitants.

Garden diversity and stone architecture on Guernsey.

The heart of Guernsey beats on the east coast, in the capital St Peter Port. The hilly old town, which is dominated by the town church first mentioned in a document in 1048, invites you to stroll and linger at one of its numerous shops and charming bars and restaurants (above). A narrow strip of land – La Coupeé – connects Greater Sark with Little Sark (opposite left).

London

London is the capital of the United Kingdom, the seat of the royal court and of the British
government, an international financial hub, and a cosmopolitan metropolis in the truest sense.
Until a hundred years ago, London was the centre of the vast British Empire that spanned the
globe, and it retains a visible presence to this day. The City of London is a city within the city;
the historic heart of London, it continues to have its own administration.

Discovering London

When the Romans founded Londinium almost 2,000 years ago, nobody suspected that it would one day become one of the trendiest and most fascinating metropolises in the world. This colourful, exciting, royal city on the Thames has so much more to offer its visitors than just the classic must-sees such as the London Eye or Westminster Abbey.

INFO ✳

LONDON

Area: 1,572 sq km
(metropolitan area: 8,382 sq km)
Population: 8.9 million
(metropolitan area: 14.2 million)
Population density:
5,667 inhabitants/sq km
(metropolitan area: 1,675 inh./sq km)

📍 ** **Tower Bridge** Opened in 1894, Tower Bridge is not only one of London's leading landmarks, when it was built it was also a prominent feat of engineering. In the mid-19th century, London's East End was so densely populated that a bridge became necessary. Until then, all new bridges had been built west of London Bridge, so as not to impede the port facilities and shipping in the east. The solution was a combined bascule and suspension bridge. Steam engines activated the hydraulics system, which opened the bridge in the space of a few minutes. Today, it is fully electro-hydraulic powered. Both bridge towers house exhibitions on the structure's history, while the now glassed-in pedestrian overpass high above the actual bridge provides sweeping views over London.

② *** **Tower of London** The mighty complex with the elaborate name of Her Majesty's Royal Palace and Fortress The Tower of London – commonly known simply as the Tower of London, stands guard by the Thames at the eastern end of the City. At its centre is the White Tower, a solid fortress erected on the orders of William the Conqueror following his coronation as King of England in 1078. It was designed not only to protect the city against attacks, but also to enable the Norman rulers to keep a watchful eye on the independent and assertive Londoners. The two ramparts and moat were built in the 12th and 13th centuries. The Tower was a royal residence until well into

London Pubs

The traditional English pub is the heart and soul of the nation. It is where people go for drinks after work, where they exchange the latest gossip, where they meet friends and colleagues. Even in a big city like London, the 'local' pub continues to play a major role – and is a great equalizer. Here different generations and strata of society come together. There is a bar with stools, a few tables and chairs or seating areas, usually a jangling slot machine, a darts board and, increasingly, a television. All orders and payments are made at the bar, with table service generally only provided when meals are served. The trend is gradually shifting towards the gastropub concept. Usually, however, the pub is a refuge for drinkers who enjoy a pint of English bitter.

the 17th century, a prison until the mid-20th century, and today remains a royal treasury where the Crown Jewels have been on display to the public for over 300 years. You may also see ravens here – legend has it that the kingdom will fall if the birds leave the Tower. They are cared for by the Ravenmaster, and should not be approached.

Tower Bridge acts as a monument symbolizing progress as the link between historic and modern London. The bridge towers are 65 metres high, the road is 61 metres long between towers and the pedestrian bridge sits 43 metres above the river. The middle section is raised several times a day to let tall ships to pass through.

The Tower is the setting for ancient ceremonies; the museum sheds light on the royals.

Tower Bridge illuminated at night.

❸ ** St Paul's Cathedral The grand dome of St Paul's Cathedral rises proudly and distinctly amongst the City's office buildings. A Christian church has stood here on Ludgate Hill for 1,400 years. The present-day English Baroque building is the fifth incarnation, and without doubt the most magnificent. The fire of 1666, which destroyed almost all of central London, ripped right through the medieval St Paul's. Its reconstruction was entrusted to architect Sir Christopher Wren, who was also responsible for designing some 50 other churches in the ruined city. While Wren's plans were rejected a number of times, the

Baroque splendour, featuring high ceilings, sculptural decorations and rich ornamentation.

foundations were finally laid in 1677, and the inaugural service was held 20 years later. Wren was the first of many greats throughout British history to be buried at St Paul's.

The elegant dome of London's finest religious building, modelled on St Peter's in Rome, is one of the city's most important symbols and landmarks.

The interior of St Paul's captivates with glittering mosaics and elaborate stonework.

★★★ Westminster Abbey This abbey, officially the Collegiate Church of St Peter, is unique not only for its grand architecture, but particularly for its rich symbolism. With few exceptions, all of England's monarchs since William the Conqueror have been crowned in this church – traditionally by the Archbishop of Canterbury – and many are also buried here. The abbey similarly houses the tombs of other historic figures, including prominent writers, artists, scientists and politicians. Being buried in Westminster Abbey has always been the highest of honours. The structure itself is a mix of several different styles: countless extensions and modifications have been added over the centuries. Nevertheless, it remains the finest example of English Gothic – and perhaps the most beautiful building in London.

★★ Chapel of Henry VII The Lady Chapel, now commonly referred to as the Henry VII Chapel, is considered the last masterpiece of English architecture in the Middle Ages. The chapel at the far end of Westminster Abbey was built between 1503 and 1519 on the orders of King Henry VII, the first monarch of the Tudor dynasty, and is separated from the main nave

The Chapel of Henry VII is adorned with a wonderful pendant fan vault ....

by a brass gate and stairs. Henry lies buried behind the altar with his wife, Elizabeth of York. The chapel's most enchanting detail is the spectacular pendant fan vaulted ceiling, the builder of which is unfortunately unknown. The walls are lined with 95 statues of saints, and the stalls of the Knights and Dames of the Most Honourable Order of the Bath, who were first appointed here in 1725. Their banners, crests and arms are displayed above the stalls. The installation is an award for high military and civil service, which is given during a ceremonial rite of investiture. Today the candidates are proposed by the prime minister.

... which is considered the best example of this type of vaulted ceiling.

While the nave of Westminster Abbey may be very narrow, measuring just 10 metres wide, it is England's tallest, making it all the more grand. The design and interior are a majestic example of medieval architecture, having been spared Henry VIII's dissolution and destruction of the abbeys.

⑤ * The Palace of Westminster The Neogothic exterior of Westminster Palace, with its distinctive towers, including the Elizabeth Tower with the world-famous bell known as Big Ben, gives the impression that it has been sitting on the banks of the Thames since the Middle Ages. The original palace had been a royal residence since the 11th century. The present-day building, with the UNESCO World Heritage site of Westminster Abbey, was, however, not erected until the mid-1800s, after the predecessor structure was destroyed in a fire. The preserved sections from the Middle Ages include the Jewel Tower and Westminster Hall, which is now only used for ceremonial purposes. Westminster Palace is also the world's largest parliamentary building, with over 1,100 rooms, 100 staircases and 3 kilometres of hallways. It is the seat of both the upper and lower houses of the British government.

**** Houses of Parliament** Both the House of Commons and the House of Lords have resided in the Palace of Westminster since the 16th century. Originally, the Lords had far more power than the elected parliamentarians in the Commons. It was not until the 19th century that the basis of power gradually shifted. The Lords, comprising the Lords spiritual (archbishops and bishops) and the Lords Temporal (secular members), can today only delay legislation, but not

A statue of Richard the Lionheart guards the palace.

prevent it. The State Opening of Parliament, an annual opening ceremony that marks each new session of Parliament, has been one of the most dazzling ceremonies in England for over 500 years. The Queen arrives in her coach and reads out a speech on the government pro-gramme written by the Prime Minister and his Cabinet in the Lords' meeting room.

The State Opening of Parliament

Queen Elizabeth II has opened this solemn ceremony every year since her accession to the throne in 1952, ususally with her late husband Prince Philip or her son Prince Charles by her side. At the State Opening of Parliament, the monarch reads out a statement drawn up by the British government. This has been the case since the 16th century. In the regional parliaments of Scotland and Wales, too, the monarch is present at the opening of parliament; in the other Commonwealth states only representatives of the royal family are present. The ceremony takes place at the start of each new legislative session. Before that, however, the Yeomen of the Guard search the basement of Westminster Palace for explosives – in memory of the Gunpowder Plot of 1605.

⑥ ** Big Ben Yet another of London's land-marks is the famous clock tower at Westminster Palace. Known as the Clock Tower until 2012, it was officially renamed Elizabeth Tower in hon-our of Queen Elizabeth II's 60th anniversary. However, it is known around the world as Big Ben – the name of the tower's first heavy bell. At a height of almost 100 metres and with a top made of cast iron, the tower broke all height records at the time of its construction. A prison was once housed in the tower, which last had an inmate in 1880. The heaviest of the tower's five bells weighed 17 tons when it was first hung in 1857, and was thus three tons heavier than had been calculated, which is why it was called 'Big Ben'. The bell cracked and was melted down. The new bell weighs just under 14 tons – and still holds up. Since 1858 it has struck the full hour with an aria from Handel's *Messiah*. The four smaller bells ring at the quar-ter hour. Since 2017, large-scale repairs of the tower have been undertaken, and Big Ben has only rung on major occasions. Work is set to be completed in 2022.

The local landmarks here are at their most striking at sunset: Westminster Baridge with Elizabeth Tower and Westminster Palace.

⑦ ** Buckingham Palace Buckingham Palace is the official residence of the Royal Family, though only on working days and outside summer holidays. The palace therefore cannot be officially visited, except in the months of August and September, when 19 of its rooms are open to the public. The magnificent residence dates back to 1705, and originally belonged to the Duke of Buckingham. In 1837, Queen Victoria decided that St James's Palace no longer catered to her needs, and moved to Buckingham Palace, which had been extended and modified in the meantime. The most recent structural work was carried out in 1913 to redesign the eastern façade, from whose balcony the Windsors graciously wave to the crowds below on state occasions.

⑧ *** Kensington Gardens Once a royal palace garden, Kensington Gardens covers 111 hectares, and is much more formal than neighbouring Hyde Park. It is particularly popular with children, who will find a number of attractions in the well-kept park. On the east-ern side near the Serpentine Lake, the Peter Pan Statue, a bronze sculpture of J. M. Barrie's famous character, enchants visitors. On the western side, the Diana Memorial Playground beckons, an adventure playground with a pirate ship, Indian tepees and plenty of space to run around. A memorial fountain and a new statue in the Sunken Garden also commemorate the close relationship of Diana, Princess of Wales, with Kensington. In addition to the park itself, adults can appreciate the Serpentine Gallery as one of the top attractions. A tea

Hyde Park is a green oasis in the city.

The white marble Victoria Monument was erected opposite Buckingham Palace in 1911.

pavilion dating from the 1930s, it presents changing exhibitions of contemporary art. The temporary summer pavilions designed by famous architects are also masterpieces.

📍 ***** Hyde Park** The Rolling Stones and Pink Floyd, to name just a few of the great rock bands, as well as the legendary tenor Luciano Pavarotti, have all performed in Hyde Park. The park also occasionally featured as a crime scene in old-fashioned British crime novels. Earlier still, gentlemen tended to duel here in the morning mist, while robbers were up to mischief. Nowadays, London's largest inner-city park, covering 142 hectares, is a peaceful and contemplative spot for office workers to enjoy their lunchbreak, for early-morning joggers and for tourists recovering from a frantic bout of sightseeing. Hyde Park was the first royal park to be opened to the public – and its north-east corner boasts one of the few public places where you can spout off on any subject under the sun without having to obtain a permit for a meeting: Speakers' Corner. An institution since 1872, you are allowed to say what you want – as long as the police believe you to be within the bounds of legality. Together with other royal parks in London, Hyde Park forms the city's green lung.

Afternoon Tea

'Tea at the Ritz' is a London institution, but not one where fatigued passers-by can simply waltz in to take a break over a cup of tea and a piece of cake. The Ritz hotel itself is so noble that its name became a term denoting somewhere extremely elegant in English idiom 'ritzy'. All guests are expected to wear formal attire. Classic afternoon tea specialties are served to dignified tea drinkers in the Palm Court, the Ritz's tea room. This includes the best tea – selected by a tea sommelier – and a cake stand packed with traditional delicacies, ranging from finely cut sandwiches topped with extremely thin cucumber slices, egg and cress, salmon and ham, elegant cakes and pastries and scones with Cornish clotted cream.

In the early hours of the morning, Buckingham Palace is still devoid of the hordes of tourists that besiege it later in the day (top left). Queen Victoria had a memorial erected to her beloved husband Albert in Kensington Gardens (above).

The Royals

The coronation of Elizabeth II in 1952 was something of a prelude to the Eurovision contest in that it was the first major TV event to be followed by millions of viewers for 11 whole hours across Europe. Today, the British Royal Family continues to stir emotions, with stories and scandals about its members stoking the tabloid press. While these headlines rock the notion of the Royals being a 'firm', as they call themselves, the media

never succeed in unhinging the House of Windsor. The Queen firmly follows protocol, but is increasingly trying to get closer to the people. For the last 40 years or so, for instance, works from the royal art collection have been put on display, and one section of Buckingham Palace is open to visitors in the summer. Some of the Queen's dresses are also exhibited there. The strategy seems to have paid off, for these insights, among other

things, prompted fashion magazine Vogue to name then-81-year-old Elizabeth among the 50 'most glamorous women in the world'. British people love their queen, and grieved the loss of Prince Philip, who died in 2021. The media interest has shifted from Prince Charles and Princess Diana, who died in a car crash in 1997, to their sons, Princes William and Harry, as well as their wives and children.

⑩ ✦✦ Trafalgar Square The entire history of the former British Empire appears to be concentrated at Trafalgar Square. Situated in the heart of the West End, the square was named after one of England's most important battles against Napoleon. It was near Trafalgar, southwestern Spain, that the British fleet defeated the armada of Spanish and French warships. The focal point of the square is the memorial column to Lord Nelson, who lost his life in said battle, while the bronze lions at the base of the monument are said to have been cast from the metal of captured French cannons. Despite, or indeed because of, all this glory, however, the square also plays host to some of the most prominent demonstrations and largest parties, such as on New Year's Eve.

⑫ ✦ Piccadilly Circus Five busy streets, including Haymarket, Shaftesbury Avenue and Regent Street, all feed into Piccadilly Circus,

The 51-metre-high Nelson's Column.

The National Gallery, with its Neoclassical exterior, lines one end of Trafalgar Square.

🅫 Covent Garden

This square has been a centre of popular entertainment since the 17th century. It all started with a large market. But soon there were all sorts of entertainments including by travelling artists. In the 18th century, *The Beggar's Opera* by John Gay, a piece which, in contrast to the then prominent courtly opera, was supposed to entertain the common people, proved to be such a great success that a theatre was built there, the Theatre Royal. It is now the world's oldest theatre site in continuous use. The area is also home to the Royal Opera House, which is one of the most important opera houses in the world. Today, Covent Garden is an entertainment district that offers a wide range of diversion for all tastes.

prompting the small square to be considered the gateway to London's West End and Soho entertainment districts and major shopping streets, but it is constantly crowded and noisy. Nevertheless, its reputation as the glittering centrepoint of London's nightlife remains secure. In 1923, giant neon billboards were added to every corner of the square, their lights flashing in the darkness promising endless options for consumers. Today, the billboards can only be found on one corner; traffic has now been reduced to parts of the square. At the south-eastern corner of the Circus stands the Shaftesbury Memorial Fountain, erected in the 1890s to commemorate the philanthropic works of Lord Shaftesbury. The central figure is the Angel of Charity but it is generally mistaken for the Greek god Eros.

Piccadilly – the street – boasts the Ritz and other elegant hotels, and is also home to the Royal Academy and Fortnum & Mason, a department store founded in 1777.

13 * The Shard This eye-catching glass edifice soars to a height of 310 metres, and is the new landmark in Southwark. It was officially opened in July 2012, and the viewing platform opened to the public in February 2013. Visible from afar, this skyscraper even towers over the London Eye, currently Europe's tallest Ferris wheel at 135 metres. In its planning phase, The Shard sparked protests, with claims that it would not fit with the rest of the city skyline. Problems with building permits, the sale of the land, and finally bailing investors led to delays in the project. Now, however, The Shard is a coveted attraction, with its 72 floors of residential units and office space, a luxury Shangri-La hotel, restaurants, bars, shops in the Shard Plaza, and access to the platforms of London Bridge train station.

15 * National Gallery** Unlike most European galleries designed for the general public, the National Gallery at Trafalgar Square was established rather late. It is the only one of

14 London Eye

The London Eye, a giant Ferris wheel situated between County Hall and the Southbank Centre, was officially opened by the prime minister at the time, Tony Blair, on New Year's Eve 1999, and has been one of the city's highlights ever since. Measuring 135 metres in height, it is so far the tallest Ferris wheel in Europe. When in operation, it spins continuously, but slowly, with a full rotation taking 30 minutes. Passengers can board or disembark without the wheel needing to stop. The 32 capsules are fully glassed-in and suspended on the outer ring of the wheel, giving passengers 360-degree views over London, stretching for some 40 kilometres. The London Eye was originally only designed to run for five years, but was so popular that it is set to spin for another 20.

its kind not to have derived from any sort of royal collection. In 1824, the British government purchased 38 paintings from the collection of deceased banker John Julius Angerstein, and displayed them in his home on the Pall Mall. The new building at Trafalgar Square was finally inaugurated in 1838 – as a place open to all sections of the population, not just privileged art connoisseurs. Its halls exhibit some 2,000 paintings from all European schools and eras, including prominent works by artists such as Vincent van Gogh, Claude Monet, Leonardo da Vinci, Paul Cézanne and Titian.

The National Gallery building was constructed in 1837 and is an attraction in itself.

🄯 *** Victoria & Albert Museum

The sprawling building houses some 4.5 million objects of art, craft and design – originating from Europe, North America, Asia and North Africa, and ranging from the earliest times 5,000 years ago to the present day. And as if that were not enough, the works encompass all forms of creativity, from sculptures, paintings, drawings and photos, to glass, porcelain, ceramics and furniture, to toys, clothing and jewellery. In short, it is the largest collection in the world. The museum was built after the Great Exhibition of 1851, from which a few exhibits were purchased. Originally intended to inspire design students as a manufactory museum, the number of exhibits grew rapidly, and more space was needed. The foundations of the present-day building were laid in 1899.

🄯 *** National Portrait Gallery

Portraits of every famous British person can be found hanging in this gallery, captured on canvas and enclosed in exquisite frames. Many can also be viewed life-sized in the National Portrait Gallery, dressed in grand regalia or sitting on a chair. The gallery has been located at St Martin's Place since 1856, later moving to its present-day building just off Trafalgar Square and directly adjacent to the National Gallery, where it has undergone two extensions. One of the first portraits to be exhibited here was that of William Shakespeare. Photography also plays a major role. The collection contains around 250,000 original photos, the oldest of which date back to the 1840s. Old black-and-white photos of stars such as Vivien Leigh and Alec Guinness alternate with modern personalities such as the model Kate Moss or the Duchess of Cambridge, Kate Middleton, and hyper-modern voice-interactive digital portraits.

🄯 *** Tate Modern

This gallery for international contemporary art, located in the former Bankside Power Station on the south bank of the Thames, which covers the period from 1900 to the present day, has blossomed into the world's most popular gallery for modern and contemporary art since it was founded in 2000. In addition to surrealism, minimalism, abstract expressionism and new figuration of the post-war period, the Tate Modern is also dedicated to contemporary trends. The oldest paintings are from the period of Fauvism, a French version of Expressionism, featuring works by Henri Matisse, Raoul Dufy, Georges Braque and Pablo Picasso. Surrealism and related currents are represented by Salavdor Dalí, but also Max Ernst, René Magritte and Joan Miró. One of the highlights is the Pop Art department, where Roy Lichtenstein is just as popular as Andy Warhol, Claes Oldenburg and David Hockney.

🄯 *** Tate Britain

This museum on the north bank of the Thames houses a unique collection of British art from 1500 to the present. The new Clore Galleries building next to the Neoclassical main entrance is home to the estate of British romanticist William Turner. The prestigious Turner Prize, named after him, is awarded annually to younger British artists.

Equally spectacular are the special exhibitions, which, in addition to being dedicated to individual artists, are often also designed as studies on a particular topic. Tate Britain was established in 1897 as the National Gallery of British Art or the Tate Gallery, named after the millionaire and sugar magnet Henry Tate. In the 19th century, he not only bequeathed his collection of contemporary art to the state, but also a sizeable amount of money to help build a suitable gallery for it.

The Tate Britain's vast entrance area is the perfect setting for the lavish collection.

As so often with major construction projects, The Shard caused all manner of controversies, but ultimately resulted in a new, popular attraction for the capital.

Discovering Outer London

A total of 32 boroughs make up Greater London. Twelve of these, together with the City of London, form Inner or Central London, the remaining boroughs are known as Outer London. Many beautiful green spaces can be found in these outlying areas of the metropolis. Great examples of this are Greenwich and Kew Gardens.

Docklands & Canary Wharf

For almost 200 years the Isle of Dogs, a large peninsula in a bend of the River Thames, had been the busiest port in London. Here, as elsewhere in the city, bombs destroyed the traditional facilities during World War II. But it was the decline of the international shipbuilding industry which eventually dealt the area the fatal blow. At the end of the 20th century, the need for office space in the financial heart of the City increased rapidly, and in 1988, despite much resistance, the expansion of Canary Wharf began on the dilapidated shipyard site. Today the post-modern ensemble of buildings, in which not only banks but also some of the media found a home, epitomises the resurrection of the city's commercial power.

** **Greenwich** Greenwich is known to every school child as the place through which the prime meridian runs, dividing our earth into eastern and western hemispheres. The determination of the district as the location of the prime meridian took place during the International Meridian Conference in 1884. Since 1997, this famous part of south-east London has been a World Heritage Site known as Maritime Greenwich, which is rightly praised for its extraordinary beauty. In addition to many historic houses, the scientific achievements and the history of England's naval power, the Old Royal Naval College and, above all, the Queen's House are all part of the UNESCO World Cultural Heritage Site. The Queen's House, a former royal residence, was the first consistently Neoclassical building in Great Britain, designed by the architect Inigo Jones at the beginning of the 17th century. When the Naval College, which was then still a Naval Hospital, was built, the view from the Queen's House was not to be obstructed by any new buildings by royal order, which in turn led to the unique appearance of the ensemble of buildings that is considered the crown of Maritime Greenwich.

*** **Kew Gardens** Botanical gardens are always a crowd magnet, but Kew Gardens, officially known as the Royal Botanic Gardens in Kew, is a garden that commands superlatives as well as a UNESCO World Heritage Site. From a small 3.6-hectare garden in the 18th century, it developed into today's 120-hectare site, housing the largest collection of plants in the world. At the centre of this are two most important greenhouses dating from the Victorian era: the Palm House and the Temperate House for plants from temperate climates. As well as these two world-famous structures made from wrought iron and glass, there are numerous other greenhouses, ornamental buildings and museums. The attractions include the small Bonsai House, the Waterlily House, boasting the hottest climate anywhere in the garden, and the Evolution House, in which millions of years of plant development are explained in a fascinating journey through time.

In Greenwich Park you can enjoy excellent views of Queen's House and the Canary Wharf office complexes in the background (above). The Palm House in Kew Gardens is the world's oldest Victorian greenhouse (right).

East of England

The idyllic landscape of eastern England has long attracted people from the Continent, with the Romans and Anglo-Saxons all leaving their traces. Later this region lost some of its prominence. Today, it is focused on farming, featuring villages, small farms, mills and pubs. Coupled with this are the vast, sandy beaches on England's driest coast, often home to more seabirds than people, and an equally vast sky, whose clouds have captivated many a painter.

Discovering Essex

Essex offers a wonderful mix of different landscapes – while the east is primarily distinguished by more than 560 kilometres of coastline, the interior is split into the rural north and the urban south. Essex is also home to Great Britain's oldest documented city, the historic market town of Colchester.

INFO *

ESSEX
County town:
Chelmsford
Area:
3,465 sq km
Population:
1.48 million
Population density:
426 inhabitants/sq km

** Southend-on-Sea Just 70 kilometres from the centre of London, and with an idyllic location on the northern banks of the point where the Thames empties out into the North Sea, Southend-on-Sea is blessed with over 10 kilometres of beaches. The little fishing village became a swanky coastal resort as early as the second half of the 18th century. The Southend Pier, at 2.16 kilometres the world's longest pier, was built here in 1889, and one of the first ever amusement parks, the Kursaal (German for health spa), followed in 1901. Today, Southend-on-Sea is a bustling town of 180,000 inhabitants, with only the picturesque main building of the Kursaal having been preserved. But there are plenty of new attractions on the seafront, as well as the opportunity to combine a beach holiday with extensive shopping sessions in the busy town centre, and a visit to theatres, cinemas, award-winning galleries and fascinating museums. The Beecroft Art Gallery, for example, showcases historic swimwear fashions among its other exhibits.

* The Kursaal While colourful neon signs both inside and outside give the Kursaal something of an American feel, the Edwardian building is very much classically British in style. Its wide variety of attractions drew many visitors to the town; even after reopening in the wake of World War II, it served as a place of entertainment, then primarily as a venue of live music hosting Queen, AC/DC and many other greats.

Now all that remains are the main building and its unmistakable dome, created by Campbell Sherrin. For a while, it housed a bowling alley (closed in 2019) and a casino (closed in 2020). Currently, a supermarket is the only occupant of the historic building.

** Prittlewell Priory The oldest preserved building in Southend-on-Sea was founded in the 12th century as a monastery for no more than 18 monks, before being used as a residential home in the 16th century. In 1922, it was eventually opened as Southend's first museum, and the historic complex has been taking visitors back in time ever since – both through its preserved buildings, as well as the well-run visitors' centre, which provides information on the history of Prittlewell Priory. The large park surrounding the entire facility is ideal for a leisurely walk.

The Kursaal is a heritage-listed building that was opened in 1901 as part of the world's first amusement park. The main hall boasts an attractive mix of styles. A supermarket chain is all that remains in the building..

The promenade of Southend-on-Sea cast in atmospheric light at sunset.

The pier at Southend-on-Sea with the new Adventure Island amusement park.

St Peter-on-the-Wall at sunset.

The interior of the St Peter-on-the-Wall chapel is as bare and unembellished as its exterior.

** Chapel of St Peter-on-the-Wall

From afar, it looks like any old abandoned farm building. Seen through the eyes of historians and preservationists, however, the plain little chapel is an exquisite Grade I-listed gem. One of Great Britain's oldest surviving buildings, it was originally part of a monastery built around 660 by the Anglo-Saxon Bishop Cedd on the remains of a Roman fort. Having long been used as a barn, the chapel was restored and re-dedicated in 1920. It hosts a church service every Thursday morning at 9 a.m., and is also used by the Othona Community, a Christian community near Bradwell-on-Sea, for its spiritual activities. It is additionally the scene of Easter dawn festivities, Taizé prayers, after-noon tea concerts as well as Christmas carols by candlelight.

*** Maunsell Sea Forts

These bizarre stilted buildings in the Thames estuary were once designed to protect London from attacks by German bombers and E-boats, or fast-at-tack craft. The cluster of artificial platforms is

Maldon Salt

Even the king in the Grimm brothers' fairy tale *Princess Mouse-Skin* learned about the importance of salt thanks to his clever daughter. Today, it is primarily award-winning chefs who give amateur cooks advice on the best salt to use in the creation of delicious dishes. And one name that often comes up is Maldon. The Maldon Crystal Salt Company was founded in 1882, although sea salt was being harvested here well before this. The company's success story began in 1955, when it exported its first batch to Sweden. To this day, Maldon Salt is extracted using the same cast-iron pans as it was when the company was first established. But that is just one of the open secrets about the salt's special properties, because it is also rich in trace elements such as selenium and zinc.

named after its inventor, British engineer Guy Maunsell. There were seven forts in total, some of which consisted of several units connected via gangways. The crews had to report imminent attacks, but also destroyed 22 aircraft and 30 bombs. The forts have been rusting away since the end of the war, and ships occasionally run into them, but their exposed location also fascinates many locals and visitors. Attempts have been made to establish hippie communes and pirate radio stations here. In 2005, the artist Stephen Turner spent six weeks living in the lighthouse of the Shivering Sands Fort – to experience personal isolation, as well as creative contemplation.

Weathered, crooked, but still there – the bizarre stilted army and navy buildings of the Maunsell Sea Forts.

Discovering Hertfordshire

Just a stone's throw from the pulsating metropolis of London is the rural idyll of Hertfordshire – the perfect place to escape the hectic, big-city hustle and bustle. Whether it be relaxing in a cosy pub in one of the quaint English villages, or admiring the majestic gardens of one of the luxurious manors, the choice is yours.

INFO *

HERTFORDSHIRE
County town:
Hertford
Area:
1,643 sq km
Population:
1.18 million
Population density:
721 inhabitants/sq km

Cathedral dates back to the 11th century, and, despite subsequent Gothic modifications, stands as a fine example of the early-Norman style. The bustling city's second historic attraction revolves around the excavations of the Iron-Age and Roman settlement, with the Verulanium Museum also providing insights into the everyday life of a Roman-British city in late antiquity.

Hatfield House was built in Elizabethan and Jacobean style between 1607 and 1611. Today, it showcases paintings, furniture and historic weapons.

*** **Hatfield House** Movie buffs will no doubt have already encountered some part or other of Hatfield House, for the sweeping estate, with its vast gardens and parklands spanning over 17 hectares, is a popular film set, and has appeared in many films, such as *Anna Karenina, The King's Speech, Shakespeare in Love, Charlie and the Chocolate Factory, Orlando, Tomb Raider, Sherlock Holmes, Batman* and the last of the *Harry Potter* movies. It was built in 1611 by Robert Cecil, the British prime minister at the time, and has remained in the family ever since. The long history and many changes are also part of the estate's charm. From its lavish Renaissance hall with its dark wood carvings to the Victorian kitchen, the artistic box-framed flower beds of the West Garden to the enchanted Woodland Garden, Hatfield House offers a veritable foray into different fashions and times..

** **St Albans** Legend has it that, shortly before the Roman Emperor Constantine the Great legalized Christianity in 313, a soldier by the name of Alban was executed in the Roman-British settlement of Verulamium for having granted asylum to a persecuted priest. As such, he became England's first martyr, and Verulamium was given the name St Albans. It grew wealthy thanks to pilgrimages, and the Abbey Church of Saint Alban, founded in 793, was for a long time considered the most important in England. The present-day St Albans

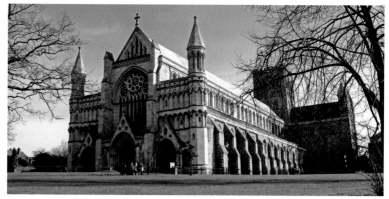

St Albans Cathedral, known as 'The Abbey', was built in 793 in honour of England's first martyr.

Norman and Gothic styles are perfectly fused in St Albans.

The mini-maze, parterres and topiary in the gardens of Hatfield House are the result of the loving work of many gardeners.

The pergola in the gardens of Hatfield House provides welcome shade.

Discovering Bedfordshire

Embark on a culinary journey in the ceremonial county by sampling a 'Bedfordshire Clanger', a pastry often filled with meat at one end, and fruit at the other. Every village has its own version.

INFO ✳

BEDFORDSHIRE
County town:
Bedford
Area:
1,235 sq km
Population:
625,000
Population density:
506 inhabitants/sq km

** **Bedford** Located at a ford of the Great Ouse River, Bedford was an important market town in the Early Middle Ages. Anglo-Saxon King Offa of Mercia, for example, was buried here in 796. Later, when the Great Ouse formed the border between Anglo-Saxon England and Danelaw, which was occupied by the Vikings, Bedford was expanded into a fortress. The townscape and life here continue to be shaped by the river to this day. The Bedford River Festival, held every second year in June, is the second largest regular outdoor event in Great Britain after the Notting Hill Carnival in London. The Bedford Regatta, the largest one-day regatta, is also held here every year in May. Equally worth a visit are the parklands lining the river, the 13th-century St Paul's Church, the 'Little Italy' festival, which celebrates the town's Italian community, and the Higgins Art Gallery & Museum. Meanwhile, Bedford Castle, Bushmed Priory and the Shire Hall, built in Gothic style by Alfred Waterhouse, all provide interesting insights into the past.

Bedford certainly knows how to show off the Great Ouse River. Here festive lighting sets off the historic bridge.

The modern Suspension Bridge takes pedestrians over the Great Ouse.

Discovering Cambridgeshire

While the university town of Cambridge traces the footsteps of Europe's great thinkers, the north of the county takes visitors back to the days when the construction of canals and windmills saw the region drained of flood waters.

CAMBRIDGESHIRE
County town:
Cambridge
Area:
3,046 sq km
Population:
651,000
Population density:
214 inhabitants/sq km

INFO ✳

*** Peterborough The city on the River Nene north of Cambridge is primarily known for its cathedral – one of the most eye-catching examples of Norman Early Gothic architecture. The wide facade, with its three gables of equal height which rise up above giant arches, is unique. Once inside, visitors find themselves in a 147-metre-long and surprisingly narrow nave. The painted medieval wooden ceiling is the largest of only four to have been preserved across Europe. In stark contrast is the dizzyingly intricate 15th-century fan-vaulted ceiling in the chancel. Another tourist magnet just a few miles northwest of Peterborough is Burghley House, a stunning estate with parklands and an art collection. The city centre, the Iron Age Flag Fen open-air museum, the Nene Valley Railway Museum and Nene Park are also worth a visit.

Burghley House

England is known for its stately manors, and one fine example of these is located some 15 kilometres northwest of Peterborough. Burghley House is considered a masterpiece of the Tudor style. It was originally built on an E-shaped plan in honour of Queen Elizabeth I. After several modifications, the building now has four wings and surrounds a large interior courtyard. Every year, the estate hosts one of the most important eventing tournaments in the form of the Burghley Horse Trials, during which the world's top riders and their horses go head-to-head over three days. Several films have also been set at Burghley House, including George Eliot's *Middlemarch* (1994), Jane Austen's *Pride and Prejudice* (2005) and Dan Brown's *The Da Vinci Code* (2006).

Numerous high windows fill the interior of Peterborough Cathedral with light.

*** Cambridge

'Silicon Fen' is the nickname sometimes given to Cambridge, which has grown to become a hub for technology and the sciences. The city's university history dates back to 1220, when some scholars from Oxford migrated to Cambridge. The oldest college still preserved to this day, Peterhouse College, was founded in 1284, while the venerable St John's College has produced nine Nobel Prize winners. Established in 1511 by Margaret Beaufort, the mother of King Henry VII, its students have included writers such as William Wordsworth and Douglas Adams, as well as the co-founder of IT, Maurice Wilkes. Cambridge boasts a high concentration of historic buildings, and the

King's College was founded in 1441 by King Henry VI, and today is one of the most advanced colleges in Cambridge.

grandest of all the colleges is King's College, established in 1441. Its chapel, completed in 1547, features a filigree fan-vaulted ceiling and magnificent glass windows..

*** King's College and King's College Chapel

The best known of Cambridge University's colleges is arguably King's College (opposite bottom). Founded by King Henry VI, it is today the place where most courses are held. The iconic chapel of the same name is considered a perfect example of Gothic architecture in the Perpendicular Style. The chapel, home to the King's College Choir, is famous for its traditional Christmas Eve 'Festival of Nine Lessons and Carols' service which is broadcast by BBC Radio every year.

** Trinity College

Trinity College boasts alumni including Francis Bacon, Isaac Newton and Ludwig Wittgenstein, and has produced an impressive 32 Nobel Prize-winners. Centuries of tradition are still palpable to this day, although the young students ensure campus life remains dynamic.

King's College Chapel is one of Cambridge's main landmarks (top).

A number of bridges span the River Cam, with punts adding a Venetian ambience.

*** **Ely** Ely Cathedral is also known as the 'Ship of the Fens', rising majestically out of the surrounding Fens moorland. And it is to the Fens that Ely owes its prominence. When the Normans conquered Anglo-Saxon England in the 11th century, they were unable to capture the Isle of Ely, which was protected by marshland. Only after William the Conqueror had guaranteed the city all its privileges did the residents surrender. In 1083, the small town, which today still only has a population of about 20,000, was given a new abbey church, one of England's largest and grandest cathedrals. The 14th-century octagonal crossing tower is an architectural gem. Its complex design features lavish partitioning in its interior, and draws eyes upwards to the superb 43-metre-high dome.

The cathedral's central nave is as impressive as the octagonal crossing tower.

It's hard to know where to look first: up at the 'star dome' ...

... or at the ornate altar.

Discovering Suffolk

Suffolk's lack of major cities means the average age of citizens here is relatively high. Yet maritime towns such as Aldeburgh and Southwold, picturesque piers, little harbours and white sandy beaches make the county worth a visit for people of any age.

SUFFOLK
County town:
Ipswich
Area:
3,801 sq km
Population:
759,000
Population density:
200 inhabitants/sq km

The Sutton Hoo Museum houses a number of impressive discoveries.

** Bury St Edmunds The modern-day market town has a significant history. A Benedictine monastery was founded here in the 11th century, and pilgrims flocked in their droves to the relics of King Edmund the Martyr, which were kept in a shrine. In 1214, English barons arranged a secret meeting and decided to force the king to sign a document that ultimately went down in English history as Magna Carta. The dissolution of the monasteries in the 16th century saw the Abbey of Bury St Edmunds destroyed, but even today, the ruins and surrounding garden continue to attract many visitors. St Edmundsbury Cathedral was erected next to the Abbey Gardens, though its striking spire was not completed until 2005. The town is also known for its Theatre Royal and the more than 200-year-old Greene King Brewery.

** Sutton Hoo It's eastern England's very own Tutankhamun. In 1939, the archaeologist Basil Brown discovered the unlooted ship burial site of an Anglo-Saxon ruler on the shores of the River Deben. It is reputed to be that of Rædwald of East Anglia, who died in the early 7th century and was buried in a 27-metre-wide ship with exquisitely decorated weapons, trinkets and armaments, originating not only in England, but also Ireland, Scandinavia, Merovingian Western Europe and the Mediterranean region. While the burial ship and treasures did not withstand the passage of time as well as the burial objects of the Egyptian pharaoh, visitors to the Sutton Hoo Museum can see the king lying in state, just as he would have done on the day of his burial, through a life-size, walk-in reconstruction of the grave.

The Sutton Hoo Helmet (centre) is covered in detailed filigree work.

St Edmundsbury Cathedral, as seen from the colourful Abbey Gardens.

One of the museum's treasures.

Newmarket

It may not play host to the most important or high prize money races, but Newmarket is certainly still the beating heart of English horse-racing. Nowhere are more racehorses bred and trained than on its heaths. Some 3,500 fine thoroughbreds are developed into future winners at 50 training facilities. One in three jobs in town is related to the horse-racing industry. There is documentary evidence of horse-racing here dating back to the 12th century, and the founding of the Jockey Club in 1750 saw Newmarket become the cradle of modern horse-racing worldwide. The sport's entire glorious history can be explored at the National Horse Racing Museum. And those preferring to witness actual races are advised to attend one of the major meets in April, May, July or October.

John Constable

Suffolk is Constable territory. It was here that the great English landscape painter was born in 1776, and it was also here that he created some of his most famous pictures. Together with his peer – and fierce rival – William Turner, Constable set new standards in landscape painting. He was one of the first to truly paint landscapes, rather than nature as an accessory to people and scenes. To achieve this, he studied

clouds and weather to such an advanced degree that meteorologist Luke Howard based his classification of various cloud types on Constable's studies. Nevertheless, Constable's motto was 'painting is but another word for feeling'. As realistic as his landscapes are still to this day, he, like the Impressionists that came after him, ultimately focused on the impression a landscape imparted on viewers at a par-

ticular moment. Unlike Turner, however, who loved to exaggerate the lighting effects in his paintings and dial up the atmosphere, Constable largely remained conservative and grounded. It is for this reason that Turner is much better known in continental Europe, while Constable is often rated more highly than his great rival in Britain. Both artists took the first step in prioritizing effect over realism.

Discovering Norfolk

Norfolk's unique natural landscape is characterized by the tides of the North Sea, which marks the northern and eastern borders of the county. With its countless dykes and historic windmills, it is somehow more reminiscent of the Netherlands than England.

Norwich City Hall and the Church of St Peter Mancroft are eye-catching even at night.

In the 15th century, Pulls Ferry was a water gate and later a ferry house.

INFO

NORFOLK
County town:
Norwich
Area:
5,372 sq km
Population:
904,000
Population density:
168 inhabitants/sq km

*** **Norwich** The lively capital of the county of Norfolk has a lot to offer. There are plenty of attractions, such as one of the most accomplished Norman cathedrals with its wonderful cloister, the great art collection of the Sainsbury Centre for Visual Arts, numerous museums and a picturesque inner city that boasts a great mix of old and new. The old Church of St Peter Mancroft, for example, contrasts fabulously with the modern cultural centre The Forum, while the glass roofs of an underground shopping centre create the impression of sophisticated greenhouses as they rise up out of the parklands surrounding the Norman castle. The many stalls at market square, a Victorian arcade and a historic department store are also great places to shop. The city is also home to several theatres – the largest being the Art Deco Theatre Royal from 1935 – and a vast array of excellent restaurants.

** **Sandringham House** Sandringham House is of particular importance to the

Sandringham House is one of Queen Elizabeth II's private homes.

British Royal Family, who typically spend their Christmas and New Year period there. Together with Balmoral Castle, it is one of the Queen's private homes. But it is also the place where the Queen's father and grandfather died, and where Prince Charles met his future first wife Diana, who had grown up at nearby Park House. Parts of the property can be visited most of the year round, as can the magnificent gardens and 240-hectare country park. In 1870, the 365-room Sandringham House replaced a smaller predecessor building, and was equipped with many blessings of the modern age, such as gas lighting, flushing toilets and an early form of the shower. But its builder, the future King Edward VII, was most fond of the great hunting grounds in the surrounding woodlands.

Norwich Cathedral (top) was built out of flint and mortar between 1096 and 1145.

The vaulted cloisters of Norwich Cathedral are an impressive feat of architecture.

The Theatre Royal seats 1,300 spectators.

** The Broads National Park

Like a completely different world, a 300-square kilometre landscape of rivers, canals and small, shallow lakes stretches between Norwich and the coast. Created when peat was dug out back in the Middle Ages, its numerous windmills attest to the efforts made to drain the marshes. Today the area attracts sailors and small motor boats, and increasingly also canoes, particularly on weekends and during the summer holidays. Hikes and bike rides in the Broads are other activities that can be enjoyed here. It was declared a national park in 1988 in a bid to protect the unique natural setting of this aquatic landscape, with its rare flora and many birds. Visitor centres exist in Hoveton, Ludham and the Whitlingham Country Park, while Wroxham is the main hub for boating tourism.

*** Norfolk Coast

The seemingly endless sky above Norfolk, with its ever-changing

The windmills of Cley-next-the-Sea.

The tricolour cliffs near Hunstanton particularly attract fossil hunters.

moods, provides a sense of calmness and relaxation for stressed-out city dwellers. The constant ebbing and flowing of the tides can be enjoyed on long beach walks, while a stroll through the marshlands reveals many rare plant species. And when it comes to seabirds, few other places in all of England offer a greater variety or better opportunities for watching them. The end-to-end coastal walk boasts impressive diversity, be it trudging through the extensive dunes at Holme-next-the-Sea, exploring vast marshland further east, or enjoying the view of the steep coast near the traditional seaside resort of Sheringham. What makes all this so beautiful is the fact that the landscape is not thrust into the foreground. The fresh breeze is instead the main protagonist here, providing perfect conditions for kite-flying.

The soft light of the rising sun dances on the River Thurne and the Thurne Windmill (top).

Norfolk's beaches

The thought of beaches in England generally conjures up images of white cliffs for visitors from the Continent. But not all its coasts look like those at Dover. Norfolk's beaches offer excellent variety. Great Yarmouth and Hunstanton are recommended for the athletically inclined, while the beaches of Winterton-on-Sea and Horsey are lesser known gems for a relaxing day trip away from the hustle and bustle. Dog owners will find animal-friendly beaches in Brancaster and Sea Palling, and the beach huts at Wells-next-the-Sea (below) make for a romantic vibe. The beaches of Norfolk are popular places for birdwatching, seal-watching and crabbing, which involves fishing for crabs with just a single line and then returning them unhurt to the water.

East Midlands

This area of central England boasts a diverse landscape, with the tall summits of the Peak District in the west, the North Sea coast with its busy seaside resorts and vast marshlands in the east, and the rolling hills of the Lincolnshire Wolds in between. The East Midlands are one of the earliest settlement areas in England, and cities like Lincoln and Leicester still testify to the important role they played as wealthy centres of the wool trade in the Middle Ages.

Discovering Northamptonshire

It would be difficult to find another region of England with as many historic houses as Northamptonshire. Many of the well-preserved mansions and aristocratic residences are open to the public, and their gardens and parklands are oases of tranquillity.

Althorp House, which has been the residence of the Spencer family for generations. .

** Northampton This city of 215,000 residents located between London and Birmingham, is not usually considered a tourist magnet, yet it is one of the oldest cities in England, with origins dating back to the Bronze Age. Its strategic location saw it play an important role in the Middle Ages, but the English Civil War and a major fire in the 17th century destroyed many of the old buildings. It was not until the Industrial Revolution that the town re-emerged as a centre of the leather and shoe industry. Nevertheless, there is a lot for visitors to explore, such as one of the best-preserved Norman round churches, the unusual baroque classical All Saints' Church, Northampton Museum, which houses one of the world's largest shoe collections, a curious 127-metre-tall tower in which lifts are tested, many parks – and, of course, a wide range of shops.

Diana's grave on the island in the Oval Lake.

*** Althorp House Of all of Great Britain's many magnificent stately homes, Althorp particularly stands out, for it was here that Lady Diana Spencer, the future Princess of Wales, grew up. Admirers can retrace her footsteps, take a pilgrimage to the lake to see the island where she is buried, and of course visit the exhibition keeping the memory of the 'Princess of Hearts' alive. But the estate northwest of Northampton has also been the home of the influential Spencer family for over 500 years, and former earls and their wives spared no expense or effort in constantly revamping the property or adding to its many treasures. The period during which the manor is open to the public begins every May with a festival showcasing regional food and drink, and ends with a literature festival in October.

INFO *

NORTHAMPTONSHIRE
County town:
Northampton
Area:
2,364 sq km
Population:
748,000
Population density:
316 inhabitants/sq km

No visitor to Northampton can miss All Saints' Church (right); it stands right in the heart of the city.

DIANA PRINCESS OF WALES   UNVEILED BY HER SONS

Diana, Princess of Wales

Beautiful, elegant, tragic and glamorous – Diana, Princess of Wales, was and remains a media icon, the most photographed woman in the world at the time, whose pictures still feature in glossy magazines more than 20 years after her death. When the ex-wife of Prince Charles, heir to the British throne, and the mother of the next in line to the throne, Prince William, died in a car accident in Paris in 1997, it sparked mass

mourning right across Great Britain and the world. Then-Prime Minister Tony Blair had the presence of mind to created the title 'The People's Princess'. She died young, thus becoming a legend. Several memorials have been dedicated to her; in addition to her grave-cum-shrine at the Althorp family estate, there is also a fountain in London's Hyde Park and the Diana Memorial Playground in Kensington Gardens. Kensington Palace, where she lived until her death, is home to the most interesting memorial of all, presenting an audio-visual photo and memorabilia exhibition, as well as some of her stylish dresses, which had been made by British designers for the fashion-conscious princess. Since 2021, it has also been home to a new statue, featuring Diana and two children, representing her universal legacy.

Silverstone Circuit

The eyes of any motorsport fan light up at the mere mention of the small town of Silverstone (population: 2000): in 1948, the A-shaped runways of a World War II military airfield straddling the border between Northamptonshire and Buckinghamshire were converted into a high-speed race track, where long straights alternated with perilously tight hairpin bends. The first-ever World Championship Grand Prix race,

attended by King George VI, was held here in front of 200,000 spectators on 13th May 1950, with Alfa Romeo taking out the trifecta. Italian Nino Farina, who was also crowned the series' first world champion at the end of the season, claimed victory in two hours, 13 minutes and 23.6 seconds, following an exciting battle with his teammates, Juan Manuel Fangio and Luigi Fagioli. Since then, most (but not all) British Grand Prix have been held at Silverstone, and are set to be held here until at least 2024. While the circuit's layout has been modified several times, the challenging corners, combined with the frequent British rain and gusty winds that sweep across the vast site, consistently ensure that a victory at Silverstone remains something very special. It also hosts vintage sports car and motorcycle races.

Discovering Rutland

England's smallest county boasts an abundance of nature and idyllic rural scenes. Outdoor enthusiasts are drawn to Rutland Water, while culture aficionados fall in love with the many picturesque, typically English towns, such as Oakham and Uppingham.

Birdlife at Rutland Water Park

It's not just cyclists and hikers who enjoy the Rutland Water reservoir; bird lovers also get their fill here, for the area around the lake has been an osprey breeding ground for more than 150 years. It is also home to lapwings, tufted ducks, Eurasian wigeons, cormorants, great crested grebes, little grebes, coots, goldeneye ducks and several over-wintering populations. The park has 31 bird-watching hides, where ornithologists and 'twitchers' (amateur bird watchers) can observe these plumed creatures. The Anglian Water Bird Watching Centre in Egleton, at the western end of the lake, provides all the information visitors need. Every August since 1989, Egleton has also hosted the British Birdfair, a renowned bird-watching event.

** Rutland Water The Neoclassical structure of Normanton church cuts a solitary figure on the banks of England's largest reservoir. But while the main part of the town of Normanton succumbed to valley flooding, there is little need for wistfulness or melancholy. Rutland Water, which extends in a U-shape around an elongated peninsula, is not only an important drinking water reservoir in England's driest region; it has long also been a much-loved recreational site and prized nature reserve. The lake is a popular place for fishing and sailing, and anyone who doesn't have their own boat can use one of the excursion boats. Lining the shore is the Aqua Park Rutland and several cycling and hiking trails. A nature reserve at the western end is heavily frequented by seabirds – and birdwatchers.

*** Oakham Castle Oakham Castle doesn't look particularly impressive at first

RUTLAND
County town:
Oakham
Area:
382 sq km
Population:
39,700
Population density:
104 inhabitants/sq km

INFO *

At Oakham Castle Museum, you can admire a collection of over 200 ceremonial horseshoes.

glance, nor does it fit the common image of a castle. But the elongated building with its high roof and the rounded arches above its doors and windows is the best and most authentically preserved residential building from a Norman castle complex in England. It dates back to the late 12th century, and was owned by the de Ferriers family. The columns and sculptures in the large great hall are thought to have been created by the same stonemasons as those who worked on Canterbury Cathedral. Among the building's curiosities is the collection of 230 ceremonial horseshoes donated by aristocratic visitors, which are displayed on the wall of the hall. The oldest came from King Edward IV in 1470.

Rutland Water (top, with Normanton Church in the background) is a popular sports and recreational destination.

The spire of All Saints Church soars up behind the Oakham Castle Museum.

Discovering Leicestershire

There's something for everyone here, with museums, exhibitions, shops and restaurants in Leicester, and impressive manor houses and abundant nature in the surrounding region.

*** Leicester Right at the very heart of this bustling industrial city, which was founded in 50 BC as a Roman military camp, is a quaint Victorian town centre bearing evidence of Leicester's long history. The skeleton of King Richard III, the hunchbacked villain from the War of the Roses, who died in 1485, was found during excavations in Leicester in 2012. He has been buried in the Norman cathedral since 2015 and a museum now provides information on the latest research findings. Also worth a visit are the National Space Centre; the Abbey Pumping Station museum of science and technology; the Jewry Wall Museum, with findings from Roman times; and Leicester Museum & Art Gallery, with paintings from the German Expressionist movement, brought to Leicester by Jewish emigrants. The city is also known for its many Indian restaurants.

** National Space Centre Young and old can learn all they ever wanted to know about the Big Bang and the history of our universe at the six interactive exhibition rooms here. You can visit the Sir Patrick Moore Planetarium, the largest in the United Kingdom, or explore the lives of astronauts in a unique 3D simulator.

** Abbey Pumping Station This museum of science and technology is dedicated to various industrial, technical and scientific achievements in the realms of health, engineering, transport and optics. There are 200 years between the invention of the first steam engines and the technical masterpieces of today. Among the museum's most special exhibits is Leicester's first pumping station.

*** Leicester Museum & Art Gallery This gallery, formerly known as the New Walk Museum, showcases German Expressionist paintings that Jewish emigrants once brought with them to Leicester. Also worth seeing are the Arts and

INFO ✳

LEICESTERSHIRE
County town:
Leicester
Area:
2,084 sq km
Population:
700,000 (without Leicester)
Population density:
335 inhabitants/sq km

Visitors can rub shoulders with astronauts at the National Space Centre.

Leicester is packed with reminders of its technological past, as evidenced by the Gimson steam engines at the Abbey Pumping Station museum.

Free tours of the town hall are conducted on the first Wednesday of the month.

Crafts Gallery and Picasso Ceramics: The Attenborough Collection.

* Guildhall This well-preserved timber-framed building is over 600 years old. Today, its historic hall hosts many different events, such as concerts, plays and children's afternoons.

Leicester city centre (opposite top) is beautifully decorated in the lead-up to Christmas, but the city has a lot to offer the rest of the year too.

If it's too wet outside, you can shop till you drop at the Highcross Centre.

** **Charnwood Forest** The name 'Forest' is misleading, for most of the hilly landscape north of Leicester has long been cleared of trees. Bare hills alternate with open meadows, picturesque rock formations, small bodies of water and light woodland, the floor of which is awash with carpets of flowering bluebells in spring. It is this variety that gives the 25-square kilometre region its charm, but also its environmental value. In centuries past, it was here, around the town of Quorn, that the most challenging foxhunts in all of England were held. Today, the Forest is primarily popular for its hiking trails and rock-climbing opportunities. Scattered throughout the area are also several old quarries where grindstones and millstones used to be mined. Not all parts of Charnwood are open to the public, however.

*** **Belvoir Castle** While the mighty complex on the edge of Belvoir Valley has the appearance of a medieval fairy-tale castle, it was actually built in the Neogothic style in the

Roses and other flowers thrive in the gardens of Belvoir.

Danish sculptor Caius Gabriel Cibber created six of the garden's statues.

This hill in Bradgate Park provides views stretching as far as Leicester.

The nature park in Charnwood Forest is home to fallow deer, among other fauna.

early 19th century by James Wyatt, one of England's most famous architects at the time, for John Manners, the 5th duke of Rutland. The castle is still owned by the duke's family to this day, but is open to the public at certain times of year. Visitors can admire magnificent rooms more reminiscent of continental European palaces than an English manor house, as well as an exquisite collection of paintings, including works by Albrecht Dürer, Peter Paul Rubens and Nicolas Poussin. The garden designs were created by English landscape architect Capability Brown, and the plans are finally being executed by the current duchess.

Visitors can explore the castle's lush garden on various garden walks, and encounter both exotic and local plants.

Discovering Lincolnshire

Lincoln offers visitors a wealth of history and plenty of exciting activities and festivals. The lively city is also the perfect place to explore this county's lovely hilly landscape and sweeping coastlines.

LINCOLNSHIRE
County town:
Lincoln
Area:
5,921 sq km
Population:
756,000
Population density:
127 inhabitants/sq km

Harlaxton Manor was built in 1837 and today serves as the campus for three U.S. universities.

Grimsthorpe Castle

Built more than 800 years ago as a defensive structure, Grimsthorpe Castle underwent several extensions and modifications that turned the former castle – of which only King John's Tower remains – into the manor house it is today. Inside, it boasts ancient tapestries and furniture, fine ceramics and prized paintings. But its surrounding gardens are also well worth a visit – take the time to stroll among the perfectly trimmed box trees and fragrant blooms. The castle's parklands, meanwhile, are ideal for longer walks and even bike rides; if you're lucky, you might even spot one of the game animals that are allowed to roam freely around the park, including red, fallow and muntjack deer, as well as buzzards and red kites. Woodland and lakes alternate with flower beds and vegetable gardens on this 1,200-hectare castle estate.

** Harlaxton Manor This is not your average university – grandiose Harlaxton Manor has served as the British campus for several American universities since 1971. It has also hosted an annual interdisciplinary medieval symposium since 1984 – but there is nothing medieval about the estate itself. The 150-room property was constructed in the mid-19th century by a wealthy businessman, who had inherited a more modest predecessor building from an aristocratic relative. Anthony Salvin, who later became famous for restoring medieval buildings, designed Harlaxton Manor in a mixture of styles featuring both neo-Renaissance and neo-Baroque elements. Its use as a university means the manor can only be visited in exceptional circumstances. Several movies have already been shot here, such as

Jan de Bont's 1999 horror film *The Haunting*, and the 2020 film version of *The Secret Garden*, directed by Mac Munden.

*** Belton House What does a typical English country estate look like? For many experts, Belton House in Lincolnshire, with its symmetry and understated décor, is the epitome, although the design of the building was based on Clarendon House, a mansion in central London. Clarendon House was designed in the 17th century and modelled on French palaces such as Versailles. The residence of the then-lord chancellor Edward Hyde, which is no longer standing, was vaunted as the 'grandest, best-conceived, most useful and most attractive house in England'. While John and Alice Bronslow, who built Belton House,

were only lower nobility, they were extremely wealthy and could afford the best tradespeople. Their new country estate was thus somewhat smaller, but still just as elegant, as the property that inspired it. Visitors to Belton House should also take a look at the extraordinary collection of maps and rare manuscripts among the 11,000 books in the library.

Exterior view of Belton House (opposite). A tomb in the church of St Peter & St Paul (above), located on the Belton estate. Image series top right: The Marble Room, library and Tyrconnel Room, at Belton House.

The Wash at low tide.

Grey seals may be spotted on the beach

The valley of the River Ancholme. The hilly Lincolnshire Wolds are popular with holidaymakers.

*** The Wash With a bit of luck, visitors can see seals here. In any case, England's largest population of small seals has chosen the sweeping bay known as The Wash as its home. Four rivers – the Great Ouse, Nene, Welland and Witham – flow into the sea at this point, located between Lincolnshire and East Anglia. They have deposited their sediments over the course of the centuries, constantly changing the shape of the bay. Low tide, particularly at the shallow southern end, exposes sandbanks and endless mudflats, creating a paradise for redshanks, sandpipers and other coastal birds. In the hinterland, salt marshes alternate with swampy fens and farmland protected by dykes. Away from the seaside resorts, it is not long before visitors find themselves in a remote, secluded landscape, where they can enjoy the peace and a panoramic view virtually unobstructed by any hedges or buildings.

** The Fens The Wash marshland was flooded between the 17th and 19th centuries, and today the landscape is criss-crossed by numer-

Lincolnshire Wolds Railway

The Great Northern Railway between East Lincolnshire and London had been in operation since 1848, before its final section closed in 1980. Today, a heritage railway has taken its place, thanks to the tireless dedication of railway enthusiasts and volunteers. It starts at Ludborough station – a stone's throw from the port town of Grimsby, the seaside resort for Cleethorpes, and the little town of Louth. Nearly every day, old steam engines judder along the early-2.5-km-long (1.5 miles) track from here to North Thoresby. The museum in Ludborough provides information on the history of the railway, transporting visitors back to the days when steam engines were a common sight.

ous streams and waterways. It is particularly attractive for walkers and cyclists. In times past, people 'fenskated' (ice-skated) on the fens, which usually froze over in winter.

*** Lincolnshire Wolds The highest point in the Wolds reaches just 168 metres, but the rolling hills that stretch southwards from the River Humber provide a great view of England's east coast, with its salt marshes, fens and sandy beaches. The Wolds used to be a wealthy area thanks to the Lincoln sheep, a large breed with extraordinarily thick, long wool. Today, the Wolds are sparsely populated and ideally explored on foot along the Viking Way, a long-distance hiking trail leading from the Humber to Lincoln. But the region is also popular among motorcyclists. The centre of the Wolds is Louth, a pretty market town, where the last remaining animal market takes place every Thursday.

The area just outside Boston (top) is heavily frequented by cockle-shell hunters.

*** Lincoln

Anyone visiting the county town of Lincolnshire needs to be light on their feet, for it was here that the Romans built their first military camp in Great Britain on a steep hill on the shores of the River Witham in 48 BC. Steep Hill is worth the climb to this day, because the narrow, sharply inclining lane is lined with some of England's finest and oldest medieval buildings. These include the home of Jew Aaron of Lincoln and the adjacent Jews' Court, both dating back to the 12th century, when Lincoln was not only the richest city in England as a result of the wool trade, but also had a large Jewish community. Other must-sees are the High Bridge topped with half-timbered houses, the ruins of the Norman castle erected here on the orders of William the Conqueror and, of course, the grand cathedral.

*** Lincoln Cathedral

Lincoln Cathedral is said to have been the tallest building in the world

Lincoln Cathedral in the historic Bailgate district is a definite must-see.

until 1549, because at that time, the mighty crossing tower had an extremely narrow, pointed pinnacle that soared 160 metres into the sky. This spire was not rebuilt after its collapse, although the cathedral still towers imposingly over the old town. The building, which was largely constructed in the 13th century and then improved until the end of the 15th century, is a unique fusion of early, middle and late Gothic styles. Adventurous master builders kept incorporating new influences, creating innovative vault structures and applying elaborate ornamentation. It was this that saw Lincoln Cathedral become one of the architecturally most interesting Gothic churches anywhere.

The spectacular interior of Lincoln Cathedral (top left); the High Bridge or Glory Hole (top) dates back to 1160.

Skegness

The British affectionately refer to this bustling resort town on the east coast as 'Skeggy', or, jokingly, 'Costa del Skeg'. Visitors can enjoy nearly 10 kilometres of broad sandy beaches and a Grand Parade, offering all the fun and revelry that make up a typical British holiday by the sea: Ferris wheels, rollercoasters and carnival rides, donkey rides for children, fish-and-chip shops, ice creams, pubs and amusement arcades. But it's just as easy to escape all the hubbub. Gibraltar Point National Nature Reserve, only 3 kilometres south of Skegness, is a haven of pure nature. Other holiday highlights in Skegness include a seal sanctuary with a small zoo and the Village Church Farm, an open-air museum hosting events such as the teddy bears' picnic and historic re-enactments.

Discovering Nottinghamshire

The home of Robin Hood, Nottinghamshire brims with culture, history and adventure: Along with Nottingham, with its castle, city of caves and England's oldest pub, it is Sherwood Forest in particular that captivates visitors.

INFO *

NOTTINGHAMSHIRE
County town:
West Bridgford
Area:
2,085 sq km
Population:
823,000
Population density:
395 inhabitants/sq km

** Sherwood Forest It was here that Robin Hood is said to have got up to his noble-minded mischief. Today, no outlaw would be able to hide in Sherwood Forest, for barely 4 square kilometres remain of what was once a sprawling royal hunting ground. The most beautiful part is the Sherwood Forest Country Park near Edwinstowe, whose main attractions are its ancient oak trees. Legend has it that Robin Hood kept his stash under the largest of them, known as Major Oak. What is certain is that it is between 800 and 1,000 years old, and has long required numerous supports to keep it upright. Anyone wanting to do more than just retrace Robin Hood's footsteps should attend the medieval festival dedicated to the famous archer every August.

* Nottingham It was in this lively university town that William the Conqueror had a castle built on a sandstone cliff. Several houses were also hewn into the rock at the time, including what is probably England's oldest pub, Ye Olde Trip to Jerusalem.

Sherwood Forest is the perfect place to take an extended stroll.

Discovering Derbyshire

Much of the county is taken up by the Peak District National Park – a paradise for ramblers and nature lovers. There are also many enchanting small towns to explore. Picturesque aristocratic estates such as Chatsworth House have inspired the likes of Jane Austen.

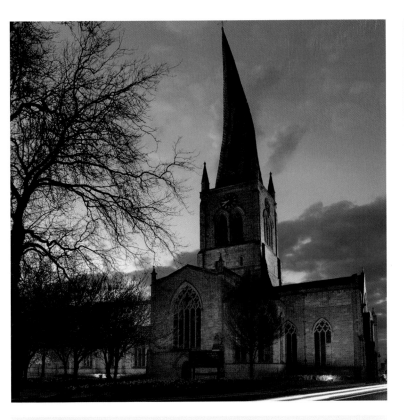

DERBYSHIRE
County town:
Matlock
Area:
2,625 sq km
Population:
1.05 million
Population density:
401 inhabitants/sq km

✻ INFO

Derwent Valley

In 1769, Richard Arkwright invented the water frame spinning machine, which was powered solely by a water wheel, without any human intervention. The invention was destined to not only change the production industry, but also the nature of work and people's lives. It was first used in the factories of Cromford, heralding the start of the Industrial Revolution. The Derwent Valley industrial region sprawls for some 25 kilometres along the River Derwent, from Masson Mill to Lombe's Silk Mill in Derby via Matlock Bath. The silk factory has been converted into an industrial museum. A cultural monument, it also includes the Darley Abbey industrial village, whose 18th and 19th-century machinery and buildings are fascinating from both a technical and historic perspective.

** **Chesterfield** Anyone seeing Chesterfield's main landmark for the first time will barely be able to believe their eyes. The tall, tapering spire of St Mary's Church is not only twisted, but also tilts perilously to one side. What looks like a dashing hennin hat is in fact a wooden structure dating back to the 14th century. There is some dispute as to how it came to look the way it does today. While the twisting may even have been a deliberate artistic move, it is more likely to have been caused by the uneven atrophy of poorly seasoned wood, combined with the pressure of heavy lead plates, which replaced oak-shingle roofing in the 17th century. Apart from the church, Chesterfield also has a quaint town centre featuring many old buildings and a historic market hall. A museum provides information on aspects such as the town's Roman origins and railway pioneer George Stephenson.

* **Derby** At the very heart of the Industrial Revolution, Derby has a rich history, which can be traced at places such as the Industrial Museum. The cathedral houses one of the world's oldest glockenspiels, while the Derby Museum & Art Gallery exhibits important works by famous painter Joseph Wright. Last but not least, Derby is also said to be home to the best ale, so make sure you sample some for yourself.

The crooked spire of the Church of St Mary's and All Saints in Chesterfield (above) is sure to attract visitors' attention.

*** Chatsworth House

Lovers of period dramas will probably have seen Chatsworth House on the silver screen. The 175-room building, designed in the Neoclassical English Baroque style, is one of the most magnificent stately homes around, and for centuries has been the residence of the dukes of Devonshire. In the film adaptation of Jane Austen's *Pride and Prejudice* (2005), actress Keira Knightley marvels at the Neoclassical sculptures amassed by the 6th duke, while in *The Duchess* (2008), she plays his scandal-ridden mother. In addition to the magnificently appointed rooms and the art collections, the gardens at Chatsworth are also rather special. It was here that the nation's most

The Neolithic complex of Arbor Low is said to be more than 3,000 years old.

The opulent interior of Chatsworth House.

inhabitants here established a complex with an oval ringfort, a moat and an irregular, egg-shaped set of standing stones, inside of which a very small inner circle still exists. An otherwise unadorned tomb has been found underneath. In the immediate vicinity is a large hill, Gib Hill, which is estimated to be even older than the stone circle of Arbor Low. Together, they form part of England's best-preserved henge complex, and are occasionally also referred to as the Stonehenge of the North. But Arbor Low is not as impressive as the world-famous site near Salisbury – because none of the large stone blocks stands upright. Whether or not they did in the past is disputed. Other smaller circle complexes can be found nearby, around Stanton-in-Peak and Chatsworth House.

famous landscape designers Capability Brown and Joseph Paxton set their hand to gardening. Paxton, for example, created a model village, the tallest fountain (90 metres) of his day, and innovative greenhouses.

*** **Arbor Low** Perched atop a limestone plateau in the south of the Peak District National Park is one of the mysterious stone circles for which England is so famous. In the second half of the 3rd millennium BC, the

The fairy-tale-like Chatsworth estate on the River Derwent (top) is the residence of the Duke of Devonshire, and has been owned by the Cavendish family since 1549.

In 2016, ballet dancers from the Claire Dobinson School of Dancing performed The Nutcracker *at Chatsworth House.*

*** Peak District National Park

The Peak District, surrounded by the industrial cities of Manchester, Sheffield and Stoke-on-Trent, is England's oldest national park. Yet the towns-people had to force their way into the country-side. It was only through an illegal mass trespass of Kinder Scout in 1932 that the private estate, predominantly owned by the 9th Duke of Devonshire, finally became accessible to the public. Rambling continues to be the most popular sport in the Peak District, though it is also a haven for cyclists, horse riders, climbers and paragliders. While the northern part around the 636-metre-high Kinder Scout (the Dark Peak) is dominated by vast heaths and raised bogs, remote peaks and spectacular rock formations (the White Peak) in the south present a scenic hilly landscape of limestone plateaus, wooded valleys and attractive small villages.

*** Mam Tor

In just under three hours, ramblers can follow a 5-kilometre-long trail up to the Mam Tor or Mother Hill. They are rewarded with one of the best and most breathtaking views of the national park. As you climb, you can also trace back the mountain's evolution based on the different layers of rock.

The impressive Winnats Pass leads through steep limestone crevices.

Losehill Pike at sunset.

The Crow Stones rock formations.

Megalith complexes in the Peak District

The 20 or so stone circles found in the part of the Peak District date back to the time of 3,000 to 1,500 BC. Barbrook I, accessed via a hiking trail, is very well preserved. The tiny circle is made up of 12 stones, the largest being 1.3 metres tall and marking the point of the winter solstice. Hordron Seven Stones on the Moscar Moor is another example of a stone circle. It comprises some 20 stones, though only half stand upright. Among the better-preserved complexes is the Nine Ladies Stone Circle in the south-eastern corner of the Peak District. It measures around 10 metres in diameter. Close by is Doll Tor, which is lined with trees and covered in grass and moss. This circle is comparatively young, dating back to 1,800 BC.

Peak District National Park

It is as if the ruins of Peveril Castle (on the left in the picture) have fused with nature. They are the remains of what is probably the oldest Norman fortress on English soil, built by Henry II in 1176.

From the top of the imposing ruins, you can enjoy breathtaking views of Hope Valley. In addition to old castles, the Peak District National Park also offers a number of other exciting experiences.

West Midlands

The region around Birmingham does not usually top the list of must-sees for visitors to England. Yet it offers an amazing array of interesting towns and buildings as well as diverse landscapes. Shakespeare was born here, the first ever cast-iron arched bridge across the Severn was built here, and Coventry rose like a phoenix from the ashes after World War II. While history has left its mark, no other region is a more vivid example of innovation resulting from misfortune.

Discovering Warwickshire

Visitors to this county can follow in the footsteps of England's most famous bard: Stratford-upon-Avon is where William Shakespeare was born and where the Royal Shakespeare Company brings his dramas to life on stage. The imposing Warwick Castle, meanwhile, will make you feel as if you've stepped back into the Middle Ages.

** Stratford-upon-Avon Nowhere else on earth is William Shakespeare more venerated by his international fan base than in his home town. Almost everything here appears to revolve around 'The Bard' – the medieval house where he was born, via the strangest souvenirs, to the modern Royal Shakespeare Theatre, where the best actors in the country show off their skills. This bustling small town would still be worth a visit, however, even without its most famous son. The old half-timbered houses have been attractively spruced up, the beautiful parklands provide the perfect place to stop and relax, and cruises enable visitors to explore the picturesque River Avon. Or they can head to Charlecote Park, the country house where Sir Thomas Lucy is said to have once caught the bard poaching and convicted him of the crime, prompting Shakespeare to immortalize him as a judge in *The Merry Wives of Windsor*.

* Rollright Stones These three prehistoric rock formations perched above an escarpment in the Cotswold Hills, on the borders of Warwickshire and Oxfordshire, are steeped in mystery thanks to an eerie folktale, making them a place of worship for modern pagans. The story revolves around a witch who, upon encountering a king passing with his army, promised him that if he continued and was able to see the village of Long Compton after seven strides, he would become the king of all England. This seemed like an easy task, until the witch suddenly conjured up a mound that blocked his view, turning all the men to stone. The king stands as the solitary King Stone, while his 77 soldiers form a circle as The King's Men. Further away are four conspirers, the Whispering Knights. The purpose of the stone circle, erected around 2,500 BC, remains unclear, for it was a closed ring, with the stones touching each other.

William Shakespeare lies buried at Stratford's Holy Trinity Church (right). If you have time to spare, take a walk along the tranquil River Avon.

WARWICKSHIRE
County town:
Warwick
Area:
1,975 sq km
Population:
571,000
Population density:
289 inhabitants/sq km

INFO *

William Shakespeare was born in Stratford-upon-Avon in 1564.

Grand Union Canal

The construction of canals to transport goods played a significant role in northern England's early economic boom. To limit costs, most canals were kept relatively narrow, securing passage for the still commonly used narrowboats, which could not be wider than 2.13 metres. As time went on, people naturally began thinking about a canal connecting the Midlands with London. In 1790, the Oxford Canal was built, linking Coventry with the upper reaches of the Thames. Its extension to Birmingham saw it become the 220-kilometre-long Grand Union Canal, featuring 166 locks. When the movement of goods progressed to road and rail in the 20th century, it no longer made sense to extend the canal further. It has been used by houseboat owners and holiday-makers ever since.

The Rollright Stones in the Cotswold Hills.

William Shakespeare

Shakespeare is an icon of Britain and the entire literary world. Many legends surround his life and works, due in no small part to the fact that none of them were preserved in manuscript form. Did he actually write all those world-renowned dramas and sonnets, or was it the nobleman Francis Bacon using a pseudonym? Some researchers believe the latter was behind historic dramas such as *King Lear*, comedies like *Much Ado About Nothing*,

and even *Romeo and Juliet*, the ultimate romantic drama. Others surmise they may have been written by Christopher Marlowe. The only thing we know for sure is that, on 23rd April 1564, a son named William was born to glovemaker John Shakespeare in the small town of Stratford-upon-Avon. Very little is known about his education or work until 1592, when he is first mentioned as being a London-based actor and playwright. In subsequent years we can reconstruct his career path: he was a member of famous acting troupes, performing for Queen Elizabeth I, becoming the co-owner of the Globe Theatre in London, making friends with influential men, withdrawing from the theatre scene around 1610, and returning to Stratford, where he died in 1616. His works had a global impact, and have even been immortalized by Hollywood.

*** Warwick What happens when one of the largest castles in England is taken over by the Tussauds Group? It becomes one of the most visited attraction in the country! Warwick Castle is today marketed as 'the greatest medieval experience' – with jousting tournaments, siege engines and re-enacted scenes from castle life. The outer courtyard is flanked by two towers – Caesar's Tower and Guy's Tower – and provides access to the medieval inner courtyard. The climb to the battlements is rewarded with a superb view over the Avon Valley. There is also a cabinet of wax figures, as is to be expected from Madame Tussaud's company, showcasing the life of the aristocracy in fully restored rooms. Those not prepared to pay the entry fees can head to the Avon Bridge to enjoy a view of the castle from afar. The buildings can hardly be seen from the centre of Warwick – which is incidentally also well worth a visit.

The Norman keep today still dominates the ruins of Kenilworth Castle, which looks back on more than 900 years of history.

View of the Collegiate Church of St Mary in Warwick.

The façade of Lord Leycester Hospital features attractive half-timbering.

* Kenilworth Castle The red sandstone towers and imposing ruins attest to the castle's importance and long history. Constantly modified and extended from the time of its founding during the Norman era until well into the Tudor age, the castle was surrounded by water for protection. It was considered the strongest fortress in central England, before being converted into a residential building in the 16th century. Kenilworth Castle was destroyed after the English Civil War, with only a farmstead left among the ruins. This farmstead soon established itself as a daytrip destination for romanticists. It was invoked in Sir Walter Scott's 1821 novel *Kenilworth,* about a visit by Queen Elizabeth I to her admirer Robert Dudley, Earl of Leicester, whom she nearly sent into financial ruin with her 19-day stay in 1575.

The Red Drawing Room of Warwick Castle is said to be haunted.

The view of mighty Warwick Castle (top) from the River Avon.

Armour and weapons are displayed in the Great Hall.

Discovering the County of West Midlands

From theatres and exhibitions, through cricket and football games, Indian restaurants and shopping centres, to enchanted forests and charming valleys – anyone visiting the West Midlands should be prepared to enjoy plenty of culture and nature.

INFO *

WEST MIDLANDS
County town:
Birmingham
Area:
902 sq km
Population:
2.9 million
Population density:
3,233 inhabitants/sq km

*** Coventry The name of this once beautiful half-timbered city is synonymous with the Coventry Blitz, the devastating air raids and fire bombs dropped by the German Luftwaffe on 14th November 1940. But Coventry equally stands for the supreme quest for reconciliation, with 26 twin towns in Europe, North

Transport Museum on Millennium Square.

America, Asia and Australia. One of these is Dresden in Germany, which suffered a similar fate through Allied bombing. There is also the symbolic Coventry Cross, whose nails come from the roof of the destroyed cathedral, although the tall spire among was miraculously preserved, and had a new cathedral built around it in 1962. Coventry's history also features the motor car, which is recounted at the Transport Museum. Opposite the museum is Millennium Square with the Whittle Arch – projects carried out as part of The Phoenix Initiative to make the city centre more attractive again.

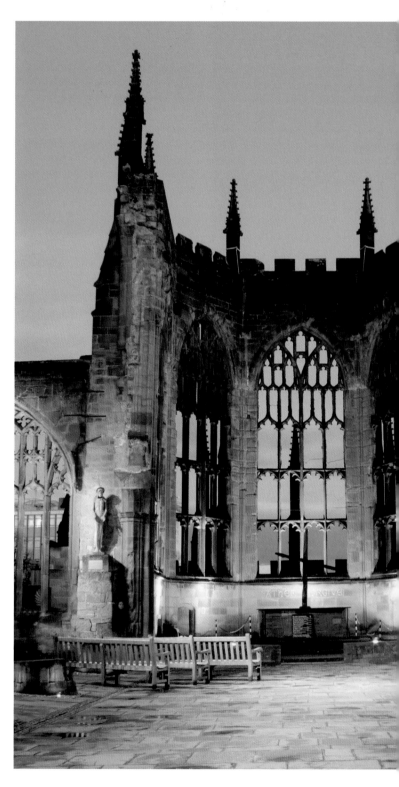

Coventry Cathedral

The official name of the modern place of worship is the Cathedral Church of St Michael. Two churches previously stood on the site, though very few traces remain of St Mary's, a 12th-century priory cathedral. It was followed in the 14th century by the Gothic St Michael's Cathedral, which was almost entirely destroyed by bombing raids in World War II. Today, its imposing ruins and two crosses – the Charred Cross and Cross of Nails – serve as a reminder of this. In 1962, architect Sir Basil Spence created the 'new' cathedral next to the old one, and it displays art and architecture from the 1950s and 1960s. Visitors can also climb the cathedral tower and enjoy the view over Coventry, or indulge in English tea and cake at the cathedral café.

The Whittle Arch at the Transport Museum is the work of MJP Architects.

*** Birmingham

England's second largest city has gone through a substantial transformation in recent decades. The city's smoking chimneys were once synonymous with its contribution to the Industrial Revolution. Today it is a modern service-providing metropolis and lively melting pot of diverse cultures. A large section of the population comes from the Indian subcontinent, the Caribbean and Ireland. In addition to historic Victorian splendour, Birmingham also offers modern shopping facilities as well as numerous theatres and art galleries. It also draws its charm from the many canals around Brindleyplace, which criss-cross 'Brum', the nickname derived from the city's local name

The Bullring was designed by Benoy architecture, planning and design studio.

The city library is one of Birmingham's most popular attractions.

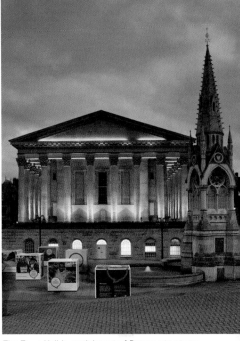

The Town Hall is reminiscent of Roman structures.

of 'Brummagem'. Riding one of the traditional narrowboats through the 60-kilometre-long canal system is an experience in itself.

** **Council House** The land on which Council House stands today was acquired by the city in 1853. Yeoville Thomason won the architecture competition to build the council house, and the adjacent art museum and old Big Brum clock tower consequently also underwent renovation work when construction began in 1874. Ashley & Newman architects further extended the building in 1911. These days, Council House at Victoria Square is one of the most impressive buildings in the historic centre.

** **Town Hall** This has been the central hub of the city's cultural scene for more than 180 years: concerts ranging from classical music to rock and pop, lectures, readings, and student graduation ceremonies all find a suitable setting here.

*** **Library of Birmingham** One of the city's flagship projects, the library is the largest in Britain and holds more than 400,000 books, including the most significant collection of Shakespeare's works in the world. The library is also a prized cultural space, hosting permanent collections, as well as regular presentations and exhibitions.

* **Bullring & Grand Central** This super-sized shopping centre – home to more than 140 different stores and 40 restaurants – will get any shopaholic excited. Trade has been the focus of activity here since the Middle Ages. The present-day complex is also an architectural highlight: only the Selfridges store in London has won more awards.

National Sea Life Centre

People of all ages can get up close and personal with the fascinating underwater world at this aquarium, designed by Sir Norman Foster and located alongside Birmingham's canal. Swimming in its giant tanks, containing a million litres of water, are more than 2,000 marine-dwellers from all over the world, including green sea turtles, blacktip reef sharks and colourful coral-reef fish. One of the aquarium's main highlights is its fully transparent, 360-degree underwater tunnel. Another unique attraction is 'Penguin Ice Adventure', which opened in 2014. There is nothing but a glass wall separating visitors from the colony of cute Gentoo penguins here. The 'Octopus Hideout' is also relatively new, and includes a giant Pacific octopus.

Birmingham boasts a fascinating mix of historic buildings and modern architecture. The town hall with The River sculpture (opposite top), locally also known as 'Floozie in the Jacuzzi', by the artist Dhruva Mistry.

*** Birmingham Museum and Art Gallery

Birmingham is particularly proud of its impressive museum, which houses a number of different galleries. This Victorian building in the heart of the city attests to the extraordinary self-confidence of the local citizens, many of whom benefited from the Industrial Revolution. The art gallery is famous for its pre-Raphaelite collection, although it also showcases a number of Old Masters. An absolute highlight of the history collections, which range from Antiquity to contemporary local history – is the Staffordshire Hoard, the largest treasure trove of Anglo-Saxon gold objects ever found. Those wanting to take a break in style – even without visiting the museum – should head to the Edwardian Tearooms on the upper level. The magnificent room hosts elegant breakfasts and traditional afternoon teas with delicious scones, sandwiches and cakes.

* Aston Hall

This impressive manor was built in the Jacobean style which characterized the second phase of the Renaissance in the United Kingdom. Aston Hall was built from red brick between 1618 and 1635, a few miles north of the city centre in the Aston district. Its variety of gables, turrets and bay windows attests to a very free and creative take on classic structures. Inside, the community museum boasts original wood panelling and stuccoed ceilings, but also a hole in the staircase, caused by a cannon ball during the English Civil War. The exhibitions are centred on the 17th century and the hall's former owners, such as James Watt Junior, who lived on the estate from 1817 to 1848 and further developed his father's steam engine inventions. And if your head starts spinning from so much

English landscape painting: February Fill Dyke *(1881) by Benjamin Williams Leader.*

The Edwardian Tearoom at Birmingham Museum and Art Gallery is perfect for a break.

The Round Room at Birmingham Art Gallery.

The Jacobean Aston Hall is one of Birmingham's splendid museums.

history, why not head to the lovely Renaissance Garden to recharge.

*** Botanical Gardens The botanical gardens in the Birmingham district of Edgbaston are a haven of rest and relaxation from what has now become a hectic metropolis. Opened in 1832, they still retain the feel of a Victorian public park with bandstand and various areas organized by theme, region or ecosystem. Coupled with this are greenhouses, which creatively showcase flora from southern climatic zones – from the tropics and subtropics, the arid zone, and the Mediterranean. Also worth a visit is the Butterfly House, whose flowers and inhabitants gleam in all manner of colours. Things get Zen in the Japanese Garden, which not only features plants and stones from Japan, but also England's most distinguished collection of bonsais. The Omiya Tree, designed in accordance with traditional ideals, is already 250 years old.

The Industrial Gallery (top) at Birmingham Museum & Art Gallery.

Lavender lines the entrance to the rose garden at Aston Hall.

Dudley Castle dates back to the 12th century.

** Black Country Living Museum

Anyone wanting to travel back in time will enjoy an exciting day out at this large open-air museum in Dudley. The Black Country north and west of Birmingham is generally considered the heartland of the Industrial Revolution due to its coal mines. It was here that the first steam engine started operation, iron and steel goods were made on a large scale, and all kinds of metal products were manufactured. Historic trolley buses take visitors back and forth between the themed centres, to old mines, metal workshops and the museum port on the canal – everything on display here comes from the region. Attractions of particular note include the true-to-original reconstruction of an early-20th-century village and a street from the 1930s, in which actors realistically portray how people lived and worked in this area during the late 19th and early 20th century. The museum was used as the setting for the TV series *Peaky Blinders*, among others.

The imposing ruins of Dudley Castle.

Perrott's Folly

Although at first glance it may be reminiscent of a 19th-century water tower, the striking structure with great views of Rotton Park was in fact erected much earlier. Also known as The Monument or The Observatory, it was built in 1758 by a certain John Perrott, who hailed from nearby Belbroughton. Stories abound as to why he had the tower built – was it to keep a better eye on his estates, to spot game or to impress his guests? Some also believe that he wanted to use the tower to see the grave of his deceased wife some 24 kilometres away. The tower is said to have influenced the tales of J. R. R. Tolkien, who grew up very close by. It is telling that it is called a 'folly' – a costly ornamental building with no practical purpose.

* Dudley Castle

This medieval castle on the eastern border with Worcestershire has been repeatedly destroyed and rebuilt. It was definitively shaped by its last redesign, initiated by the ever-active John Dudley, who was the virtual ruler of England from 1549 to 1553, during the minority of Edward VI. After Edward's death, Dudley bit off more than he could chew by plotting against Edward's half-sister Mary Tudor – an act for which he was executed. In 1646, after the English Civil War, all of the castle's fortifications were destroyed. What was left of the buildings was used for agriculture, before these too were burned down in 1750. The picturesque ruins soon attracted romanticists, who used them as sets for all kinds of historical spectacles in the 19th and 20th centuries. The visitors' centre presents the castle's history in a captivating manner, including ghost walks and a virtual tour of the castle as it was in 1550.

Discovering Worcestershire

The county best known around the world for its Worcestershire sauce boasts a number of recreational facilities in a spectacular natural setting, with picturesque towns and majestic manor houses nestled amongst the romantic English landscape.

This unusual Chinese bridge can be found in Croome Park.

** Worcester Established as a Roman military camp on the eastern banks of the River Severn, the town of Worcester experienced a new heyday during Anglo-Saxon times, and by 680 it was already a priory with a bishop's see. Over the centuries, the cathedral then acquired features from different eras, ranging from the Norman crypt, via the round Chapterhouse, Gothic chancel and chapels, to the Perpendicular cubicles that existed at the time when the monastery was dissolved and converted into an Anglican diocese. The final battle of the English Civil War, in which Oliver Cromwell defeated King Charles II, who narrowly escaped to France, took place near the city in 1651. Worcester also became best known for its spicy sauce, which chemists John Lea and William Perrins first made through systematic fermentation in 1838. Royal Worcester porcelain is also well known.

Although it is no longer made in Worcester, you can admire it in a collection at Worcester Porcelain Museum.

* Croome Court & Park The former home of the 6th Earl of Coventry, Croome Court exhibits historic objects, such as furniture, ceramics and paintings that once formed part of this country estate. The mansion is also

Malvern Hills

The Malvern Hills, reaching a height of some 400 metres, sprawl picturesquely between Gloucester and Worcester, their silhouettes providing a foretaste of the rugged terrain that lies further west over the nearby Welsh border. The jagged contours stand out sharply from the low-lying valleys of the meandering River Severn, contrasting starkly with the gently rolling Cotswolds. The Malvern Hills were originally volcanic, and were created some 650 million years ago. They acquired their present-day form through the weathering of softer rock. The 'bare hills', as their name likely means in Breton (Celtic origin), offer a wide variety of rambling trails. The town of Great Malvern is famed for its excellent spring water, which amongst others attracted royal visitors, including the family of the German emperor more than 100 years ago.

INFO *

WORCESTERSHIRE
County town:
Worcester
Area:
1,741 sq km
Population:
592,000
Population density:
340 inhabitants/sq km

home to contemporary works of art and sculptures, which are housed in the Long Gallery, designed by Robert Adam. The mansion perfectly combines Croome Court's historic interior with the modern art on display, allowing visitors to experience its history through a unique fusion of old and new. After spending time exploring the inside, the Walled Gardens and vast parklands are a wonderful place to enjoy a relaxed walk. The attractions here include the Panorama Tower, Dunstall Castle and the Park Seat.

Croome Court (above) is dwarfed by the surrunding borders and woodlands. The park invites you to take long walks.

A postcard picture – Worcester Cathedral dominates the banks of the River Severn.

Discovering Herefordshire

Both nature and culture lovers will get their fill here – whether it be participating in various sporting activities, discovering the lovely half-timbered houses on the Black and White Trail, or learning interesting facts about cider on the Cider Route.

HEREFORDSHIRE
County town:
Hereford
Area:
2,180 sq km
Population:
192,000
Population density:
88 inhabitants/sq km

* Hereford The region where the River Wye curves eastward through the heart of England has always been characterized by agriculture, and known for good cider and Hereford cattle, the most commonly farmed breed of beef cattle in the world. So it is no wonder that strategically important Hereford, whose name is said to come from Anglo-Saxon *here* (army) and *ford* (place for crossing a river), and which is located near the Welsh border, soon became a wealthy city. This is evident in its beautiful half-timbered buildings and burgher houses, as well as its Norman cathedral and valuable collection of books. It is indeed home to the largest preserved medieval world map, the *Mappa Mundi* (1290), and it is fascinating to see how Europe, Asia and Africa are depicted in a circle, with Jerusalem at its centre, in keeping with salvation history.

*** Hampton Court Unlike the royal palace of the same name, this estate presents an epoch-spanning penchant for medieval scenes, coupled with classic English horticulture that appears to attract couples on their wedding day. Hampton Court was created as a result of two properties being merged under Henry IV, who had his knight, Sir Rowland Lenthall, erect the castle-like buildings in 1427. They were not intended to serve a military purpose, but still had battlements that had to be specially approved by the king. In the early 18th century, the property was taken over by the Arkwright family of textile entrepreneurs, who, in the 1830s and 1840s, had it modified and fitted

The golden autumn season is the perfect time to visit Hampton Court and its parklands.

out in the popular Neogothic style of the time. To this day, the fairy-tale-like estate, with its award-winning gardens, remains privately owned, with diverse offerings for visitors.

Hereford is still home to 17th-century half-timbered houses (opposite top). The city's amnazing cathedral (top) dates back to the 12th century.

Dore Abbey

A fascinating abbey in Herefordshire's Golden Valley, Dore Abbey was once a Cistercian abbey, and it is still possible, to this today, to make out precisely where the former living quarters and chapter house once stood. The abbey garden is a place of rest and recreation. The first monks lived here in 1147, and, in the 13th and 14th centuries, Dore became known across large parts of Europe for its top-quality sheep's wool. The church building was saved following the Reformation under Henry VIII, and was restored in 1630 by John Scudamore. Today, Dore Abbey remains one of the few places of worship to be characterized by 17th-century Laudianism. Sections of the medieval altar, the stained-glass windows and wall murals are among the original elements to have been preserved.

The garden at Hampton Court.

Discovering Shropshire

The cradle of the Industrial Revolution and modernity, Shropshire is home to the first cast-iron bridge, and Shrewsbury was the birthplace of Charles Darwin in 1809. Far from bustling cities, the idyllic county offers plenty of opportunities for rest and recreation.

INFO*

SHROPSHIRE
County town:
Shrewsbury
Area:
3,487 sq km
Population:
498,000
Population density:
143 inhabitants/sq km

The remarkable Stiperstones.

* Stiperstones Legend has it that the devil did not like good people, especially children, so he scattered countless rocks across Shropshire to impede agriculture and cattle farming. One day, a giantess came along, liked the look of the stones, and consequently placed them all in her apron to take them home. But the furious devil cut the fabric, causing the stones to fall out of the giantess' apron and be scattered across the landscape once more – where they remain to this day.

** Caer Caradoc During the Iron and Bronze Ages, a defence fortification was built atop this iconic hill, giving it its name. The volcanic mound soars steeply out of the otherwise flat landscape, and can be climbed from both Church Stretton and Cardington. Parts of the ascent involve very sharp inclines.

* The Wrekin A popular hiking destination, this hill lies 16 kilometres north-east of Caradoc. Its geology is fascinating, with the rock made up of 600-million-year-old layers of lava.

The green hills of the Batch Valley in the Long Mynd near Church Stretton.

*** Shropshire Hills The hills in south-west Shropshire continue to be considered quiet and largely undiscovered today, in stark contrast to the rest of the farming-centred region. A long-extinct volcano, the Long Mynd and its narrow valleys, rises up near Bishop's Castle. The market town of Church Stretton, with its fascinating Carding Mill Valley, nestles so picturesquely amongst the hills that it proudly bears the nickname of 'Little Switzerland'. The Stiperstones rock formations, created by weathering, are another striking sight, lining an 8-kilometre-long ridge. An attractive rambling trail leads to Devil's Chair and Shepherd's Rock, perched at a height of 536 metres and providing a spectacular view of the mythical hill landscape. The Shropshire Hills are designated an Area of Outstanding Natural Beauty.

The iconic hill of Caer Caradoc gave its name to the Iron Age hillfort.

Caer Caradoc in the Shropshire Hills offers dramatic views of the surrounding landscape.

Shropshire Hills

The weather in the Shropshire Hills is often grey and rainy. But that doesn't bother the local sheep; on the contrary – the plentiful rainfall means the grass on the hills is lush and green.

*** Stokesay Castle

Power relationships in the 13th century were known to shift rapidly. Wealthy wool trader Laurence of Ludlow wanted to fortify his new manor in Stokesay for this very reason, receiving official permission to do so from the king in 1291. And so it was that a complex with two towers and high outer walls was built around a central courtyard, though, from a military perspective, it never achieved the status of a fort. The name Stokesay Castle was not adopted for another 200 years. After the English Civil War, only the front ring of walls was demolished, making the complex the best preserved of its kind today. Interesting examples of medieval craftsmanship abound here, such as the original roof beams of the Great Hall. In the 17th century, these were joined by the amazing half-timbered gatehouse and the authentically furnished private quarters.

Stokesay Castle includes a gatehouse (top, on the left) and two fortified towers (opposite top, on the right).

Stokesay is a jewel of medieval fortified manors, and its Solar Room displays wonderful wood carvings on its walls.

* River Severn The 354-kilometre-long River Severn and its tributaries have shaped western England since prehistoric times. Celts, Romans and Anglo-Saxons all settled here. And people and goods have been transported along it since time immemorial. Great Britain's longest river starts in Wales, bringing water from the Cambrian Mountains to rural Shropshire. In many of its sections, it meanders leisurely through quaint valleys, although it can also pick up the pace, such as in the UNESCO World Heritage Site of Ironbridge Gorge. In Worcester, the Severn then resumes its leisurely flow past the cathedral standing on its banks. It incorporates the River Avon in Tewkesbury, before reaching Gloucester, which was long the most important maritime trans-shipment port. The enormous 15-metre tidal range in the Bristol Channel becomes apparent here, and is the reason why, on its final section heading towards the Atlantic, the Severn is accompanied by a tide-independent canal. The Severn thus has the second-greatest tidal range in the world.

The River Severn forms a horseshoe as it winds its way through the valley near Newnham in Gloucestershire.

*** **Ironbridge Gorge** Ironbridge Gorge with the town of Coalbrookdale in Telford, near Birmingham, is one of the pioneering sites of the industrial age, and a World Cultural Heritage site since 1986. Ironbridge Gorge owes its name to the bridge built here on the orders of ironworks owner Abraham Darby III in 1779. It is home to the 'Stonehenge of the Industrial Revolution': the first iron bridge in history, which spans the Severn Valley here near Coalbrookdale, and which can still be used by pedestrians today. The nearby mines and coking plant are also open to the public, as are the railway installations that were built to enable nationwide transportation. These well-preserved systems form a vast museum landscape which vividly documents the start of the industrial age in England.

** **Wroxeter** The little village of Wroxeter lies in the heart of the country near the River

The hypocaust and a basilica wall have been preserved from the Roman settlement in Wroxeter.

Severn. It is hard to believe that the Romans first established a military camp here and then, in the early second century, Viroconium, the fourth largest town in Roman Britain. With as many as 15,000 inhabitants, it was both a front-line town and also an important trading centre for the entire region. Following the Romans' withdrawal, the town held its own under the Celtic Cornovii people until the end of the 7th century. A 7-metre-high wall of the basilica survived all the different eras, as did the foundations of the forum, market hall and thermae, which were unearthed during excavations. The true-to-original reconstruction of a Roman townhouse, along with a small exhibition on everyday life at the time, rounds off the perfect foray into the past.

The world's first iron bridge still stands and is in use today. It has spanned the River Severn near Coalbrookdale for nearly 250 years (top).

Ironbridge Gorge Museums

The following ten museums are run by the Ironbridge Gorge Museum Trust: Blists Hill Victorian Town, Enginuity, Jackfield Tile Museum, Coalport China Museum, Coalbrookdale Museum of Iron, Museum of the Gorge, Darby Houses, Tar Tunnel, The Iron Bridge & Tollhouse and Broseley Pipeworks. They all have one thing in common: England's industrial development in the late 19th and early 20th century. During the Victorian era, countless innovations and ground-breaking inventions were produced here. The settlements of Ironbridge, Coalport, Jackfield, Coalbrookdale and Broseley were shaped by a time in which human life sped up faster than it ever had before. This area is the cradle of the Industrial Revolution.

*** Attingham Park

This Neoclassical palace with its mighty portico stands solitary in a sprawling country park, as if in a landscape painting. Built on the country estate of politician Noel Hill in 1772, the palace's present-day appearance was largely the work of Hill's son Thomas, the 2nd Lord Berwick. The taste-fully appointed rooms are full of references to the ancient world – not least in the form of a vast collection of paintings. Few Englishmen have lived out their passion for Italy with such abandon as he did – to the great chagrin of the family, whom he sent into financial ruin in the process. In 1827, a large proportion of the palace's contents had to be auctioned off, which was not actually uncommon among English aristocracy. Fortunately, some pieces found their way back or were added later in the same style. Now perfectly restored, Attingham Park is today one of England's most popular historic houses.

Robert Clive's statue outside the market hall.

Shrewsbury Music Hall is lit up beautifully at night.

** Shrewsbury

The old town is almost entirely surrounded by a sweeping loop of the River Severn, and access has been protected by a castle since the 10th century. The well-fortified city played a key role in the wars against the Welsh. Edward I had his headquarters here when he eventually defeated the Welsh sovereigns in 1283 and had the last remaining princes executed. Heirs to the English throne have borne the title of Prince of Wales ever since. Over 600 half-timbered houses, some from the Middle Ages, attest to the days of the lucrative wool trade. They, along with St Mary's Church and its beautiful stained-glass windows, make for an enjoyable stroll through the town. Outside the library stands a monument to commemorate the city's most famous son: Charles Darwin.

Look into Attingham Park's painting gallery (large picture) from the entrance hall. Blue drawing room and Octagon (opposite). Painting gallery and dining room (top right).

Whittington Castle

The history of this castle begins in the 12th century, when Whittington was, for a time, part of the Kingdom of Wales. The region promptly rejoined England in the 13th century. Repeatedly destroyed and rebuilt, the castle was declared a ruin in 1392, and was not restored until the 18th/19th century under the ownership of Londoner William Lloyd. Since then, the gatehouse has been leased out to farmers, who today independently take care of the castle within the community. Evidence of a garden was recently discovered near the gatehouse, and attempts are now being made to replant it in the original style. While the moated Whittington Castle may be one of the lesser known English castles, it is definitely worth a detour.

Mammalia Pl. 1.

Charles Darwin

Charles Robert Darwin (1809–82) is considered one of the most prominent naturalists of the 19th century. After completing his theology studies, he undertook a five-year trip (1831–36) on the research ship *Beagle* at the recommendation of his botany professor John Henslow. The trip took him past the islands of Cape Verde, around the east and west coast of South America to the Galapagos Islands, and onwards to Tahiti, New

Desmodus D'Orbignyi.

Zealand, Mauritius, Cape Town and St Helena. During the trip, the young researcher made observations and collected samples of rocks, plants and animals. Darwin spent the rest of his life analysing his collections, which led to a wealth of new findings in the fields of geology, botany and entomology. His most outstanding achievement, however, was his theory of evolution, centred on a process of natural selection through different abilities to adapt to an environment. Darwin waited until 1858 to publish his revolutionary theory – the same year naturalist Alfred Russel Wallace published similar ideas. His groundbreaking work *On the Origin of Species* was released the year after, and *The Descent of Man* and *Selection in Relation to Sex* in 1871. Darwin died in 1882, and was buried in Westminster Abbey in London.

Discovering Staffordshire

While the Alton Towers theme park provides fun for the whole family, Stoke-on-Trent offers insights into the long tradition of ceramic production, and the nearby Trentham Estate and Gardens delights all those with green fingers.

View of Lichfield Cathedral through the Skidmore Screen (also on the right).

** **Lichfield** Unlike in most of the other nearby cities, industry never played a major role in Lichfield. To this day, the quaint town of half-timbered buildings is considered the intellectual and spiritual centre of the Midlands – in sharp contrast to Birmingham some 25 kilometres away. Lichfield owes this reputation to St Chad and the Christianization of the Kingdom of Mercia in the 7th century. The clever, devout bishop is buried in the Gothic cathedral, which replaced a predecessor building here in 1085. With its three striking spires, it is rightly considered the symbol of the city, though its interior is just as impressive, with chapels and the decagonal Chapter House. The beautiful Lichfield Angel and the Book of Chad, containing prayers and illustrations, date back to the 8th century. The handwritten notes are among the oldest to exist in the Welsh language. Also worth seeing are Christ Church and Lichfield Clock Tower.

INFO *

STAFFORDSHIRE
County town:
Stafford
Area:
2,620 sq km
Population:
875,200
Population density:
334 inhabitants/sq km

The Ancient High House on Greengate Street in Stafford.

* Stafford whose name translates as 'ford at the landing place', can trace its origins back to a sand and gravel bank in the middle of a large wetland area of the River Sow, a tributary of the Trent. Despite all conceivable measures having been taken, the market town today continues to struggle with flooding. Its strategic importance saw a stone castle erected here in the 14th century although this repeatedly fell into disrepair and had to be rebuilt.. The town became a centre of shoe production, mostly employing Irish families. These factories, and later also industrial production, propelled Stafford to international prominence, before the last of its factories closed in 2001. The Elizabethan Ancient High House, built in 1594, is a must on every visitor's list. England's largest half-timbered house is four storeys high and contains an impressive display of the history of Stafford. King Charles I briefly lived there in 1642, and the original Tudor furnishings can still be seen today.

National Memorial Arboretum

This arboretum at Alrewas, near Lichfield, is a place of remembrance, but also of looking ahead to the future. The gigantic country park is home to thousands of memorials to fallen soldiers and task forces, as well as 30,000 trees. An audio-guide takes visitors through the park, explaining the stories behind 90 of the 330 memorials. Guided tours can also be booked. At the same time you will learn interesting facts about the plants thriving here. Exhibitions, such as 'Landscapes of Life', provide people of all ages with background information on plants from all over the world. Particularly worth seeing is the Armed Forces Memorial, dedicated to all those who have been victims of war or terrorism since World War II, and the new Remembrance Centre.

*** Trentham Estate and Gardens

This sprawling recreational and country park, is located in a suburb of Stoke-on-Trent, a city famed for its pottery industry. The 120-hectare garden complex, boasting exquisite landscaping, has effectively become a pilgrimage site. Famous garden designers worked here and created the Upper Fower Garden, the Floral Labyrinth and Rivers of Grass. The large Italian Garden was painstakingly restored to its formal design from 1840 and refurbished again in the 21st century. The magnificent manor is still waiting its turn to be renovated. The park offers a number of different recreational facilities, including close-up encounters with wild monkeys in the Monkey Forest and precarious excitement thanks to the Treetop Adventures. The stylish Garden Centre and the Trentham Shopping Village of timber log cabins also attract many visitors.

* Alton Towers Theme Park

Founded in 1814 by the 15th Earl of Shrewsbury, and acquired in 1990 by the Tussauds Group, this theme park offers fun and games for young and old. It is the largest of its kind in Great Britain, and the summer months draw tens of thousands of visitors seeking to enjoy the more than 40 rollercoasters rides and attractions, including Wicker Man, The Smiler, Nemesis, Galactica, Oblivion as well as the most recent: Gangsta Granny: The Ride. One of the rollercoasters even includes an almost vertical drop. The waterpark is also popular.

Trentham's landscaping is influenced by Italian garden styles. Flower beds and water features, mazes and statues all make for an exquisite garden visit.

View of the Old Conservatory.

The Italian Garden in Trentham.

David Austin roses thrive in the gardens.

Yorkshire and the Humber

Windswept moors and heaths, wealthy industrial cities and bustling seaside resorts, ancient
culture and modern art: England's rugged north-east, between the mouth of the Humber and
the Tees Valley, is a land of contrasts. The ancient city of York, with its grand cathedral, is just as
captivating as the vibrant cultural scenes of the former industrial hubs of Leeds and Sheffield.
Ramblers will discover idyllic national parks and the ruins of mighty abbeys and castles.

Discovering South Yorkshire

Sheffield, the fourth largest city in England, has a lot offer its visitors. And the surrounding area is also home to aristocratic country estates and mighty castles.

** **Sheffield** This old steel metropolis with a population of half a million people rarely even gets a mention in the travel guides. But this is unfair, because today Sheffield is a lively university town that boasts a lot of exciting offerings for visitors. The parklands outside the imposing Neogothic town hall are home to large modern sculptures, while the city centre has the Winter Garden, a public greenhouse containing exotic plants, and the

Graves Gallery presents classic and contemporary masterpieces. The Millennium Gallery, meanwhile, houses artworks made from the material that brought the city its prosperity: metal. The Gothic cathedral is also worth a visit, although the Kehlham Island Museum and Abbeydale Industrial Hamlet are perhaps even more fascinating. Located some way out of the city, they both bring Sheffield's industrial past back to life.

** **Town Hall** Sheffield's Town Hall was opened in 1897, after seven years of construction. While the ornamentation on the façade drew criticism at the time, today the building is considered a fine example of Victorian architecture. The interior is generally not open to visitors – unless you are getting married there.

** **Sheffield Cathedral** Sheffield Cathedral doesn't stay stuck in the past; it is constantly

∗ INFO

SOUTH YORKSHIRE
County town:
Barnsley
Area:
1,552 sq km
Population:
1.4 million
Population density:
904 inhabitants/sq km

An egg-shaped Bessemer converter at the Kelham Island Museum.

changing. The first building, constructed in the 12th century, displays Norman style, can still be seen on sections of the eastern wall. Parts of the cathedral were rebuilt in the 15th and 19th centuries, and further modifications and extensive renovations are planned for the years to come.

** Millennium Gallery und Winter Garden Concrete and glass are the main materials used to build the Millennium Gallery, which opened in 2001. Housed inside are exhibitions on art, crafts and design. The award-winning Sheffield Winter Garden is also located in the centre of the city adjacent to the railway station, and is particularly popular on rainy days.

The Town Hall (top) is one of Sheffield's architectural highlights. The city offers its guests excellent theatres, including the Lyceum Theatre and the Crucible Theatre (right) designed by Burrell Foley Fischer. The Sheffield Christmas Market (opposite top).

Conisbrough Castle's watchtower is visible from afar.

*** Brodsworth Hall

Sylvia Grant-Dalton, the last chatelaine of Brodsworth Hall, died in 1988, leaving behind an exceptionally elegant country house whose interior and exterior had hardly changed since one of her husband's uncles had it built in the Italian style in the mid-19th century. In some of the rooms, however, it was hard to overlook the fact that the ravages of time had taken their toll. The charity English Heritage purchased the Grade I listed building, located about 8 kilometres north-weat of Doncaster and decided to preserve the estate in the condition it was in at the time. This allows visitors to witness the former grandeur, as well as its impermanence, and gain an impression of how many a wealthy family once lived in this ageing and excessively large house. No compromises were made with the elaborate gardens though; these have been recreated based on their original Victorian-era plans.

Cusworth Hall

This elegant Georgian manor was built in the mid-18th century for the Wrightson family, who were local landowners and politicians. In 1961, they handed over ownership to the regional district council, which decided to turn Cusworth Hall into a museum dedicated to life at every level of society in South Yorkshire. The grand estate hosts changing exhibitions and events on social history and everyday life. Its collection encompasses some 10,000 photographs and more than three times as many historic garments, household objects, tools, children's toys and other exhibits. The Hall attracts visitors with country fairs, historic re-enactments and wildlife events. The magnificent garden and a sprawling country park around the house are ideal places to take a walk.

** Conisbrough Castle This mighty castle on the southern banks of the River Don was erected in the 12th century to secure the Norman conquest of England. The 28-metre-high tower house – the donjon – is particularly worth mentioning. A hexagonal floor plan not found anywhere else in England gives the hefty building a surprising elegance, and earned Conisbrough Castle the reputation of being one of the finest examples of Norman defensive architecture in the UK. But neglect meant the castle began to fall into disrepair as early as the 16th century. In the early 19th century, the writer Sir Walter Scott renewed public focus on the romantic ruins by making them the setting for his world-famous novel *Ivanhoe*. Today, the ruins have been extensively restored and visitors can explore the rooms and walls without any concern.

You can immerse yourself in all the facets of the often fateful world of the English aristocracy at Brodsworth Hall (top).

Discovering West Yorkshire

The fact that this region was once the centre of coal, iron ore and wool production can be seen in much of its architecture. Cities such as Leeds and Bradford, along with the villages and landscapes that inspired the novels of the Brontë sisters, all vie for visitors' attention.

*** Yorkshire Sculpture Park A bare iron tree by Ai Weiwei, a one-eyed Buddha by Niki de Saint Phalle, the ambiguous interplay of *Two Large Forms* by Henry Moore, along with half a dozen other large sculptures, as well as black heads and bodies by Joan Miró, which contrast greatly with the Spaniard's trademark vibrant works, but are still distinctly 'Miró' – all of these can be found in Great Britain's first modern sculpture park, which was opened in the sprawling parkland of a historic 18th-century house south of Wakefield in 1977. Today, there are more than 100 large works of art by the masters of modern sculpture, including Barbara Hepworth, Eduardo Paolozzi and Damien Hirst, waiting to be explored on the 2 square kilometre site. In addition, there are temporary exhibitions, some of which take place outdoors, some in a former chapel or in modern galleries.

** National Coal Mining Museum Coal was the driving force behind the Industrial Revolution. Coal-mining in Great Britain reached its peak in 1913, with a haul of 287 million tonnes. Nearly 1.2 million people worked underground as miners. The south of Yorkshire was also a coalfield. When the Caphouse mine near Wakefield produced its last coal and closed in 1985, it was decided that a monument would be erected there to commemorate British coal-mining. The most exciting offering for visitors of any age are the various underground tours conducted by former miners, although the original machinery and exhibitions on social and industrial history also provide a vivid insight into the heyday of the coal industry. Encounters with pit ponies are an additional highlight for children of all ages!

The site of the National Coal Mining Museum contains many preserved relics from the prosperous coal-mining days (top). The Small Lie Stands Out (right) is a sculpture by the American artist and designer KAWS at the Yorkshire Sculpture Park.

INFO *

WEST YORKSHIRE
County town:
Wakefield
Area:
2029 sq km
Population:
2.3 million
Population density:
1143 inhabitants/sq km

Ten Seated Figures *by Magdalena Abakanowiczat in the Yorkshire Sculpture Park.*

Exquisite shops in magnificent arcades epitomize the Victoria Quarter in Leeds.

*** Leeds

A walk through Leeds city centre, with its many ornate Victorian buildings, reveals the wealth that the textile industry brought to the city in the 19th century. But unlike many other former industrial cities, the largest city in West Yorkshire managed the structural change very early on. Today, Leeds is a university town and the centre of a metropolitan area, home to around 3 million people who are able to enjoy a cultural scene unrivalled by any other town in northern England. Its many cultural spaces includes the Leeds Art Gallery, the City Museum and the Henry Moore Institute, as well as some first-class theatres. Industrial history is brought back to life at Armley Mills, which

nearby Kingston upon Hull. They had insisted on having a 61-metre-high bell tower, which remains one of the main landmarks of the city. The magnificent Neoclassical building has long ceased to be used as a town hall, however. Only the registry office still holds weddings here. Otherwise the building is used as a prestigious concert hall and exhibition centre.

*** **Victoria Quarter** The abundant use of colourful marble and gilded mosaics, as well as many wrought- and cast-iron features, coupled with the many columns, arcades, fountains and balconies, make this shopping area reminiscent of an Italian city. They all sit under colourful domed glass roofs that protect visitors from bad weather. The glamorous shopping arcades of the Victoria Quarter were created in the late 19th century by theatre architect Frank Matcham, exemplifying his flair for dazzling productions. It is definitely worth a stroll through the quarter, even if only for a window-shopping experience – the 70-odd stores comprise many expensive luxury brands such as Louis Vuitton, Vivienne Westwood, Mulberry and Tommy Hilfiger. Leeds also boasts a large pedestrian zone and half a dozen other shopping centres catering to people on less elevated budgets.

Leeds' former Town Hall is an imposing monument and impressive venue.

The magnificent organ in the Town Hall.

*** **Grand Theatre** When Scottish architect George Corson was commissioned to build a prestigious music theatre in 1877, he relied on his assistant, James Robinson Watson, who had visited continental Europe and seen the great opera houses there, such as Milan's La Scala. The result – as was so often the case in the late 19th century – was a vibrant mix of styles. Today you can take guided tours of the Grand Theatre and admire the Victorian grandeur, although perhaps even more highly recommended is a visit to the theatre for a performance by Opera North. One of England's best opera companies, it is known for its repertoire which includes both classical operas and extraordinary stage productions. The Northern Ballet enjoys a similarly excellent reputation.

was once the world's largest wool-spinning mill. Coupled with this are excellent shopping facilities and a wide range of high-quality restaurants, pubs and cafés.

** **Town Hall** When Queen Victoria inaugurated the new town hall in Leeds with great pomp and circumstance on 7th September 1858, the construction costs were nearly three times as high as originally planned. But it was the largest town hall in England. To achieve this feat, the city councillors had continually requested modifications to the design by the relatively young and as yet unknown architect Cuthbert Brodrick, who hailed from

Corn Exchange

Not even two years after his Town Hall had opened, architect Cuthbert Brodrick was commissioned by the city councillors to build a new, prestigious corn exchange. To do so, he drew inspiration from the *Halle aux blés* (Wheat Exchange), which the French architects Nicolas Le Camus de Mézières had designed as a 'temple of commerce' in the style of a Roman rotunda in 1763 and which had been retained in the later Commodities Exchange on the same site. For his Leeds project, Brodrick designed a large oval space surrounded by two galleries and topped with a spectacular, partially glazed domed roof. These days, the 60 rooms around the galleries contain shops rather than trading stations, although these shops are not chain outlets, but rather independent boutiques, stores and galleries.

** **Kirkstall Abbey** The imposing ruins of Kirkstall Abbey are located on the banks of the River Aire, in the Leeds district of the same name. During the Middle Ages, the Cistercian monastery was one of the largest landowners in England, but, like all English abbeys, it was dissolved following the establishment of the Anglican Church. Although the buildings were plundered and left to fall into disrepair, they are nevertheless much better preserved than most other abbeys, and today are still able to convey to visitors that a medieval monastery was not just a place of prayer, but also a complex enterprise that had to feed and look after hundreds of people. Another museum in the former gatehouse features a replica of a Victorian street, taking visitors on a journey back in time to experience the daily lives of ordinary people over the last few centuries.

*** **Royal Armouries Museum** As early as the 15th century, anyone curious to see the inside of the royal armoury at the Tower of London was able to do so for a fee. The Royal Armouries Museum in London became Great Britain's first museum, and one of the oldest museums anywhere. Over time, however, the British kings collected so many weapons and armaments from all corners of their empire that these could no longer be adequately presented at the Tower. In 1996, most of the collection was moved to a spectacular building at Leeds' old docklands, where visitors are now able to view impressive armaments rang-

This helmet was made for Henry VIII.

Display at the Royal Armouries Museum.

ing from German frog-mouth jousting helmets to Indian elephant armour and thousands of wartime, jousting and hunting weapons.

Thick columns support the vaulted stone ceiling at Kirkstall Abbey (opposite).

Roundhay Park

Spanning an area of nearly 300 hectares, Roundhay Park is considered one of the United Kingdom's largest city parks, and its diversity is appreciated by both locals and visitors alike. Each part of the park has its own theme, including the Canal Gardens, Friends Garden, Alhambra Garden and Monet Garden. It also has two lakes, and it is possible to fish in the larger of these. There is a whole host of other recreational offerings – a castle folly, playgrounds for children, a sledging hill, rowing lakes, as well as tennis courts, golf courses and sporting grounds, plus a skate park and various cafés. Equally popular is Tropical World, where colourful butterflies flutter through exotic plants, and koi carp splash about in pools formed by mini waterfalls.

*** Saltaire

The village of Saltaire is the largest fully preserved model settlement of the early industrial age. It reflects the 'philanthropic paternalism' of the Victorian era, when factory owners wanted to take care of their workers. On 20th September 1853, the industrialist Sir Titus Salt (1803–1876) opened his textile mill, known as Salts Mill, here on the River Aire, where all manner of wool was combed, spun and woven. Sitting at some 1,200 looms, the workers produced around 27 kilometres of fabric every day. Even more extraordinary was the workers' settlement that Salt went on to build around the factory; the industrial village featured well-equipped houses, a church, a school, a hospital, a park, a bathhouse and an establishment containing a library, meeting rooms and gym. The factory workers had access to all of these facilities. Saltaire, a historic example of humane industrialization, has been a UNESCO World Heritage Site since 2001.

** Cliffe Castle Museum

The museum housed in Cliffe Castle, which was built around 1880, covers a wide range of topics and exhibits. Visitors can learn about minerals and archaeology, as well as Victorian clothing and traditional crafts. Egyptian mummies are also displayed here, as are stained-glass windows designed by William Morris. In short, the castle has something for everyone's taste and interests, rounded off with changing exhibitions and a programme of courses and work-

These faces at the Cliffe Castle Museum date back to Celtic times.

The imposing main staircase inside Cliffe Castle.

Harewood House

The furniture in Harewood House is by Thomas Chippendale, the family portraits by Joshua Reynolds, the interior design by Robert Adam, and the landscaping by Capability Brown – when Edwin Lascelles began building his new country house in 1759, he hired the best artists and designers of the time. Money was not an issue, for Lascelles' father had accumulated great wealth through his Caribbean plantations and the slave trade. Even Queen Victoria was impressed by her visit to Harewood House and when, in 2016, ITV filmed *Victoria*, a series about the queen's younger years, Harewood House was given the honour of acting as a double for Buckingham Palace. Besides, what other English stately home can claim to have penguins?

shops. The greatest exhibit of all, however, is probably Cliffe Castle itself, a successful fusion of Victorian and Neogothic architecture. Outdoors, the parklands and playground are a great place to take a stroll or recharge after a visit to the museum.

The architecture in Saltaire Village (top) significantly influenced the development and design of parkland complexes.

Discovering North Yorkshire

England's largest county features picturesque towns and spectacular natural settings, while the city of York itself boasts quaint cobbled lanes and oodles of charm. The Yorkshire coast is home to stunning beaches and tranquil villages, and the scenery in the Yorkshire Dales, North York Moors and Herriot Country is utterly unique.

INFO

NORTH YORKSHIRE
County town:
Northallerton
Area:
8,053 sq km
Population:
615,000
Population density:
76 inhabitants/sq km

A red grouse on the moor.

The unusual karst landscape typical of Malham Moor.

*** Yorkshire Dales National Park
Anyone seeking solitude and views as far as the eye can see will love the Yorkshire Dales. The barren, hilly landscape of the Pennines, criss-crossed by river valleys, or dales, is characterized by sprawling pastures lined with ancient dry-stone walls. Climbing over these via one of the stiles or gates takes visitors into a rugged landscape of moors and heaths, with the odd windblown tree or bizarre rock formation protruding in between. Most of the area has been designated a protected national park. One of the best experiences to be had here is a hike along one of the many long-distance or circular footpaths in late summer, when the blossoming heather covers the hills in a deep purple. Among the more popular valleys is Wensleydale, home to the cheese of the same name, the ruins of Bolton Castle, and the television series *All Creatures Great and Small*.

** Gaping Gill
This cave was first discovered back in 1842, but it was another 53 years before it was explored in full by Edouard Martel. The subterranean cavern is one of the largest in England, and can only be visited during two periods each year, one week in May and one week in August, by prior appointment.

*** Cautley Spout
England's highest above-ground waterfall is located in the north-west area of the national park. But it's not just the 175-metre-high waterfall that makes the hike there worthwhile. On a clear day, the summits of the Howgill Fells provide panoramic views extending as far as the Lake District.

The Yorkshire Dales National Park has green hills, criss-crossed by grey limestone and a few gnarled trees. Two east-west valleys characterize the north of the park, while the tourist-magnet valleys stretch from north to south. View of Ingleborough mountain from Twistleton Scar End (above).

Haworth and the Brontë family

The year 1847 saw the release of a novel that sparked fierce discussion in Victorian England: *Wuthering Heights*. A family drama set in a desolate, inhospitable region of West Yorkshire, whose heroes are just as cold, wild and indeed forbidding as the landscape and unusual narrative style. While some critics were fascinated by the power of the tale, the majority were shocked by the destructive passions of the heroes, who

were not condemned by the author. The novel was published under the pseudonym Ellis Bell – the fact that this scandalous book had been penned by the reclusive daughter of a priest only became known later on. Even as a child, Emily Brontë had immersed herself in the fantasy worlds she, with her sisters Charlotte and Anne and her brother Branwell, conjured up in the loneliness of Haworth parsonage. Today, the three sisters' works rank as classics of English literature. Several films have been made of Emily's *Wuthering Heights* and Charlotte's *Jane Eyre*. The town of Haworth, where the sisters grew up, is home to the Brontë Parsonage Museum, and the hilly landscape west of the town is considered 'Brontë country'. Ramblers can follow in the footsteps of the protagonists from *Wuthering Heights*.

*** Studley Royal Park and Fountains Abbey

The Cistercian Fountains Abbey was founded by monks from York, and it ended up becoming one of the largest and wealthiest monasteries in the country through sheep farming and the wool trade. The 123-metre-long church, the 55-metre-high tower above the northern transept, and the adjacent monastery buildings have been largely preserved, albeit without a roof. The cloister, dormitory, refectory, the 100-metre-long undercroft (storage cellar) and other storage rooms give an idea of the size of the complex. After King Henry VIII dissolved all the monasteries in England in the 16th century, the complex fell

Fountains Abbey, one of the largest and best-preserved monasteries in England, has been a UNESCO World Heritage site since 1998.

into disrepair, before becoming part of the Studley Royal Park in the 18th century. Created in 1727, the Georgian park with its Octagon Tower, Temple of Piety and Moon Pond is one of the most magnificent in the country.

** Skipton Castle This grand castle complex, with its six mighty defence towers, on the southern edge of the Yorkshire Dales is one of the best preserved castles in all of England. It was built in the 12th century to secure the Norman conquest of England, and later served as an important base in the wars against the Scots. During the English Civil War, Lady Anne Clifford succeeded in keeping Oliver Cromwell's troops away from the castle for three long years, before finally negotiating a controlled handover. After Cromwell's death, Lady Anne had the castle renovated, without changing its fundamental character as a medieval fortress. The pleasant market town of Skipton is home to many artisanal shops, lovely cafés and restaurants as well as boat rides on the Leeds-Liverpool Canal.

Fountain Abbey's nave continues to impress visitors with its former grandeur– despite its grassy floor and open-air ceiling.

The entrance to the medieval Skipton Castle.

The interior courtyard of the castle complex.

*** York

This city on the River Ouse has been the heart of northern England since Roman times. It fell somewhat out of the spotlight during the Industrial Revolution of the 18th and 19th centuries, although this only makes it all the more attractive to tourists. The best place to start a visit it to take a walk along the almost completely preserved city wall, which provides a wonderful view of the skyline, with its great minster and 20 other medieval churches. Then allow yourself to get lost in the narrow lanes and alleyways between the half-timbered buildings that have grown warped and crooked over time, and which today house cafés and lovely little shops. York also has top-class museums, such as the world's largest railway museum, the Castle Museum with replicas of historic residential streets, and the Viking Centre, which provides insights into the days when York was the capital of the Viking kingdom of Yorvik during the 10th century.

*** The Shambles

Most of the buildings lining the historic lanes around The Shambles date from the 14th and 15th centuries, when butchers lived, worked and sold their wares in the timber-framed houses, and the alleyways were

The Shambles oozes medieval charm.

known as The Great Flesh Shambles. Today, a visit is a must for all tourists.

*** Low and High Petergate

The best places to take a city stroll in York are Low Petergate and

The National Railway Museum

The National Railway Museum has been a magnet for visitors ever since it opened in 1975. Over the years, railway collections from right around the country have been assembled here, and a separate branch was opened in Shildon in 2004 to provide more space for displays. More than 100 historic locomotives from around the world are housed at the museum, along with another 100 railway vehicles, as well as the saloon carriages of various kings and queens. Exhibits such as signs, uniforms, models and technical drawings provide an authentic insight into the history of rail transport and its impact on society in Great Britain. Free entry and special children's activities make the museum well worth a visit.

High Petergate, where the streets are lined with interesting shops and great restaurants and bars housed in Georgian buildings. During the summer months, the air is filled with the sounds of street musicians, while in winter, both locals and tourists alike head out to shop for Christmas gifts for their loved ones.

** **Bootham Bar** Anyone thinking that Bootham Bar is some kind of pub would be wrong: it was a gate that formed part of the city wall, and served as the main northern entrance to York. The medieval structure remains well preserved. Today, it is primarily the starting point for an exploration of the inner city on foot, as the gate is located at the start of High Petergate.

A festive atmosphere in High Petergate (opposite top). Bootham Bar is a popular starting point for city strolls (top).

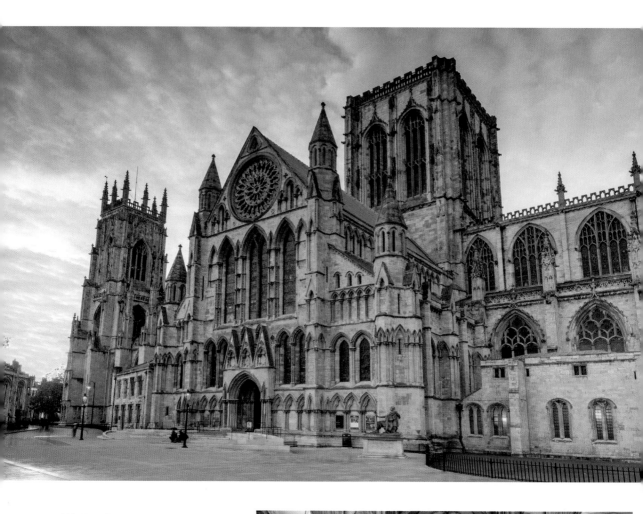

*** **York Minster** The minster, measuring almost 160 metres in length, is England's largest Gothic church. Its sandy-coloured buttress rises majestically and elegantly above the red rooftops of the old town. Its light interior features ceilings higher than those found in most other medieval churches. The different Gothic styles that were in fashion during its 250-year construction combine to form one harmonious whole. The stained-glass windows play an important role here: York is home to the greatest number, as well as the largest, medieval church windows in all of England. If you can, you should definitely climb the 72-metre-high central tower, and enjoy the breathtaking views over much of the county of Yorkshire that unfold between elegant battlements and curious gargoyles.

A bluish light filters through the stained-glass windows of York Minster.

** **York Castle Museum** In the 1930s it was John Kirk's vision to create a vibrant and interesting museum as an alternative to the very clinical museums that existed at the time, and he finally found the perfect space for it in the building that housed York's former women's

View of the illuminated York Castle Museum at night.

Jorvik Viking Centre

In the 1970s, a spectacular excavation took place in York, uncovering a number of arte-facts such as pottery and metal objects as well as bones and structural remains of tim-ber buildings from the Viking city of Jorvik. The discovery shed an important light on the way people lived more than 2,000 years ago. It prompted the launch of a project that laid the foundations for a very unique museum. Replica Viking homes and work-places were built, and lifelike mannequins added a face to that period of history. Bear-ing fictitious names, animated characters and actors talk about their life and work. A large part of the museum is also dedicated to the excavations. One of Britain's most popular attractions, not only does it present the finds, but it also allows visitors to see the reconstructed excavation site through a glass floor.

prison. His vision continues to impress visitors to this day in the changing exhibitions and, in particular, Kirkgate, a reconstructed Victorian street.

The largest Gothic cathedral in Britain, and seat of the Archbishop of York, the minster still manages to appear light and airy.

** Helmsley Castle

Among the previous owners of Helmsley Castle are the Earl of Rutland, the dukes of Buckingham, and the man who would later become King Richard III (1452–1485). But in 1644, during the English Civil War, the Parliamentarians were able to conquer the castle following a three-month siege. They destroyed the walls, towers and gates, meaning the castle could no longer be used as a defence fortification. In 1687, the Duncombe family bought the old castle, built a luxury manor in the immediate vicinity, and eventually left Helmsley Castle to decay and become a romantic ruin. The castle is now owned by English Heritage, and can be visited. Also worth seeing is the former kitchen garden of Duncombe Park next to the castle, which has been redesigned into an absolute showpiece, with spectacular gardens, parklands and a nature reserve.

Castle Howard

England is without doubt the land of magnificent historic houses. And Castle Howard, some 20 kilometres north-east of York, is a unique example from the Baroque period. The castle served as the home of the aristocratic Howard family for several generations. Today, visitors can explore the manor on their own, taking a step back in time as they do so. If you have any questions, you can consult the experienced guides who stand guard in the various rooms and are more than happy to explain the history of the castle and the family. As is so often the case, the property also includes vast parklands featuring rose gardens, fountains and a nearly-30-metre-high mausoleum.

*** Rievaulx Abbey Located in the picturesque Rye Valley, not far from Helmsley Castle, and easily accessible on foot via a
4-kilometre-long signposted hiking trail, are
the romantic ruins of Rievaulx. England's oldest Cistercian abbey, it was founded in 1130
and, like Helmsley Castle, was deliberately
allowed to fall into romantic disrepair in the
17th century. But its decay also provides new
insights because, not only are the majestic
ruins well worth a visit, but the adjacent
museum houses some of the finest stonemasonry that is usually not visible as it is hidden
far up in the buttresses or adorning the vaults
in the form of keystones. The fascinating artworks include friezes depicting intricate
scenes, bizarre figures and filigree ornamentation – all crafted with the utmost precision,
as, at the time, people firmly believed God
could also see what was hidden to the human
eye. The museum also houses chess figures
and gold coins, providing an idea of how the
monks may have lived at the time.

*Rievaulx Abbey (opposite and right) has only
survived as a ruin. Here, the sunrays cast
their atmospheric light on the remains of
the former Cistercian abbey and the beauty
of its dilapidated state.*

Helmsley Castle seen from Duncombe Park.

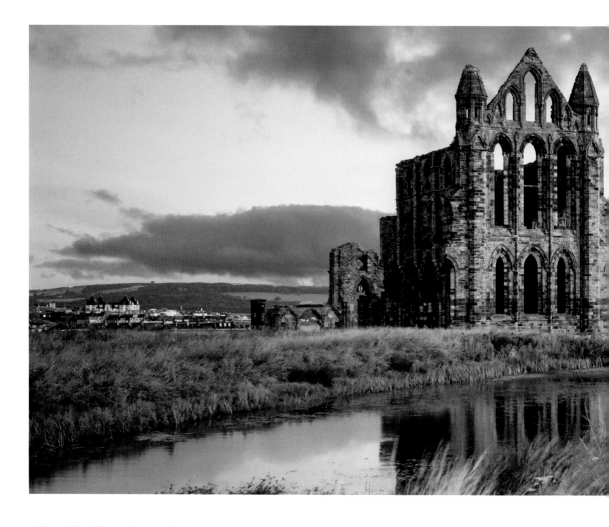

** North York Moors National Park

In the west, the hills of the North York Moors fall away sharply into the sea. Anyone following the coastline along the Cleveland Way from Scarborough to Redcar will be constantly rewarded with spectacular views stretching far out into the distance. But the inland region is also a great place for ramblers. Over 2,000 kilometres of signposted trails criss-cross the national park. It is a desolate land-scape of vast moors and endless heathland, repeatedly carved up by land fissures and rug-ged rock formations. Travelling by car here can be an extremely arduous exercise; steam trains from the York Moors Historical Railway operate regularly between Whitby and Picker-ing during the summer and are a more con-venient option. Mountain-bikers will enjoy the Moor to Sea Cycling Network, which enables them to plan their own rides along the coast and through the national park.

Strange rock formations on the moors.

The picturesque landscape around Robin Hood's Bay and the fishing village of the same name.

Scarborough

Founded by Danish settlers, the town first became famous in the Middle Ages for its fair, which was immortalized in the traditional English ballad *Scarborough Fair* and made famous by Simon and Garfunkel. In the early 17th century, a woman by the name of Elizabeth Farrow discovered a spring of acidic water, sparking Scarborough's career as a spa and seaside resort. The town's unique topography also contributed to its success: the old town lies at the base of a line of cliffs on a small headland surrounded by two large sandy bays. Ritzy old resort facilities are clustered around the South Bay, these include the Grand Hotel and Joseph Paxton's Spa complex, which today has its own orchestra and annual jazz festival. The Victorian Cliff Tramway connects the spa area with the South Cliff.

*** **Whitby Abbey** Almost every castle in England is haunted, but when this will not suffice, the literary world is quick to invent a few scary figures of its own. Bram Stoker, author of *Dracula* (1897), was so inspired by the ruins of Whitby Abbey that he set part of his vampire story in the seaside resort town of Whitby. 'It is a most noble ruin, of immense size, and full of beautiful and romantic bits', he wrote, describing the remains of the Gothic Benedictine abbey, whose origins date back as far as the 7th century. He also praised the wonderful view the abbey provides of the town located at the base of the cliffs. Whitby returned the favour to Stoker posthumously in the form of a Dracula museum and two annual Gothic festivals. Today the former fishing port is also a popular seaside resort with a picturesque old historic centre.

The romantic aspect to which Bram Stoker alluded in his description of the Whitby Abbey ruins becomes evident at sunset.

Discovering East Riding of Yorkshire

Yorkshire's east is a haven for ramblers. Walks through the hilly, river-etched landscape are a great way to unwind, and medieval towns such as Beverley and coastal cities like Kingston upon Hull make for equally relaxing destinations.

INFO ✱

EAST RIDING OF YORKSHIRE
County town:
Beverley
Area:
2,479 sq km
Population:
600,260
Population density:
242 inhabitants/sq km

Christmas decorations in the nave of Beverley Minster.

Burnby Hall

The garden at Burnby Hall is particularly well known for its wide variety of waterlilies, with some 100 different European species growing in its two lakes. This collection, and the entire garden complex, is the creation of Major Percy Marlborough Stewart and his wife Katharine. Stewart loved travelling and nature. He undertook an impressive eight trips around the world, often bringing exotic souvenirs back with him. Today these are exhibited in Burnby Hall Museum, which is dedicated to the Stewarts' travels. The grounds also include an Aviary Garden, Victorian Garden, Rock Garden and a Stumpery as well as a visitor centre and sometimes even an open-air theatre. The fish-feeding sessions are another highlight – for all ages. Carp and goldfish splash about in the lakes, enjoying treats from visitors.

** Kingston upon Hull For many visitors to England, the 'king's town', founded by King Edward I at the mouth of the River Hull as a base for his wars against the Scots, is just a ferry port that they use purely as a transit point. Heavily destroyed by German bombers in World War II, the city admittedly does not cut the most attractive of figures at first glance. But the historic centre is still worth a look, and Hull, as it is usually known for short, also has a number of other attractions, such as the Maritime Museum, which highlights the city's long seafaring tradition; Wilberforce House, the birthplace of abolitionist William Wilberforce which is home to an exhibition on the history of slavery and its abolition; the converted docklands, which are now parks, shopping centres and an entertainment precinct; one of the world's longest suspension bridges; and, of course, The Deep, a large and truly spectacular aquarium, designed by architect Terry Farrell.

*** Beverley and Beverley Minster

Although Beverley Minster is actually just a parish church, it outshines many Gothic cathedrals in terms of both size and appearance. This is due to the fact that its founder, John of Beverley, who later became the bishop of York, was canonized in the 11th century. The pilgrims flocking to the city brought money, but they also needed a space to pray, so, in 1220, construction began on the more than 100-metre-long minster which, in many respects, influenced the English Gothic style. The beautiful western front, for instance, was said to be the model for the front of London's Westminster Abbey. It is remarkable that, despite having a population of just 30,000, Beverley is also home to a second large and fascinating church. The historic town centre is equally worth a visit.

Farrell's impressive architecture at The Deep, Kingston upon Hull's huge aquarium complex.

The Hull Maritime Museum (opposite top) focuses on the city's seafaring history.

North West England

England's north-west is shaped by the Irish Sea. The ports had an important role in Roman times, and overseas trade and the Industrial Revolution marked the region later on, bringing great wealth and many problems. A constant wind of change meant that new ideas took root here earlier than elsewhere. Vibrant cities like Manchester and Liverpool are joined by two of the country's most popular holiday regions: the Lake District and the coastal resorts.

Discovering Cheshire

North-west England is the birthplace of Lewis Carroll, whose Cheshire Cat we are familiar with from *Alice in Wonderland*. Attractive English landscape gardens and the elegant town of Chester are sure to put a big grin on every visitor's face.

INFO ✳

CHESHIRE
County town:
Chester
Area:
2,343 sq km
Population:
1.03 million
Population density:
440 inhabitants/sq km

*** **Chester** Rightly considered one of the most beautiful cities in Great Britain, Chester is sometimes affectionately known as 'a slice of Elizabethan England in aspic', and anyone who strolls along The Rows – the famous two-level shopping arcades set among well-maintained half-timbered buildings – will quickly see why.

Bentley

When the Queen is chauffeured around, it's a Bentley that she is sitting in. And not just any old Bentley, of course. The vehicle took three years to be tailored perfectly to Her Majesty's requirements. The brand was created by Walter Owen Bentley, who began designing sports cars after World War I. His best customers were known as the Bentley Boys and Girls – young men and women from wealthy families with a weakness for car racing. But the Great Depression saw business collapse, and Bentley sold to Rolls-Royce in 1931 and became part of the VW Group in 1998. The headquarters and production facilities in Crewe, Cheshire, are open to visitors.

Chester Cathedral has stood here since the 11th century. The chancel dates back to 1380.

Architecturally, the buildings feature a mix of Tudor and later Victorian design elements. And while not everything is original, this does not ruin the effect in any way. Today there is no evidence that Chester was a major port in the Middle Ages. When the bed of the River Dee began silting up, the port lost prominence, and was superseded by Liverpool in the 18th century. Today, Chester lives off tourism, and is also world-famous for the local Cheshire cheese.

*** Chester Cathedral In keeping with its medieval look, Chester boasts an impressive red-sandstone Gothic cathedral, which was built over the shrine of St Werburgh of Mercia, an Anglo-Saxon princess. But is it really Gothic? As with the other buildings in the city centre, considerable effort went into cultivating its medieval appearance in the 19th century. Between 1868 and 1875, the cathedral was under the charge of George Gilbert Scott, the most prolific architect of the Gothic Revival, and he made a number of changes to give the building a more uniform look. Scott's supporters believed he had done this with extreme care, and had enhanced the existing structure. On the other hand, critics such as William Morris, founder of the Arts & Crafts Movement, accused him of sacrificing historic buildings to modern styles. Be that as it may, the cathedral is definitely worth a visit.

The Eastgate Clock dates from the year 1897.

Christmas lights on a shopping street in the beautiful city of Chester (opposite top).

Half-timbered buildings opposite Chester High Cross.

Cheshire's canals

It all began when a planned wedding was called off. Having had his proposal rejected by the beautiful widow Elizabeth Hamilton, Francis Egerton, 3rd Duke of Bridgewater, turned his back on London and devoted himself entirely to his country estates. In 1759, he decided to have a waterway built from his coal mines to Manchester. Completed two years later, the Bridgewater Canal is considered England's first arti-

ficial waterway to be created from scratch rather than as a channelled river. And the aqueduct, on which engineer James Brindley guided the canal over the River Irwell, was greatly admired. The construction was also a tremendous success economically, causing the coal price in Manchester to drop significantly. Brindley's plan was to connect all of England's major rivers through canals – and his many innovations sparked a veritable 'canalmania' in the late 19th and early 20th centuries. Today, tourism is booming on the canals. They are filled with the colourful, standardized narrowboats introduced by Brindley to enable the construction of narrow, low-cost canals and locks. One of the most popular routes is the Cheshire Ring, which includes sections of six canals in and around Cheshire and Greater Manchester.

Discovering Greater Manchester

Manchester has a proud football history. As well as its legendary sporting status, the city is an attractive, modern metropolitan region boasting numerous museums and exhibitions, top-class restaurants and a buzzing nightlife.

INFO *

GREATER MANCHESTER
Area:
1,276 sq km
Population:
2.81 million
Population density:
2,204 inhabitants/sq km

*** **Manchester** Manchester vies with Birmingham for the title of England's second most important city. While Birmingham is larger, the vibe in the metropolis of Manchester is more reminiscent of that found in cities like Barcelona. Nowhere else has the decline of tra-ditional industry, with which Manchester was once synonymous, been overcome better than in this cultural and financial hub east of Liver-pool. The Town Hall still attests to the city's for-mer splendour, while The Lowry, the cultural centre dedicated to the painter L.S. Lowry (1887–1976), sets a futuristic tone. The Man-chester Art Gallery houses rich artwork treas-ures, and the Museum of Science and Industry provides information on industrial history. But it's not just art and culture that flourish here: the city boasts two football heavyweights: Manchester United and Manchester City.

❶ ** Castlefield The district draws its name from the Roman fort of Mancunium that once stood here, and which was the starting point for both the name and the city that would later become Manchester. But that wasn't the only reason why the city councillors declared the area an Urban Heritage Park in 1982. Castle-field is the heartland of Manchester's indus-trial history. It was here that the canals that brought important raw materials into the city converged. It was also where the first ware-houses were built, and where the first railway line, which started in Liverpool, ended. Castle-field still has its train station from 1830, which is one of the oldest in the world, and the area continues to be dominated by red-brick ware-house buildings, as well as ancient cast-iron and stone bridges. Restored and carefully enhanced with modern structures, they have become showpieces in one of the city's most attractive districts.

The Bridgewater Canal (top) connects Manchester with Leigh and other locations.

The Albert Square Christmas market.

Manchester's Gothic cathedral is a must-see in the city.

2 ★★★ **Manchester Museum** Stan is the name of the giant Tyrannosaurus rex whose replica skeleton is one of the top highlights at Manchester Museum, but it has long ceased to be the only attraction there. Created 200 years ago out of a rich factory owner's scientific collection, the museum is today Great Britain's largest university museum, housing a collection of 4.5 million objects that not only serve as exhibits but also assist with research and teaching. The museum's collection spans an extraordinarily vast spectrum, providing information on the creation of the earth, flora, fauna and humans. There is an extensive ethnology collection, as well as archaeological treasures and artefacts collected in Europe, Asia, Egypt and Sudan, some of which are now being repatriated to their original countries and museums. And which other museum can claim to have an exhibit on the history of archery in the world's most diverse regions, ranging from Brazil to Japan?

3 ★★★ **Manchester Art Gallery** In the early 19th century, some of Manchester's leading businesspeople, citizens and artists decided to take a stand against the city's reputation of being an industrial metropolis devoid of any culture and good taste. They had an impressive Neoclassical building erected, and began organizing art exhibitions and buying paintings. This collection would serve as the basis for Manchester Art Gallery, whose exhibits today fill three interconnected buildings in the

The Imperial War Museum North was designed by Daniel Libeskind.

city centre, as well as several external branches. The extensive fashion collection, for example, is housed in a manor in the suburb of Fallowfield. The original building is known for its prestigious collection of European paintings, including several works by the English Pre-Raphaelites led by Dante Gabriel Rossetti.

♀ ** Whitworth Art Gallery The name Whitworth is primarily synonymous with a screw thread for piping. But the thread named after British engineer Joseph Whitworth (1803–1887) – the first in the world to be standardized – was just one of his many inventions. Whitworth went from being no more than an apprentice fitter to one of the leading machinery developers of Victorian England, endowing, among other things, a hospital and the gallery named after him. The latter is now owned by the University of Manchester, and was reopened in 2015 following large-scale renovation and expansion. The renovation work was so impressive that the 'Whitworth' was promptly named Museum of the Year. In addition, when she was director of the Whitworth, Maria Balshaw, who went on to be the director of the Tate Gallery in London, helped ensure the museum also gained a modern profile beyond its exquisite classical collection.

** Salford Quays Friedrich Engels once cited Salford as an example to describe the squalid situation of the working class, and folksinger Ewan MacColl dedicated his 1949 song *Dirty Old Town* to the city. With only a canal separating it from Manchester, Salford was one of the hotspots of the Industrial Revolution. One of the lasting legacies of this time is the extensive port facilities known as the Quays, which began to fall into disrepair in the 1970s. In 1983, however, Salford became the first city to transform its industrial wasteland into a new, hip urban district. The construction of promenades, bridges and canals saw the system of paths and waterways adapted to the area's new purpose. Today the cinemas, restaurants, numerous outlet stores and water-sport facilities are hugely popular with the many visitors. Spectacular stages and museums, as well as an amazing lift bridge, have all been created by renowned architects.

The Tyrannosaurus rex is one of the main exhibits at Manchester Museum.

Works by the Pre-Raphaelites at Manchester Art Gallery.

The Lowry Bridge (Salford Quays Millennium Lift Bridge), designed by Carlos Fernández Casado.

The Lowry, which comprises two theatres and art galleries as well as an outlet mall, was designed by Michael Wilford.

Manchester football

There are few things people outside of England associate more with Manchester than its football. Headed by manager Alex Ferguson, and with celebrity players like David Beckham, Wayne Rooney, Cristiano Ronaldo, Eric Cantona, Gary Neville and Paul Scholes, Manchester United dominated European football in the 1990s and 2000s. While the club has now lost some of its shine – due in no small part to a

sheikh's injection of cash into local rival Manchester City to boost competition – it continues to command a global fan base. It is impossible to imagine Manchester without football. Yet it was actually university students in Cambridge who discovered football in the mid-19th century and initially infected their classmates with the bug. Manchester United was founded in 1878 as a union of footballing railway workers in the district of Newton Heath, and Manchester City two years later as a parish team. But it was not until the 1950s that United, and its team of youngsters – known as the Busby Babes – began to dominate the English league. In 1968, Manchester United brought the European Cup back to the home of football for the first time, making the city synonymous with top-level football ever since.

Discovering Merseyside

Merseyside is renowned as the birthplace of The Beatles – the most successful music group ever. Yet this metropolitan and ceremonial county, which includes the city of Liverpool, also offers a fascinating history as a prosperous port.

INFO *

MERSEYSIDE
Area:
645 sq km
Population:
1.42 million
Population density:
2,200 inhabitants/sq km

*** Liverpool Liverpool received its town charter as early as 1207, but it remained a fishing village for 500 long years. Only when the slave trade began was the first dock built in 1715, after which Liverpool played a strategic role in the transatlantic slave-trade triangle. It was here that weapons, alcohol and textiles were loaded and transported to West Africa where they were exchanged for slaves, who in turn were taken to the Caribbean and America. There the ships were reloaded with tobacco, cotton and sugar for transportation to Liverpool. Even after slavery was abolished in 1807, docks continued to be built – for purposes such as shipping emigrants, primarily to America. Liverpool experienced a significant boom following the arrival of immigrants from the Caribbean, China and Ireland, during the Irish Potato Famine of 1845. Six areas of the city centre and port were declared World Cultural Heritage sites in 2004 but lost their status in 2021..

** Liverpool Cathedral Who would expect Liverpool of all places to have one of the world's greatest cathedrals? Measuring nearly 190 metres in length, it is surpassed only by St Peter's Basilica in Rome and Notre-Dame de la Paix in Yamoussoukro in the Ivory Coast. It also ranks among the top few in terms of overall size. Yet Liverpool was only declared a diocese in 1880. The young Giles Gilbert Scott, grandson of Gothic Revival icon George Gilbert Scott, was commissioned to build an imposing cathedral in 1903. The younger Scott modified his design several times during a protracted construction period, incorporating elements of the Arts & Crafts Movement, creating a church interior that, on closer examination, is extraordinary. Modern art continued to be integrated, such as Elisabeth Frink's *The Welcoming Christ* above the cathedral's western entrance in 1993.

With its impressive buildings and docks, Liverpool attests to Britain's rise to the rank of a world power. The docks were used until the mid-1900s. After an economic downturn, the historic centre and docks were rebuilt with EU aid. Today, the warehouses contain shops, bars, restaurants and museums.

Liverpool Metropolitan Cathedral

'Paddy's Wigwam' is one of the nicknames Liverpudlians have given their Catholic cathedral. 'Paddy' is a common English nickname for the Irish, and it was decided that a distinguished Catholic church would be built, particularly for those who had fled to England during the Great Famine of the mid-19th century. This was, of course, to be done in Gothic Revival style, though there was only enough money for a chapel. The grand 1930s plans of erecting a Neoclassical building in the style of St Peter's Basilica in Rome – and almost of the same size – in response to Scott's Gothic-Revival cathedral failed when World War II broke out, and it was not until the 1960s that the Catholics got their cathedral – in the form of a highly modern rotunda.

Liverpool, music, The Beatles and more

Liverpool is where it all started. It was here that the G.I.s arrived for their D-Day mission during World War II, and they had more than just chewing gum in their bags: they also brought music with them. The new rhythms and sounds found fertile ground in Liverpool. With The Beatles, the city created a new cultural beat: the birth of British pop music. From 1962 to 1970, the Fab Four epitomised the growth of pop and rock

music, exploring new realms of musicality. English bands dominated the evolving trend. The Rolling Stones, The Kinks, The Who, and all-round artists and singers like Elton John and David Bowie shaped the music tastes of young people all over the world. These musicians' songs consistently topped the charts worldwide. And the punk movement, originally a form of protest against the commercial aspects of pop cul-ture, also has its roots here. The Sex Pistols and The Clash soon started setting trends too. Today, British pop music remains a highly successful export, thanks largely to the pioneering work of the Beatles. Former Beatle Paul McCartney was knighted in 1997 in recognition of his ser-vices, and Liverpool is now one of 47 cities that have been designated City of Music by UNESCO.

Discovering Lancashire

This county virtually has it all: historic buildings and medieval castles, interesting museums and an exciting offering for families, lush parks, blossoming gardens, rambling trails and cycle routes in stunning natural settings – the list is endless.

** Blackpool Blackpool is England's largest seaside resort, and the epitome of British recreational bathing. Worker associations in the surrounding industrial cities began organizing excursions for their members as early as the mid-19th century. Whereas other seaside resorts have one pier with shops and amusement arcades, Blackpool boasts three. The amusement park is one of the largest anywhere, with ten rollercoasters, and the vast and opulent Victorian stages offer a dazzling array of musicals, variety shows, cabaret, plays and concerts. The world's largest magic festival is held here in February, while the oldest and largest competitive dancing festival is staged in May. In late summer, the Blackpool Illuminations bring night-time colour to the town. And there are, of course, also some beautiful beaches. The water quality is good, and the sandy North Shore Beach is a haven of rest and relaxation.

INFO *

LANCASHIRE
County town:
Preston
Area:
3,079 sq km
Population:
1.5 million
Population density:
487 inhabitants/sq km

Lancaster Town Hall dates back to 1909.

.* Lancaster The top of the Ashton Memorial offers the finest view of Lancaster and the sweeping Morecambe Bay. This 50-metre-high Neobaroque temple was built by a millionaire industrialist in memory of his second wife. He opened the surrounding parklands to the public as a gift. At the foot of the memorial is a university town filled with historic buildings, because Lancaster's location on the River Lune made it a prominent base even in Roman times. In the late Middle Ages, the marriage between heiress Blanche of Lancaster and Prince John of Gaunt saw it become the seat of the House of Lancaster, which waged the War of Roses with its York rivals. In addition to the castle and medieval abbey church, the city's other attractions include the 18th-century port facilities and Maritime Museum.

Blackpool Central Pier (opposite top); Ashton Memorial; Blackpool Tower Ballroom (top).

Lancashire Folk

Morris dancers used to feature prominently in many places, especially during Wakes Week. Costumed groups and musicians would move through the streets, the wooden soles of the dancers' boots clopping to the rhythm against the cobbles. Scarves, sticks and even swords would sometimes be twirled in the air. The name Morris Dance is a reference to the dance's roots in the *moresca*, a dance which was performed in Moorish costumes and which was widespread in many parts of medieval Europe. The tradition never totally died out in Lancashire, and a revival began with a festival in Leyland on 29th May 1889. The dance was a revelation to the young men and women who worked in the factories. Today, Lancashire is one of the regions of England where the folk-song and folk-dance scene is thriving.

Despite their fallow appearance, the West Pennine Moors boast great biodiversity.

* West Pennine Moors The seclusion of the West Pennines starts only about 25 kilometres north-west of Manchester's city centre. The vast moor landscape, which stretches to the outskirts of Blackburn, contrasts starkly with the industrial cities surrounding it. Anyone travelling through this region may encounter peregrine falcons and short-eared owls, Stone-Age burial mounds and the ruins of abandoned villages. In addition to rambling, mountain-biking is also becoming increasingly popular, though it is important to stick to the tracks if you want to avoid getting stuck in a bog. While the hills are not high, many of them provide fantastic views of the surroundings, often thanks

Enchanted ruins in the Rivington Terraced Gardens.

stone bridges are the main highlights of the climb. The Rivington Terraced Gardens are like a maze, with hidden paths, caves and smaller lakes all waiting to be discovered. Together with Thomas Mawson, Lord Leverhulme, the soap baron and founder of Lever Brothers (today's Unilever), created the gardens between 1905 and 1925, though the estate fell into disrepair after Leverhulme's death. The Rivington Heritage Trust has overseen major repairs of this hidden gem in recent years.

** **Furness Abbey** The Furness Peninsula, which juts into Morecambe Bay from the north, is home to the remains of an abbey which, when dissolved by Henry VIII, was the second richest in England. It is said to have inspired the poet William Wordsworth and painter William Turner in the 19th century. The monks who lived there in the Middle Ages even built a separate port on offshore Walney Island to enable the produce grown on their sprawling estate to be shipped. It cannot have been easy to build the mighty red sandstone abbey on the soft coastal marshland. Recent restoration work has revealed a foundation of oak trunks which the former master builders had used to construct the walls. The grave of an abbot, bearing precious insignia, has also been discovered. This, along with fragments of the artistic stonemasonry, are now exhibited in a little museum next to the impressive abbey ruins.

Steep steps lead up to the Rivington Pike Tower.

to specially erected viewing towers. But the West Pennines not only serve as a place of recreation; they also encompass a drinking-water reservoir, and are home to a series of dams, some of which even cater to water sports.

** **Rivington Pike & Terraced Gardens** Scaling these hills is one of the moorland's attractions, and arguably the most popular route heads through the beautiful Rivington Terraced Gardens. A Japanese garden and the Lever

Remains of the former Cistercian abbey of St Mary of Furness (opposite and top).

Discovering Cumbria

Home to the Lake District, arguably one of the United Kingdom's most beautiful landscapes, and a UNESCO World Heritage Site, Cumbria inspired the works of Wordsworth, Coleridge and Southey – the Lake Poets – and continues to enchant visitors today.

Buttermere Lake is a popular day-trip destination in Lake District National Park.

*** Lake District National Park This impressive landscape of mountains and lakes was made famous by 'Lake Poets' such as William Wordsworth in the 18th and 19th centuries. Spanning some 2,300 sqare kilometres, and usually known simply as The Lakes, the area stretches for around 130 kilometres north-west of Manchester. Several ice ages, particularly the Last Glacial Period that ended about 15,000 years ago, produced trough valleys with numerous lakes, and it is these that gave the national park its name. With the Cumbrian Mountains making up much of the landscape, the upper regions are home to many cirques with ponds, while the lower areas are dominated by sprawling raised bogs covered in bracken and heather. Romanticist artists had been inspired by the scenery here from the 18th century, dedicat-

ing their paintings and writings to the beautiful surroundings they so loved.

*** Crummock Water & Buttermere Lake Crummock Water, a lake between Loweswater and Buttermere, is rather unfairly overshadowed by Buttermere Lake, which is one of the

Lake District's visitor magnets. Yet Crummock also boasts an attractive combination of remote lakes and dramatic mountain scenery.

** Scale Force Waterfall Measuring some 100 metres) in height, Scale Force is the largest waterfall in the national park, and is best

INFO

CUMBRIA
County town:
Carisle
Area:
6,768 sq km
Population:
499,000
Population density:
74 inhabitants/sq km

accessed from the village of Buttermere. Even the likes of William Wordsworth hailed it as a 'lofty, though but slender fall of water' cascading over several stages.

*** **Scafell Pike** Scafell is one of the 214 so-called 'Wainwrights' – the Lake District mountains described in the writings of Alfred Wainwright and known locally as fells. At a height of 978 metres, this is also the tallest mountain in the country. Several routes can be taken to climb it. A highlight here is the Broad Crag Tarn, England's highest standing water body, located around 800 metres south of the summit.

* **Helvellyn** The third highest peak in the Lake District is often climbed by mountain bikers during the summer months. Its summit is also the end point of a triathlon held every year in September. The mountain has been memorialized in literature since the days of William Wordsworth, Sir Walter Scott and Benjamin Robert Haydon; in 1805, a friend of Wordsworth, Charles Gough, lost his life in a tragic accident on the Striding Edge.

Coast to Coast Walk

This varied long-distance hiking trail was devised in the 1970s by Alfred Wainwright, a British fellwalker, guidebook author and illustrator. It spans 306 kilometres (190 miles), running in 15 day-long stages from St Bees in Cumbria, along the Irish Sea, and ending in Robin Hood's Bay in North Yorkshire. The Coast walk comprises a mixture of asphalt roads and dirt tracks, country lanes and meadows. Also known as the 'C2C' – short for 'Sea to Sea' –, it is hugely popular, and is one of England's most extensive long-distance trails. What makes it unique is the fact that it passes through the Lake District, Yorkshire Dales and North York Moors national parks. Each day of hiking is different from the day before, with landscapes proving to be as fickle as the weather. The stages in the Lake District are, however, among the most scenic.

Tranquil lakes in Buttermere Valley, Lake District. Soaring up behind Wast Water lake and the Western Fells is the snow-capped Scafell Pike (below).

Lake District National Park: Loughrigg Tarn

The idyllic Loughrigg Tarn is a small natural lake north of Lake Windermere, located near the tiny village of Skelwith Bridge and at the foot of the eponymous Loughrigg Fell.

Beatrix Potter

Peter Rabbit is the name of the protagonist in Beatrix Potter's first children's book. Unlike his well-behaved sisters, Peter runs riot in the McGregor family's vegetable garden, and is only able to narrowly escape at the end. Beatrix Potter was only 27 years old when she invented the character for the young son of her former governess, sending the illustrated stories in a series of letters to little Noel. She later also sent illus-

trated letters to other children. This enabled Potter, who lived the sheltered life of an unmarried daughter of an upper-class family, to live out her passion for animals, as well as her talent for drawing. Encouraged by Noel's mother, she took the plunge and published *The Tale of Peter Rabbit* in 1902. The book captured the spirit of the age and became an instant hit. With some 45 million copies sold since, it is today one of the most successful children's books of all time. Her other animal protagonists, such as Samuel Whiskers (a rat) and Jemima Puddle-Duck, were similarly well received, not only as books but also as merchandise. Potter went on to buy an old farm in the Lake District, became a sheep farmer, protested against the construction of an aircraft factory at Lake Windermere and campaigned for rural healthcare.

*** Castlerigg Fell

The 40 starkly different stone blocks arranged into one of England's largest and probably also oldest stone circles on Castlerigg Fell in Cumbria look as if they are dancing. Many people consider this stone circle to be the most beautiful in the country, as the fell is surrounded by some of the most striking peaks in the Lake District. But why the people who lived here some 5,200 years ago went to the effort of setting up the boulders, which reach heights of up to 2.5 metres and weigh up to 16 tonnes, remains a mystery. As is the case at other Neolithic complexes, the positions of some of the stones tie in with certain phases of the sun or moon. Excavations under a stone formation inside the ring in 1882 only uncovered coal. So visitors can further speculate on the circle's secrets as they gaze upon it.

** Carlisle

The mighty and largely intact 12th-century fortress is arguably the main attraction of the old border town in England's far north. An exhibition details the turbulent

Carlisle Castle is over 900 years old.

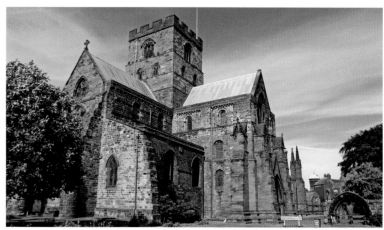

Carlisle Cathedral is a gem of a medieval church.

Levens Hall

Levens Hall has been exuding Elizabethan charm for more than 500 years. The estate has been owned by the same family since 1590, who transformed it from a fortified castle to the present-day manor house. Every era has left its mark; the interiors feature magnificent stucco ceilings, fine oak-clad walls, antique furnishings and several centuries' worth of remarkable paintings. Levens Hall's gardens date back to the 1690s, boasting lush floral splendour and landscaping influenced by more than three centuries of horticulture. Adjacent to the property is another park, which is perfect for long walks. Levens Hall has also been used as a set for various film and television productions, such as the BBC's *Gardners' World* and *Antiques Road Trip*.

history of the over-900-year-old Carlisle Castle and its predecessor buildings, which originated as a Roman military camp. The many, skilfully crafted pictures carved into the walls by bored watchmen are a fascinating detail. The pretty town centre within the largely preserved city walls also boasts a number of historic buildings, including the imposing Gothic cathedral from 1133, the Guildhall (14th century), Tullie House Museum and Art Gallery that features an exhibition on the town's history, and the train station. Today, the centre of Carlisle is largely a pedestrian zone which makes it even more enjoyable to explore.

The stone circle of Castlerigg (top) is one of the largest in England, and dates back to the early Stone Age. Soaring up in the background are Helvellyn and High Seat.

Traces of the Celts in Cumbria

As the famous English nursery rhyme goes, 'Old King Cole was a merry old soul'. According to a medieval Welsh source, King Cole is said to have ruled Hen Ogledd, the old north, following the Romans' retreat in the 5th century. Whether or not such a person existed is questionable. What is for sure, however, is that, after the Romans' military retreat, several Celtic principalities with a Romanized, largely Christian, upper class

stayed behind. They may even have brought Saxons, Angles and Jutes to the country as mercenaries to resist invasions by the Scottish Picts, but they soon fell victim to the Anglo-Saxon invasion themselves. The Celtic kingdoms in the north, however, were able to offer resistance for some time. Welsh epics particularly glorify King Urien of Rheged, who is likely to have resided in the present-day area of Carlisle, and even appears in

Arthurian Legend as a great warlord. He is said to have been murdered by a rival, prompting Oswiu of Northumbria, king of the Angles, to take over Cumbria in the early 7th century. The Cumbrian language died out in the 12th century, apart from among the shepherds, who are reported to have still been counting their animals in Cumbrian – yan, yan, yhetera, methera, pimp – into the 20th century.

Discovering the Isle of Man

Shrouded in legend and boasting exceptional beauty, the Isle of Man offers more than just breathtaking views of the surrounding sea and romantic sunsets. Castle ruins and little towns reflect the isle's eventful history.

INFO *

ISLE OF MAN

Area: 572 sq km
Highest mountain: Snaefell (621 m)
Longest river: Selby (17 km)
Population: 84,500
Population density: 148 inhab./sq km
Capital: Douglas (28,000 inhabitants.)
Currency: Isle of Man Pound
Form of government: British crown dependency

*** Isle of Man The inhabitants of the 572-square-kilometre Isle of Man – the Manx – are proud of their picturesque glens, some of which have a wild side. At the entrance to the Dhoon Glen gorge, for example, moss-covered cliffs rise up at an almost totally vertical angle to heights of around 140 metres, while two waterfalls plunge down the steep rock face. Locals call the larger of the two 'Big Girl'.

Some say it is possible to hear the whimpers of the little girl who once drowned here. In any case, the isle is said to be inhabited by numerous spirits, trolls and fairies, such as Moddey Dhoo the black hound that allegedly causes mischief in the ruins of Peel Castle on the west coast. The highest peak of the hilly island is the 621-metre-tall Snaefell, and its summit provides stunning views over seven kingdoms: Man, Ireland, Scotland, Wales, England, Heaven and the realm of Neptune.

* Peel Castle Built by the Vikings, this castle has stood on St Patrick's Isle, off the coast of Peel, since the 11th century, and is connected to the town by a dam. The castle is open to visitors in the summer.

* Bradda Glen & Milner's Tower Bradda Glen is the starting point for the climb up to Bradda Head and the 40 steep steps up Milner's Tower, where a monument (1871) is dedicated to wealthy philanthropist William Milner. The commanding view of Port Erin, Port St Mary,

Isle of Man TT

The world's likely oldest and most dangerous motorcycle race has been held annually on the Isle of Man since 1907. Over 260 riders have lost their lives on the approximately 60-kilometre-long Snaefell Mountain Course. The curves are extremely tight, and the public roads, which weave through villages and under bridges, demand particular care. Memorizing the route to the last detail is a matter of life and death. Joey Dunlop is arguably the most famous rider of all time, having held the Tourist Trophy (TT) aloft 26 times. Ranking second is John McGuinness, who has won the race 23 times and even set a track record in 2015 with an average speed of 214 kilometres per hour! A pure adrenalin rush – and not just for the riders...

Langness, Calf of Man and the Sound from the top is simply beautiful.

** Tynwald Hill The sessions of the Manx parliament – the Tynwald (Manx: Tinvaal), or to give it its full name: the High Court of Tynwald – were held atop this 3.5-metre-high hill in St John's in the 1st century AD, making it the oldest, continuously existing parliament in the world. Every third Tuesday, the government convenes in the nearby Manx capital of Douglas. And every 5th of July (the national holiday), an open-air session is held on Tynwald Hill, during which the previous year's laws are officially read out in Manx (a Goidelic language) and English. After all, the Isle of Man is independent, a direct dependency of the British Crown and is not a part of the United Kingdom.

The south of the Isle of Man is home to the villages of St Mary, Calf of Man and Port Erin (above).

Peel Castle stands on St Patrick's Isle, and is connected to the mainland by a dam.

Milner's Tower dates from 1871.

North East England

England's north-east is great for secluded walks. There are no bustling seaside resorts, and the long beaches are often deserted. Nature presents itself at its most striking along Hadrian's Wall in the North Pennines and in Northumberland National Park. Imposing castles and monasteries attest to this border region's turbulent history. The twin city of Newcastle and Gateshead attract visitors with their great architecture, vibrant cultural scene and pumping nightlife.

Discovering County Durham

The city of Durham, with its mighty cathedral and castle, is a must-see. But the quaint market towns and villages of the Durham Dales and the coast have a few attractions of their own – and outdoor enthusiasts can go rambling or mountain-biking in the North Pennines.

INFO *

COUNTY DURHAM
County town:
Durham
Area:
2,721 sq km
Population:
867,000
Population density:
324 inhabitants/sq km

The eastern window of Egglestone Abbey (12th century) at Barnard Castle is well preserved.

*** Barnard Castle

While the small town of Barnard Castle on the Tees is named after its castle, it is actually dominated by the Bowes Museum. What looks like a gigantic manor house in the style of a French château was designed by John Bowes in the late 19th century. It was conceived as a new home for his art collection, which the heir of ultra-rich coalmine owners wanted to make accessible to the public. Today, the Bowes Museum is considered the most eminent art gallery outside London, and also displays a wide range of Arts & Crafts objects, historic costumes, furniture and fully furnished rooms. Another must-see are the ruins of Barnard Castle on the riverbank, immortalized by Charles Dickens in his novel *Nicholas Nickleby* (1839).

*** North Pennines

The northern foothills of the Pennines are England's third-largest nature reserve, and also the country's first geopark, due to their interesting and often exposed layers of rock. They are a haven for all outdoor enthusiasts – not just ramblers, cyclists, anglers or bird-watchers. Special facilities are also available for horse-riders, climbers, kayakers, sailors, survival experts, cavers, geologists, biologists, stargazers and even skiers. Towering over the entire scene are the highest peaks of the Pennines: Cross Fell, Great Dun Fell and Little Dun Fell. Despite not even reaching heights of 900 metres, these hills are covered in rare alpine vegetation, frequently shrouded in clouds, or buffeted by strong local winds. Anyone climbing them in fair weather, however, will be rewarded with a fabulous view extending as far as the Solway Firth and Scotland.

Teesdale

The River Tees is one of the most spectacular rivers in England. Its waters spring from the eastern slope of Cross Fell, at an altitude of 750 metres above sea level in the North Pennines, and are dammed on a plateau in the Cow Green Reservoir, to supply water for the industries on Teesside. Construction of the reservoir, between 1967 and 1971, was highly controversial, although the lake remains surrounded by a variety of alpine habitats not found anywhere else in England: moors and heaths, low juniper shrubs, chalk meadows, calcareous grassland and alpine pastures. Upon leaving the reservoir, the water cascades down from rapids into the valley, and is positively catapulted out of the wall at High Force, England's most bountiful waterfall, before disgorging over the wider Low Force into a torrent channel perfect for high-speed kayaking.

The Bowes Museum in Barnard Castle (below) holds a major collection of European paintings, textiles, ceramics and clocks. The North Pennines (opposite bottom).

River Tees

The River Tees flows along the border between County Durham and North Yorkshire. At Middleton, it disgorges over rugged rocks as the High Force waterfall. A few miles further on is another waterfall, Low Force. It's wise to watch your step here as legend has it that the Tees is inhabited by the water-spirit Peg Powler, who grabs inattentive passersby by the ankles and drags them into the river!

*** **Durham** The Norman castle and three-storey Anglo-Norman cathedral in the city of Durham in the county of the same name in north-east England are examples of Norman architecture and the power of the bishops. They have been a UNESCO World Cultural Heritage site since 1986. Towering over the River Wear are the fort-like complexes of the bishops of Durham. A castle was built here in 1072; it was intended to serve as a bastion against the Scots. It ultimately became the centre of a Benedictine monastery settlement and a residence for the bishops, who were also the secular rulers of the region until 1536. Construction of the cathedral began in 1093, with a view to it housing the relics of the Venerable Bede and St Cuthbert. The church is considered one of the very first structures erected by the Normans during the transition from Romanesque to Gothic styles.

** **Durham Castle** People are said to have lived in the area around Durham over 4,000 years ago. The town's location on the hill above the River Wear was strategically ideal; the river provided a natural barrier, and the lords of the castle had a good view of the surrounding region. So it is no wonder that a picture-post-card fortress was built in the form of Durham Castle. It was constructed in the 11th century on the orders of William the Conqueror, and remains well preserved. The defence tower's floor plan is just as discernible as the distinct motte design introduced by the Normans. They had skilfully devised a structural style in which they could pre-fabricate individual wooden parts and simply fit them together on site. The present-day complex is made entirely of stone, and is partly used as a university.

*** **Durham Cathedral** Even churches had to be prepared for attacks from the north, for people in Scotland and Northumberland were anything but thrilled about the Norman Conquest. And Durham Cathedral, whose construction began in 1093, was suitably well-fortified. The Norman cathedral is unique in that its roofing was the first to feature rib vaults and buttresses, which later became commonplace in Gothic churches. The cathedral is home to the tomb of St Cuthbert and a miners' monument. At its northern end is an entrance with a door knocker for those seeking refuge.

The ribbed vault above the choir is the oldest of its kind, securing the cathedral an important place in architectural history.

Durham Miners' Gala

Every year, on the second Saturday of July, Durham buzzes with excitement, for that is when the city celebrates its mining heritage – more specifically, that of its workers' movement. The first Miners' Gala was organized in 1871 by the Durham Miners' Association, whose members worked in Durham's coal-mining district. The area had over 100 mines, with more than 200,000 workers. None of these mines is in operation today, although at the gala, you could be forgiven for thinking mining was still booming. Former miners march proudly behind colourful trade union flags, while dozens of brass bands play workers' songs. The local miners are joined by fellow miners from all over England and by other trade union groups, making the Miners' Gala one of the largest political gatherings in Europe.

St Cuthbert of Lindisfarne is buried in Durham.

Durham Cathedral is one of England's most prominent Romanesque churches.

Discovering Tyne and Wear

Newcastle and Gateshead is a cosmopolitan hub, with museums and entertainment options, while its environs boast historic castles and superb examples of nature.

TYNE AND WEAR
Area:
2,104 sq km
Population:
1.14 million
Population density:
540 inhabitants/sq km

on the shores of the River Tyne like a silver caterpillar, was designed by star architect Sir Norman Foster, and is considered the showpiece of computer-generated blob architecture (also known as blobitecture). Boasting some 330 shops and an amusement park, the MetroCentre is the largest shopping centre in Europe. And overlooking the city is Europe's tallest statue, the crimson Angel of the North designed by Antony Gormley, with a wing span of more than 50 metres.

*** **Newcastle upon Tyne** During Roman times, it was here at Hadrian's Wall that civilization ended. Today, Newcastle offers a wide variety of rich cultural pickings. The façades of grand old buildings, blackened by a long industrial history, have been cleaned; the quays transformed into modern, vibrant urban districts; and striking new buildings erected. But Newcastle's biggest draw is its rich cultural scene. Anyone who comes to the city should not only visit its museums, but also explore its music and theatre venues. And Newcastle's dizzying mix of nightlife, with its many bars, pubs, clubs and restaurants, is considered by many the most exciting in Britain outside London.

** **Gateshead** The twin city on the other side of the Tyne, Gateshead is connected to Newcastle by 10 bridges. The most spectacular of these is the Millennium Bridge, whose semicircular tread section lifts diagonally whenever larger ships need to pass through. But this city, whose centre fell victim to a devastating two-day fire in 1854, also boasts ultra-modern architecture. The Sage events centre, which stands

Shopping in the Victorian Central Arcade (top) in Newcastle is a real treat.
The Millennium Bridge (right) was designed by Wilkinson Eyre Architects, and the Sage by Foster + Partners and Arup Acoustics.

A number of bridges lead over the Tyne in Newcastle.

Gray's Monument in the centre of Newcastle upon Tyne is a popular meeting place.

Marsden Rock south of South Shields ...

... can only be reached on foot at low tide.

* Marsden Bay The mighty Marsden Rock, which sits in the water off the coast, once formed an arch, though this collapsed some 100 years ago. Today, it provides a nesting ground for thousands of seagulls, cormorants and fulmars. The tall, solitary rock pillar bears the name Lot's Wife, after the biblical figure who, after looking at Sodom and Gomorrah, turned into a pillar of salt. But it's not just the picturesque rocks and many birds that make Marsden Bay near South Shields a popular day-trip destination. As early as the end of the 18th century, a miner blasted the shoreline rocks to create a cave dwelling, and Marsden Grotto later became one of England's most famous pubs. It is easy to believe the stories of smuggling here – but less so the fact that mining was taking place in this idyll until 1968. Yet the remains of a mine and a mineworkers' village can still be visited.

** Tynemouth Castle and Priory The coast of northern England was once among the country's most fortified areas. The towers, gatehouse and peel are located adjacent to the remains of a 7th-century Benedictine priory containing the graves of the first kings of

Arbeia Roman Fort

When you stand in front of the imposing gate structure, it is hard to believe that the Arbeia South Shields Roman Fort was only one of many forts that dotted Hadrian's Wall in a bid to protect Roman Britain from invasions by northern tribes. Located at the mouth of the River Tyne, the fort was the easternmost outpost of the Roman Empire in England, and was partly reconstructed following excavations in the 1970s. Today, for example, the rebuilt gate is joined by the Commandant's House and a crew barracks, which have also been reconstructed on their original foundations. Together with the artefacts exhibited in the adjacent museum, they provide a fascinating insight into Roman garrison life on the border.

Northumbria. The priory was attacked by the Danes in around 800, prompting the monks to fortify their property. That same century, however, the attackers destroyed the priory completely. It was re-established in the 11th century, and surrounded by a more than-900-metre-long stone wall in the 13th century, with a gatehouse and barbican also being added. The 'Life in the Stronghold' exhibition recounts the history of the complex, explaining how the Anglo-Saxon settlement became an Anglican monastery, a royal castle and a defence fortification.

The Collingwood Monument in Tynemouth (top) commemorates Admiral Lord Collingwood (1750–1810), who fought in the Napoleonic Wars as vice admiral.

Discovering Northumberland

England's northernmost county boasts the rugged natural world of the North Pennines, Northumberland National Park and the North Sea coast. The castles here attest to the border battles that were waged over centuries.

INFO *

NORTHUMBERLAND
County town:
Alnwick
Area:
5,013 sq km
Population:
320,000
Population density:
64 inhabitants/sq km

*** Hadrian's Wall In a bid to better protect the Roman Empire against the peoples in the north, border fortifications were erected in the 2nd century, stretching across Europe for more than 5,000 kilometres. Hadrian's Wall runs from Newcastle via Carlisle near the English-Scottish border to Bowness-on-Solway 120 kilometres away on the Irish Sea. It is part stone wall, part earth wall. The Roman Emperor Hadrian ordered the construction of the 5-metre-high and almost 3-metre-wide wall in the years 122–132 to protect local people against Scottish tribes. The fortification included the actual wall, built along a military road, as well as a military camp, smaller mile-castles and larger castles, towers and gates. A moat ran along both sides of the wall. After the Romans' retreat in around 410, however,

View at sunset from Windy Gyle over the Cheviot Hills in the northern part of the national park (top).

the wall fell visibly into disrepair. Its stones were taken for other sites, and it was not until the 18th and 19th centuries that historians started to study and protect the wall. Hadrian's Wall was made a World Heritage Site in 1987.

*** Northumberland National Park

The area north of Hadrian's Wall was once a dangerous place characterized by the many frontier battles waged here in bygone times. Today, it provides an idyllic antidote to everyday stresses. Northumberland National Park, located between the wall and the Scottish border, is one of England's most remote regions. Hikers, nature-watchers and mountain-bikers all have ample room here. At the centre of the park is the Kielder Water reservoir, and ramblers will be surprised by the large, open-air art installations punctuating the 44-kilometre-long Lakeside Way. There are also

observatories, and so the national park is equally popular among astronomers. Here, far away from any cities and other artificial light sources, the dark sky is filled with thousands of twinkling stars.

A summertime heath blankets the hills of Dove Crag in Northumberland National Park (above). Hadrian's Wall is very well preserved in some parts. Milecastle 39 with Crag Lough Highshield Crags and Hotbank Crags (below).

Northumberland National Park: Sycamore Gap with the Robin Hood Tree

The Robin Hood Tree, also known as the Sycamore Gap Tree, grows in the eponymous Sycamore Gap, a dip formed out of meltwater near Hadrian's Wall. It is probably the most photographed tree in the North-umberland National Park, having become famous thanks to the film Robin Hood: Prince of Thieves (1991), *starring Kevin Costner. The Woodland Trust designated it 'Tree of the Year' in 2016.*

*** Alnwick Castle
Anyone wanting a perfect medieval experience will find just that in Alnwick. The little town is dominated by its giant castle complex, the second largest in the country still to be inhabited. It was once home to the Percy family, the powerful sovereigns of Northumberland. The most famous of them, Henry Percy Hotspur, rebelled against his former friend, King Henry IV, and was killed in battle – a story recounted by William Shakespeare in his dramas, albeit with some creative licence. Today, the castle offers a plethora of interactive offerings for visitors, especially children; there are even training sessions on a flying broomstick – after all, this was where parts of the Harry Potter films were shot. Coupled with this are magnificent rooms decorated in the Italian Renaissance style. Keen gardeners can admire the gorgeous sprawling gardens of Alnwick Castle.

*** Bamburgh Castle
Located right on the sea, Bamburgh Castle is something very special indeed, and boasts a fascinating history. The present-day, essentially Norman fortress was erected on the site of an older castle where it is presumed the Celtic kings of the

Kings Hall at Bamburgh Castle was first created during Victorian times.

Bamburgh Castle bathed in evening light.

Romano-British empire of Gododdin first ruled, before the castle was then conquered by King Ida of Bernicia in 547. It was bought and restored by a steel magnate in the 19th century, and it is still owned by his family to this day. The state rooms, appointed in the opulent, fanciful style of romantic Victorian castles, are open to visitors. The gardens, delighted the 15th-century writer Thomas Malory so much that he incorporated them in his Arthurian work, can also be viewed. The beach beneath the castle is also stunning.

The iconic Alnwick Castle (above) was used as the set for the first two Harry Potter films, as well as for Christmas editions of the British television series Downton Abbey.

Alnwick Castle is the second largest aristocratic estate in all of England.

*** Lindisfarne

The name Lindisfarne is synonymous with tragedy. On 8th June 793, this little island off the coast of Northumberland was attacked by Vikings, who killed or abducted all its inhabitants. The attack is considered the start of the Viking age that sent Europe into a state of terror for more than 200 years. It also resulted in the destruction of the monastery founded by St Aidan, and which had been famed for the Lindisfarne Gospels, a superb illuminated manuscript. The picturesque monastery ruins open to the public on the island today, however, date back to the 11th century, while the castle perched atop a conical hill was built on the orders of King Henry VIII following the monastery's dissolution. If you wish to visit the Holy Island, beware of the tides: at high tide, the sandy track that runs for some 5 kilometres from the mainland to the island becomes submerged.

*** Lindisfarne Priory

In 635, King Oswald took Irish monk Aidan to Northumbria and made him the bishop of his kingdom. Aidan built a priory on the island of Lindisfarne

A converted fishing boat on Lindisfarne beach.

where, in the early 8th century, a manuscript of the New Testament, known as the Lindisfarne Gospels, was created. Abbot Cuthbert, who tried to mediate between the

ongoing Irish and Roman-Catholic conflicts in the 8th century, is equally famous. Cuthbert later lived as a hermit near Lindisfarne, and is buried in Durham Cathedral. The present-day priory, which only remains as ruins, was built between 1120 and 1150. It is managed by English Heritage. The Benedictine abbey was finally disbanded in 1536.

** Lindisfarne Castle

The castle on Lindisfarne Island is much newer than the priory. Located in the fiercely disputed border region between England and Scotland, it was built in the 16th century at the same time as the priory was being dissolved, and faced many battles. Publisher Edward Hudson bought the building in 1901 and had it redesigned in the Arts & Crafts style. Today, the castle is looked after by the National Trust. Visitors can also enjoy the nearby garden, which writer Gertrude Jekyll designed in the Arts & Crafts style.

Ruins of the Roman abbey on Holy Island.

Lindisfarne Castle (top) is immortalized in several works by painter William Turner.

WELSH HIGHL

Wales

The smallest country in the United Kingdom, Wales has preserved its cultural independence to this day. Celtic traditions remain alive and well – in the Welsh language, festivals and customs. And yet there are equally clear signs of English rule. After conquering the province of Gwynedd in the 13th century, King Edward I ordered that a series of mighty fortresses – the so-called Iron Ring – be built there. These are now a UNESCO World Cultural Heritage site.

Discovering Torfaen

Blaenavon tells of the early days of industrialization and mining; today the town and its industrial landscape are listed as UNESCO World Heritage Sites. The ruins of Tintern Abbey are another highlight of this Welsh county

*** Tintern Abbey Tintern Abbey was founded as the first Cistercian monastery in Wales in 1131. The Cistercian Order was one of the most influential in Europe in the 12th and 13th centuries. The abbey was redesigned in the late 13th century, and the present-day ruins date back to that time. Monastic life came to an end in 1536 following the founding of the Church of England; anything of value found its way into the royal treasuries. The buildings were given to the Earl of Worcester, who stripped the lead from the roofs and sold it, initiating the abbey's decline. Ruins came into vogue in the 18th century, with many making pilgrimages to the crumbling, ivy-covered walls. Artists and poets such as William Wordsworth drew inspiration for their work here.

View westwards through the nave of the remains of Tintern Abbey.

INFO

WALES

Area: 20,779 sq km
Coastline: 1,400 km
Highest mountain: Snowdon (1,085 m)
Largest lake: Lake Bala (4.8 sq km)
Longest river: Severn (354 km)
Population: 3.1 million inhabitants
Population density: 150 inhab./sq km
Capital: Cardiff (361,000 inhab.)
Currency: Pound Sterling

INFO

TORFAEN
County town:
Pontypool
Area:
126 sq km
Population:
93,000
Population density:
740 inhabitants/sq km

Blaenavon Industrial Landscape

In 1789, three entrepreneurs from England had three blast furnaces built near the village of Blaenavon, in the mining landscape of South Wales. They produced pig iron based on the latest iron-making technology of the time using steam power. The blast furnaces were built into a slope to enable them to be supplied with raw material from above. A residential settlement for workers was established next to the hill slope, the simple stone structure resembling cottages. At the eastern edge of the old industrial region of Blaenavon is one of the largest collieries, known as 'Big Pit', where the coal needed for the furnaces was mined. The complex fell into disrepair when iron production ended at the start of the 20th century.

Discovering Monmouthshire

Apart from the impressive landscape, it is the many castles in particular that delight visitors here. Both are best explored on a long walk through the Monmouthshire countryside.

** Wye Valley The Wye Valley is located in south-east Wales, right on the border with England. With its river and sprawling green forests, the valley is a veritable idyll that has inspired many an artist. William Wordsworth described the wonderful natural landscapes here in his verses, while William Turner captured them in his paintings. The valley bears traces of human settlement dating back over several millennia. West of the river mouth, for instance, are footprints from around 3,720 BC, and Caerwent has ruins of a Roman city wall. A number of footpaths, such as the Wye Valley Walk, also lead through the river landscape and picturesque forests. The region, which is popular among ramblers, mountain-bikers and canoeists, is additionally an important nature reserve, and is known officially as the Wye Valley Area of Outstanding Natural Beauty.

The River Wye flows calmly through the valley of the same name. It is an ideal place for long walks and fully appreciating nature.

MONMOUTHSHIRE
County town:
Newport
Area:
850 sq km
Population:
94,000
Population density:
111 inhabitants/sq km

* INFO

Discovering Newport

The harbour city of Newport has been the region's focal point since the 19th century. The surrounding area, with its quaint villages, is still dominated by agriculture.

** Newport Transporter Bridge Rising above the River Usk, just before it opens out into the Bristol Channel, is a masterpiece of engineering, visible from afar and more reminiscent of a giant crane than a bridge. In essence, the Transporter Bridge is both. A delicate platform hangs on the spanning steel structure, and floats from one riverbank to the other via an electric slide, rendering it unaffected by the tremendous tidal variations. At the time of its construction in 1906, transporter bridges were still quite popular; today, only seven remain in use around the world. The Newport Transporter Bridge is run by an association as a monument. Plucky visitors can climb inside the bridge's supporting structure and cross the River Usk from a vertiginous height of 54 metres.

INFO *

NEWPORT
Unitary authority:
Newport
Area:
218 sq km
Population:
153,000
Population density:
795 inhabitants/sq km

The Newport Transporter Bridge in southern Wales crosses over the River Usk, taking cars and pedestrians safely from one side of the river to the other.

Discovering Caerphilly

Caerphilly is known for two very different things: its crumbly cheese and its giant castle, which happens to be the largest in all of Wales.

*** Caerphilly Castle The castle north of Cardiff dates back to Gilbert de Clare, one of the most powerful men during the reigns of Henry III and Edward I. Between 1268 and 1280, he ordered the construction of a mighty complex to protect the southern plains against the Welsh princes from the mountainous regions. In the United Kingdom, only Windsor Castle is larger. The initial design was for a concentric castle with two curtain walls, protected by two artificial lakes. This then served as the blueprint for all castles built under Edward I in northern Wales. But Caerphilly Castle soon lost its importance and fell into disrepair. The intact corner towers were demolished in 1649. The wealthy marquesses of Bute had much of the castle restored, starting in 1870, and with the re-damming of the lakes the castle has begun to regain its former imposing appearance.

INFO *

CAERPHILLY
County town:
Caerphilly
Area:
278 sq km
Population:
181,000
Population density:
653 inhabitants/sq km

Caerphilly Castle, the largest castle in Wales, has been vacant since the 14th century, though legend has it that the Green Lady, the spirit of the former wife of Gilbert de Clare, can be spotted here during the full moon, roaming the castle dressed in green.

Discovering Cardiff

The capital of Wales boasts great museums, attractive cultural events, a fascinating castle, lots of green spaces and a giant stadium. Cardiff is also a perfect base for day-trips into the surrounding area.

*** **Cardiff** Cardiff, the largest city in Wales, has also been its capital since 1955. The town was still small and insignificant at the start of the 19th century, before industrialization saw it experience a rapid boom. The port became an important transshipment site for what was considered the fuel of progress at the time: coal. Following the decline of heavy industry, Cardiff evolved into a centre of science and culture, with a university and prominent theatre and opera house. Another famous site is the Red Castle, Castell Coch, in Cardiff's north – an opulent, Neogothic-inspired building from the 1870s. The flipside of the region – the steel works, coal mines and abandoned sites of the Industrial Revolution – can be visited at the UNESCO World Heritage site in Blaenavon.

*** **Cardiff Castle** Originally consisting of several Roman forts, the castle has been modified and expanded multiple times over the course of its turbulent, centuries-long history. Today, the complex comprises a medieval castle and fairy-tale-like Neogothic manor built in the Victorian style. Its impressive dining hall hosted the banquet for the 2014 NATO summit, involving various heads of state and government. Tom Jones, Green Day and the Stereophonics have performed here. The castle is also home to the National College of Music and Drama.

** **Bute Park** This magnificent park once formed part of Cardiff Castle, and was owned by the aristocratic Bute family for generations. It was handed over to the city in 1947, and, in combination with Cardiff Castle, is today a popular excursion destination.

** **Llandaff Cathedral** Located south of the River Taff, in the suburb of Llandaff, the cathedral is considered one of the oldest Christian sites in Great Britain. It was severely damaged in World War II, but has been rebuilt, and was further renovated in the 1990s. Dante Gabriel Rossetti painted a triptych for the cathedral between 1858-64.

** **Llandaff Palace** Between the Middle Ages and 15th century, the palace served as the residence for the bishops of Llandaff. The palace was then leased out, before lying vacant in the 18th century. It has been home to the Cathedral School since 1958.

* **The Senedd** The Welsh Parliament building stands right by the sea. It was here that the National Assembly for Wales was founded in 1998, and the first elections were held in 1999.

INFO *

CARDIFF
County town:
Cardiff
Area:
140 sq km
Population:
1.1 million
Population density:
653 inhabitants/sq km

The Senedd, the home of the Welsh Parliament, was designed by Richard Rogers.

The Parliament is able to establish certain regulations for Wales.

*** **Wales Millennium Centre** The imposing building in Cardiff Bay is one of the city's main landmarks. Its two large theatre stages host performances such as musicals, cabaret, opera and other cultural events.

The Wales Millennium Centre, designed by Jonathan Adams, is one of city's landmarks.

Mari Lwyd

The name of this Welsh custom translates as 'Grey Mare'. On New Year's Eve, small groups of people head to the south of Wales with a 'mare' – a hobby horse on a stick – and go from house to house wassailing – singing songs in a bid to be invited in for food and drink. The head is usually made of wood or cardboard, with a white sheet acting as a cover for the pole and its bearer. The custom is said to bring good luck, and became controversial during the temperance movement during the Industrial Revolution. The Catholic Church did not look favourably upon the pagan ritual either. The tradition had all but been lost by the first half of the 20th century, although, these days, small townships in particular are attempting to revive it.

Entrance to Cardiff Castle.

Welsh Traditions

All-male choirs are one of many Welsh traditions; they developed out of the singing in Nonconformist chapels and by groups of workers in the country's mines, factories, docks and shipyards. Singing is popular in general – including after rugby matches when everyone in the pub spontaneously bursts into song. Wales is the only country in the United Kingdom which is not represented on the Union Jack flag, but it has its own national standard

featuring the Welsh dragon. Today the creature appears on badges, bumper stickers and as rugby fans' face paint at international matches. Its origins go back to Roman times but are shrouded in mystery. The Welsh began to wear a leek in their caps every St David's Day (1st March) but the country is also associated with daffodils. British prime minister and Welsh statesman David Lloyd George wore the daffodil on St David's Day and encouraged its use at the investiture of the Prince of Wales in 1911. National dresses help build an identity – and Lady Llanover (1802–1896) may have shared this line of thinking when she propagated her ideas about authentic Welsh dress. In any case, today the combination of a lace-trimmed black hat, a pinafore, lace collar and scarf, in the national colours of red, white and green, continues to be considered the authentic Welsh women's costume.

Discovering West Glamorgan

Any Welsh holiday should include a visit to West Glamorgan and Swansea. This bustling coastal city delights visitors just as much, if not more, than the beautiful Swansea Bay and the stunning Gower Peninsula.

*** Gower Peninsula The peninsula is one of the most popular tourist destinations in Wales. It is located in the county of West Glamorgan, and is an exquisite natural paradise – featuring a spectacular coastline and ideal conditions for ramblers and nature enthusiasts. Gower also has many caves. The most beautiful beaches and bays are within easy access of the city of Swansea, and surfers will love Swansea Bay or Llangennith at the western tip of the peninsula. The bays of Langland, Caswell and Limeslide make for relaxing beach holidays – all three have been recognized for their excellent water quality and exemplary infrastructure. Inland, Gower is still characterized by farming. The peninsula was named an Area of Outstanding Natural Beauty as early as 1956 – the first landscape in the United Kingdom to officially receive this distinction.

INFO ✳

WEST GLAMORGAN
County town:
Swansea
Area:
380 sq km
Population:
685,000
Population density:
601 inhabitants/sq km

.*** Swansea Anyone who ventures into Swansea is in for a pleasant surprise. The port at the mouth of the River Tawe was a central transshipment site for coal as early as 1700, acting as a magnet for heavy industry – first with the copperworks, then steelworks and chemical plants, and, from 1918 onwards, crude-oil refineries. The industrial centre was almost totally destroyed in World War II, but has been rebuilt. It is thanks to structural change and many town-planning projects that Swansea today boasts a rich cultural scene and many delightful areas, such as the Trevivian workers' district and the Maritime Quarter by the port. The birthplace of Dylan Thomas, Wales' most famous poet, is also worth a visit.

A jewel of nature: the Gower Peninsula with Three Cliffs Bay (opposite). The modern city of Swansea (below).

Worm's Head

Rhossili on the Gower Peninsula provides an excellent view of the Worm's Head headland. Its name comes from the Old English for dragon, and it is indeed shaped like a dragon's head. There are, in fact, three islands: The Outer Head, Middle Head and Inner Head. At low tide, and for two hours before and after, the long, thin island group is accessible on foot from Rhossili via a rocky coastal path. But it is not an easy walk, because, just before the end, hikers must climb over the famed Devil's Hole, a gate formed by erosion. The tip of the island offers a view of the entire Rhossili Bay, as well as stunning vistas of the southern and western stretches of the coast. As inexperienced walkers and hikers have been known to misjudge the tides, helicopters frequently fly over the island to assist stranded day-trippers.

Discovering Pembrokeshire

Boasting natural gems such as the Pembrokeshire Coast National Park, cultural treasures such as St David's Cathedral, and picturesque Victorian coastal towns like Tenby, Pembrokeshire is an outdoor paradise and cultural hotspot in one. Whether it be hiking, surfing, swimming or simply taking a break, it's all about enjoyment and recreation here!

INFO ✳

PEMBROKESHIRE

County town:
Haverfordwest
Area:
1,590 sq km
Population:
125,000
Population density:
77 inhabitants/sq km

*** Pembroke Castle The far south-west of Wales – particularly the sprawling inlets of Milford Haven. One of the world's largest natural harbours, it has been considered the gateway to Ireland since prehistoric times. This fact was even recognized by the Norman conquerors, who built a fort and settlement here in 1090, laying the foundations for what would become the new county. In 1170, it became the starting point for the Norman conquest of Ireland, and 1189 saw the establishment of a castle surrounded by water on three sides – a mighty outpost where Henry VII, the first Tudor king, was born in 1457. Pembroke Castle retained its importance for centuries, until the town switched sides during the English Civil War and was besieged by Oliver Cromwell. After 48 days, the citizens were forced to capitulate due to a water shortage, whereupon the castle was destroyed. This turbulent history is presented in various exhibitions, including in the Great Tower and immense gatehouse.

*** Carew Castle The stories that are told on a tour through the magnificently located castle ruins by the River Carew, one of the tributaries that enter the inlets of Milford Haven, are

Kidwelly Castle

Few castles were so hotly disputed, and changed owners as often, as Kidwelly Castle. Roger of Salisbury, lord chancellor under Henry I, first had a fortress built on the strategically important hills here in around 1110. These hills fall steeply towards the River Gwendreath yet, even if besieged, the castle would still be accessible from the nearby sea. But despite constant expansions, the border-straddling castle fell into Welsh possession on numerous occasions, constantly being reconquered and surrendered. A modern castle was built in 1275, and reinforced with a gate complex between 1408 and 1422. Thereafter, however, the castle's role in military activities was negligible. It gradually fell into disrepair, and was abandoned completely in the 17th century. A watercolour by William Turner depicts the romantic ruins before they were restored.

thrilling and varied. The large 11th-century stone cross, with its stunning knot and loop patterns, today remains as evidence of the former Celtic ringfort. The complex was taken over by the Normans in 1100 as the dowry of Nest ferch Rhys, the daughter of a Welsh king. The legendary beauty was kidnapped and married several times, so it is no wonder she is said to still haunt the castle walls as the White Lady. Her castle was repeatedly modified and – like so many others – ultimately fell victim to the English Civil War. A reconstructed mill not far from the ruins is also open to visitors.

Historic Pembroke Castle is located on the river of the same name (top).

Carew Castle, on the southern banks of the River Carew, is part of the Pembrokeshire Coast National Park.

*** St Govan's Chapel

There are few places as atmospheric as St Govan's Chapel. The stone chapel, providing spectacular panoramic views over the sea, has been partly hewn out of the cliffs. It is only accessible via 52 stone steps, and is a rare gem in this barren region. The legend surrounding its construction states that the monk Govan lived in a cave nearby. When he eventually died, he was buried at the exact point where the altar stands at the eastern end. But many details still remain unclear when it comes to the chapel. Some parts are said to date back to the 6th century, while the current building is likely to be from the 13th century. The limestone walls enclose a 5 by 4 metre space. It is particularly important to check out up-to-date opening information before you go, for St Govan's Chapel should only be visited when the nearby shooting range is closed.

** Tenby

This little corner of southern Wales on Carmarthen Bay has been a popular seaside resort since the 19th century, largely due to the three magnificent beaches stretching in and around the town along the sea. Colourful houses, narrow lanes and countless cafés and souvenir shops add to the holiday feel. It was the Vikings who first established a settlement here, with the town gaining prominence in the Middle Ages, primarily due to the maritime trade and fishing. Its main showpiece is its little harbour, from where boats regularly set sail for Caldey Island. Little St Catherine's Island

Tenby's colourful little harbour makes for a picture-postcard scene.

Solva

Postcards of the fishing village of Solva (or Solfach) blow visitors away, because in one sense, the town appears to sit right on the water, and in another, it appears inland. Both are correct, and the reason for this is the tides. The narrow bay is usually completely dry at low tide, while at high tide, the water sloshes against the port walls. In the Middle Ages, lime-burning was one of the main sources of income here, and some of the furnaces have been preserved and are open to the public. In the 19th century the focus shifted to maritime trading. The town is extremely picturesque. The many colourful houses are popular among tourists, who are now the main source of income. Surfers and other watersport enthusiasts feel at home in Solva – perhaps thanks to its attractive beach.

is also accessible at low tide. Offshore, and perched atop Castle Hill in the middle of the sea, are the ruins of Tenby Castle – only one tower remains today. Built by the Normans in the 12th century, the castle was almost totally destroyed during the English Civil War.

The spectacularly located St Govan's Chapel (top) was carved into the limestone cliffs. Its origins date back to the 6th century, when a monk lived at this remote site.

*** St Davids

St Davids is the westernmost city in Wales, situated on the north coast of St Brides Bay. The reason the small town qualifies as a city is thanks to its cathedral – a church of such stature can only stand in a city, no matter how small the town's population. And it is not just any old cathedral; it is the largest in Wales. In the Middle Ages, it was an important centre for pilgrims; St David (circa 512–587), the patron saint, worked there as an abbot and missionary. The present-day church building dates from the 12th century. Despite its Gothic elements, the interior is essentially Norman. The carved wooden ceiling from the 16th century is an imposing sight, and the choir stalls and Bishop's Throne also display artistic carvings – including scenes from everyday farming life.

** Whitesands Bay

This is where St Patrick is said to have had a vision prompting him to evangelize Ireland, and it was from this very bay that he is said to have set sail to convert the people there to Christianity. Just nearby is St Patrick's Chapel, the excavation site of a former cemetery. According to inscriptions on a stone, this is also likely to be the place where the ruins of a chapel dedicated to St Patrick were found in 1924. Over time, Whitesands Bay has become a seaside resort, well known and loved by surfers in particular. It has two cafés, a lifeguard service and a surfboard-hire facility. The immediate vicinity also includes a camp site, a youth hostel and a golf course. The Pembrokeshire Coast Path, which leads straight past it, provides stunning views of the bay.

Welsh Cakes

This traditional cake is a cross between a scone and pancake. The ingredients – flour, sugar, milk, butter, dried fruit such as raisins and spices, usually cinnamon and nutmeg – were originally baked on a hot stone, and later also on a cast-iron griddle. Today, Welsh cakes are cooked in a frying pan. They were typically served for afternoon tea or given to mine workers and school children as small, filling snacks. Welsh cakes are relatively easy to make, but they are even easier to buy – look for them at baker's shops, market stalls and supermarkets or enjoy them in a café or tea room. The cakes are tossed in sugar before serving, and they are delicious warm or cold. They are also very tasty when split and spread with butter or strawberry jam.

Apart from its cathedral (opposite), the city of St Davids boasts a pretty centre with winding lanes perfect for leisurely strolls. St David's Head (bottom).

*** Pembrokeshire Coast National Park

If you find yourself passing street signs with names like Fford Cilgwyn, Llwyngwair, Feidr Cefn or Gellifawr – unpronounceable to English speakers – it means you are in the wondrous world of the Pembrokeshire Coast National Park. And just as these names conjure up images of fairies and elves, so the landscape also creates the feel of a magical nature kingdom. This is particularly the case along the snaking Pembrokeshire Coast Path, one of Great Britain's most breathtaking coastal hiking trails, where cliffs, bays and sandy beaches alternate in rapid succession. Here, 50 different species of flower, from hyacinths to plumose anemones start blooming as early as January due to the mild climate. And later in the year this sea of colour also becomes the breeding ground for thousands of seabirds, including puffins, oystercatchers, cormorants and razorbills.

*** Pentre Ifan
Though very little is known about Neolithic megalith culture, many people find its millennia-old monuments fascinating – perhaps also because these are usually found at striking locations. One such example is Pentre Ifan, a chambered dolmen above the Nevern Valley, with a fantastic view of the Preseli Mountains. It is one of the largest and

Pentre Ifan is one of Great Britain's most famous megalithic monuments.

The Green Bridge of Wales, formed by the waves of the Atlantic.

best known burial chambers of its kind in Wales, measuring 2.5 metres high and featuring a 5-metre-long capstone weighing some 16 tonnes. The central entrance to the portal is blocked by another stone standing at an angle. Information panels show how the chamber of this communal tomb was originally completely covered with a cairn, and how the stones in the forecourt had to be removed for every burial.

The Blue Lagoon near Abereiddy in the Pembrokeshire Coast National Park.

The enchanting landscape of the Pembrokeshire Coast and the Stumblehead Lighthouse (left).

The view extends far down the coast of Penbwchdy.

Pembrokeshire Coast Path

In 1953, natural historian and author Ronald Lockley presented plans for a route along the Welsh coast, and consequently the Coast Path was inaugurated in 1970. Largely divided into 15 stages, the long-distance walking trail essentially follows the upper edge of the cliff line for some 300 kilometres. The many bays provide spectacular views. In some areas, the path climbs over steep basalt cliffs, and the odd stretch can

only be covered at low tide. Part of the route heads over extremely flat terrain, while other sections take in pebbly and sandy bays or head past inlets reminiscent of natural harbours. Tall rock formations also frequently provide views of lighthouses, little fishing villages and the coast far below. And everywhere the lush Welsh green of the grass constantly stands in eye-catching contrast with the weathered rock. Seals, bottle-nose dolphins and harbour porpoises can be observed at the coast, and the area is also home to various species of bird. Nearly 60 Iron-Age coastal fortresses line the route, and the beautiful beach of Amroth near Tenby is the perfect place to bathe in the sea at the end of the hike. The charming coastal fishing villages have accommodation available for anyone wanting to stay the night.

Discovering Powys

Wales' largest county is one of lovely green hills and the natural idyll of the Brecon Beacons National Park. A visit to Powis Castle, meanwhile, transports visitors back to the Middle Ages.

Carreg Cennen Castle in the Brecon Beacons National Park.

The national park is characterized by mystical landscapes.

*** Brecon Beacons National Park It is not uncommon for hikers in the remote Brecon Beacons to suddenly find themselves face to face with a billy goat who refuses to move out of the way. He appears to size hikers up quizzically, and once he has won the power play, he magnanimously steps aside. That is when it becomes clear who the goat is. It is Merlin, of course – the Druid from King Arthur's Round Table, who is buried here in the south of Wales, and who occasionally appears to people as a goat. And given Merlin was also a mystic, it is no wonder he tends to roam around the mystical landscape of the Brecon Beacons. The mountain range is the centre-piece of the national park that was founded in 1957. The hike along the 'horseshoe' of the four peaks of Pan y Fan, the highest mountain (886 metres) in the Brecon Beacons, takes around six hours from Storey Arms, the old stagecoach station.

*** Hay-on-Wye Literature plays a major role in the book town of Hay-on-Wye. The Hay Festival of Literature & Arts held there annually at the end of May and the beginning of June since 1988, was once labelled the 'Woodstock of the mind' by former U.S. President Bill Clinton. Today, bibliophiles from all over the world meet in this small town at the northern tip of the Brecon Beacon National Park all year round. Many buildings are literally packed to the rafters with books. The village boasts some 25 second-hand bookshops, despite a population of not even 2,000 residents. Hay-on-Wye has existed as a literary place since 1961, when bookseller Richard Booth opened his second-hand bookshop and spread the idea of the 'book town', attracting many more such stores. The town is also home to the ruins of Hay Castle, which today doubles as a marketplace for – what else but – used books.

INFO

POWYS
County town:
Llandrindod Wells
Area:
5,179 sq km
Population:
132,000
Population density:
26 inhabitants/sq km

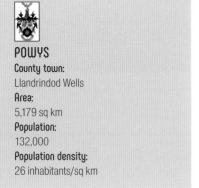

The amazing views from Pant-y-Creigiau (565 metres).

*** Powis Castle

This castle's erd sandstone towers and walls glow as it sits atop a mountain ridge. The blossoming terraces with their ancient arborvitae trees majestically cascade down to the manicured lawns and hedges and a small country park. The castle was built in 1200 and boasts elements of all architectural styles until the late 19th century. Henrietta Herbert, the daughter of the then-Lord Powis, was responsible for the gardens, while her husband, Baron Edward Clive, as Commander-in-Chief of British India, collected treasures which are today exhibited in the museum.

The Sgwd Ddwli Uchaf waterfall in the Brecon Beacons National Park (top).

One of the magnificent terraces at Powis Castle.

Brecon Beacons National Park: Llangattock Escarpment

These days, the slopes near Llangattock are incomparably idyllic. Only the limestone cliffs and a few abandoned mines still serve as visual reminders of the region's industrial past.

Discovering Ceredigion

In Cardigan Bay you can watch porpoises play, and you can also admire art or visit the National Library in the town of Aberystwyth, locally known as Aber.

INFO

CEREDIGION
County town:
Aberaeron and Aberystwyth
Area:
1,783 sq km
Population:
73,000
Population density:
41 inhabitants/sq km

** **Aberystwyth** The university town of Aberystwyth is the administrative centre of the west coast of Wales. Known by its residents simply as 'Aber', the town stretches between three hills and two beaches. One of the hills, Pen Dinas, today still bears the ruins of an Iron Age fort, while on Constitution Hill, a café has been joined by a camera obscura showing the town and landscape as a projection, for the view from up here provides a spectacular panorama of Aberystwyth and the coast. The port, into which the rivers Ystwyth and Rheidol flow, once played a key role in trade with Ireland, and sometimes even in trans-Atlantic trade, although this is no longer the case. Penglais Hill is home to the National Library of Wales and the university, whose most famous former student is Prince Charles.

Aberystwyth Cliff Railway
The Aberystwyth Cliff Railway has been in operation since 1st August 1896. It was designed by engineer George Croydon Marks, and, with a route length of 242 metres, it is the second longest funicular railway in Great Britain, and the only one in Wales. Originally operated by a sophisticated system involving water tanks, it has been electrically powered since 1921. In the space of just a few minutes, passengers are transported to Constitution Hill, which soars up at the end of Aberystwyth's bay. It provides a stunning view of the city, the bay and – in clear weather – more than 20 of Wales' other peaks. A look through the camera obscura allows you to enjoy panoramic vistas spanning some 2,000 square kilometres.

Aberystwyth University with Aberystwyth Cliff Railway in the background (top). Aberystwyth cuts a romantic figure in the late-afternoon sun (opposite right).

Discovering Gwynedd

Nowhere else have Welsh traditions been better preserved, and nowhere else do so many people still speak Welsh, than here in Gwynedd. Visitors enjoy interesting towns like Caernarfon and Bangor, and nature lovers head to the Snowdonia National Park.

** Harlech Castle High above the golden sandy beaches, a fortress clings to the cliffs like an eagle's eyrie. Harlech Castle once guarded the port here at Tremadog Bay, which is widely considered the place where English troops led by Otto de Grandson landed in 1283. King Edward I spared no expense in ordering the rapid construction of a fortress system to fight the insurgent Welsh and re-integrate Wales into English territory. So it was that the medieval complex was completed in just six years, and has remained virtually unchanged to this day. Only the landscape has ceased to be the same. At the time, the castle's inhabitants accessed the sea, which used to be right under the cliffs, via a staircase. But the coast increasingly silted up over the centuries, and the ocean is today more than 1 kilometre away.

** Portmeirion Some find it odd, others see it as genius. Regardless, everything here fol-lows the illusion of an Italian village – as if Portmeirion were on the Mediterranean rather than a headland of the stormy Welsh coast. It was established as a holiday village of sorts in 1925 by eccentric architect Clough Williams-Ellis, who converted the handful of houses into accommodation. He spent 50 years working on this fantasy world, with many construction elements coming from demolished buildings. Upon closer examination, almost everything turns out to be a colourful backdrop and con-siderably smaller in real life – a fascinating play of sight lines and optical illusions. The village stretches from the gatehouse to the cathedral and piazza, and down to the bay with its hotel and lighthouse. Portmeirion has served as a location for many TV series and films. The surrounding parklands, on the other hand, are 100 per cent real, with enchanting pathways and great views.

** Porthmadog This little town in north-west Wales boasts a proud history. It is considered to have been founded by William Madocks, who had an embankment built here in 1811. The River Afon Glaslyn sent considerable volumes of water through the town and into the bay, forming a natural harbour capable of easily han-dling ocean-going ships. During the 19th cen-tury, Porthmadog consequently developed into a tremendously important port and trading base for slate. It was here that the material was loaded and then exported to various towns in Great Britain and countless cities worldwide. Following the collapse of the slate industry, Porthmadog gradually became a shopping and holiday destination, and is still visited frequently for these purposes even today.

Harlech Castle (top left), a UNESCO World Heritage site, played a key role in many historic events. Wales or perhaps Italy? Portmeirion looks amazingly like a Mediterranean coastal town (opposite).

Wales' slate industry

During the age of industrialization in the 19th century, the slate industry was the most important and successful industrial sector in Wales. The largest production sites at that time were the Penrhyn and Dinorwic quarries in the north-west of Wales (the world's largest slate quarries) and the Oakeley mine, which was then the world's largest slate mine. Anyone who worked in slate mining faced tough conditions. In the 1880s, the industry's success was halted by a recession, coupled with workers' strikes and unrest, and later the two World Wars. Today, slate mining is limited solely to a few mines and quarries. The former Dinorwic quarry is now a museum, and several mines have become tourist attractions.

INFO

GWYNEDD
County town:
Caernarfon
Area:
2,548 sq km
Population:
124,000
Population density:
49 inhabitants/sq km

Welsh Steam Trains

Grown men instantly become young boys again as soon as they hear the hissing and clattering of traditional steam trains. The plumes of white, or sometimes jet-black, smoke, the smell of coal and axle grease, and the sight of the restored train slowly setting into motion sends them to cloud nine. The fact that the abandoned narrow-gauge and traditional railways have been reconstructed and put back in operation is largely

thanks to museum associations and volunteers. The Welsh Highland Railway from Porthmadog to Caernarfon was totally rebuilt, with work being completed in 2011. The narrow-gauge railways once transported shale and coal to the local centres and along the main tracks. The trains were small to keep costs low, and they look like toys by today's standards, but they are capable of handling even steep climbs. The mountainous region of Snowdonia is home to the most breathtaking sections which lead all the way up to Snowdon itself. The Ffestiniog Railway from Porthmadog to the mountains is the oldest, and the steam trains dating from 1863 operate along it again today.. The Rheidol, Fairborne and Talyllyn Railways head further south along the coast, while the Brecon Mountain and Welshpool & Llanfair Railways unlock areas of great beauty.

*** Snowdonia National Park

Once upon a time there was a giant named Rhudda, who lived on a mountain and wore a coat made from the beard hair of kings he had slain – until King Arthur killed him. Legend has it that, ever since, Rhudda has been resting on his mountain, which the Welsh thus call Yr Wyddfa or 'the tomb'. In English, it is known as Snowdon, and it is both the name-giver and highlight of this national park in northern Wales. Its mountain lakes are deep blue, and its slopes a ghostly green. Often, however, all the colours are blotted out by the mist and clouds. The area gets more than 5 metres of rainfall every year; the summers are hot, the winters are bitterly cold, and there is no shelter from the wind. Visitors to Snowdonia need to be on their guard, particularly against mountains like Cadair – because, according to legend, anyone who spends the night on it goes either blind or insane.

*** Snowdon, Y Lliwedd and Cnicht

As manageable as the three main peaks of the Snow-

View of the Cnicht mountain.

Snowdonia National Park is an enchanting sight in the early morning fog.

donia National Park may seem, no one should underestimate a mountain hike in this rugged terrain. Coupled with this is the fickle weather, which can make for unforgettable moments, but often also obscures any views with fog. For the seven hiking trails on the 1,085-metre-high Mount Snowdon, at least, there is also a convenient alternative, with a cog railway that

has transported visitors from Llanberies to just below the summit since 1896. Not far away is the striking Y Lliwedd (898 metres), whose steep rocky slopes make it the most popular among climbers. Rising up some way farther south is the distinctive peak of the Cnicht (689 metres), which thanks to its shape – at least when viewed from Porth-

madog – lives up to its nickname of 'the Matterhorn of Wales'.

Mountain streams tumble through the wildly rugged rocky landscape. The lakes, such as Llyn Gwynant (top) here in spring, are popular with kayakers and canoeists.

The legendary landscapes of Snowdonia can be explored on various routes.

Snowdonia National Park: Snowdon Horseshoe

A total of seven routes lead to the summit of Mount Snowdon, Wales' largest mountain. The Horseshoe Route, which crosses the entire chain of peaks – Crib Goch (923 metres), Crib y Ddysgl (1,065 metres), Snowdon (1,085 metres) and Y Lliwedd (898 metres) – is extremely challenging. Surefootedness and a head for heights are prerequisites for anyone wanting to properly enjoy the fantastic panorama.

The dining hall at Penrhyn Castle.

* Glyder Fawr At a height of 1,001 metres, Glyder Fawr is the highest peak of the Glyderau mountain range, and the fifth highest in the Snowdonia National Park. The Glyder Fawr is characterized by its cragged rock walls, making it very popular among climbers. Several hiking trails also lead up the mountain, many of them additionally taking in the neighbouring peaks. One particularly impressive circuit heads to the Glyder Fawr, as well as the adjacent Glyder Fach and Trfan peaks, and past 'Devil's Kitchen' – the mountain knoll resembles a chimney, and, in cloudy weather, 'smoke' appears to rise out of it, almost as if the devil were in the process of cooking something. The region's harsh climate, coupled with the seemingly innocuous hiking trails, poses a particular challenge for visitors. Extreme caution is required in fog or snow.

*** Caernarfon Castle Gwynedd is a rugged region in northern Wales which was governed by small noble families for centuries. Construction on Caernarfon Castle at the mouth of the River Seiont began in 1283 on the orders of Edward I, once his troops had subordinated the previously independent Wales. Located around 13 kilometres south of Bangor, the structure, with its octagonal towers, is one of the most impressive castle complexes in Wales. Not only was it designed to be part of the 'Iron Ring' of defence, the castle was also the king's residence and the seat of his government. It was there that, in 1284, Edward's eldest son was born, who later became the first Prince of Wales and then King Edward II. In 1969, this title was officially conferred upon the current heir to the throne, Charles Mountbatten-Windsor (Prince Charles), at the castle.

** Bangor The cathedral in this small town is particularly worth a visit. Its construction dates back to the 6th century. Bangor also offers ample opportunities for shopping, as it boasts the longest high street in all of Wales. Another attraction that draws many tourists to

the town is, without doubt, Penrhyn Castle, located on the outskirts. Today the property is managed by the National Trust.

*** Penrhyn Castle and Garden This is one of the largest country houses in Great Britain. But behind the picture-postcard façade lies an unsavoury reality, with the grandiose Victorian interior and sprawling parklands the result of profits gained by the Douglas-Pennant family through the sugar and slave trade in Jamaica, as well as compensation for his many slaves after the abolition of slavery in 1833. The family purchased the castle in the 17th century, and modified and extended it over the subsequent centuries.

Caernarfon Castle (top) was intended to demonstrate power and command respect, and architecturally it is indeed one of the most impressive castles in Wales.

National Slate Museum

The National Slate Museum is housed inside the Victorian workshops of the former Dinorwic slate mine, with a stunning location amongst impressive slate mountains. The museum provides detailed insights into the lives of the workers and their families, as well as the working conditions at the time and the workers' strikes. An informative film, Great Britain's largest working waterwheel and daily slate-splitting demonstrations bring the history of the slate mine and the skill of the quarry workers to life. Visitors are also transported back in time as they tour the reconstructed miners' homes and the former iron and brass foundry and forges. Another highlight is the field railway with its original working steam engine.

Caernarfon Castle

Caernarfon Castle was designed to demonstrate power and respect, and architecturally it is indeed one of Wales' most impressive castles. Comprising several portcullises and gate wings, plus - unlike other castles in Wales - octagonal towers and solid walls decorated with sandstone and limestone, the castle ruins are listed as a UNESCO World Heritage Site.

Edward I, Conqueror of Wales

Edward (1239–1307) began demonstrating his fighting spirit right from his time as crown prince. The English royalty's main adversary was Simon de Montfort – leader of the rebelling English barons and ally of the Welsh Celtic prince Llewelyn ap Gruffydd. Prince Edward had in turn struck a deal with Welsh noblemen whom Llewelyn wanted to topple, and managed to annihilate the Montfort camp in 1265. This marked a temporary

end to the battles, at least in England. Edward I was crowned king in 1274 but Llewelyn's refusal to bow to him prompted Edward and his army to invade Wales. All previous conquerors had steered clear of the wild peninsula, but Edward besieged Llewelyn in the Snowdon Massif and forced him to capitulate. It was only after a second campaign (1282–83), however, that the Welsh surrendered. To secure the new sovereign territory, the king ordered the construction of mighty fortresses in Gwynedd. And he appointed his son, the future King Edward II, as the prince of Wales. The English heir to the throne has borne the title of Prince of Wales ever since. Edward I was also known colloquially as the 'Hammer of the Scots' and 'Longshanks', because he not only had a mighty stature in terms of warfare, but also measured a stately 1.88 metres in height.

Discovering Anglesey

This island in north-west Wales is separated from the mainland by the Menai Strait. It is also known as the island of the Druids, for Celtic heritage remains strong here. Megalith complexes, as well as a mighty castle built by Edward I, attract many visitors.

Beaumaris Castle is a fine example of a medieval castle complex.

*** Anglesey In the north-west of Wales, near the Snowdonia mountain ridge, lies the island of Anglesey, connected to the mainland by two bridges. The fertile island was considered the breadbasket for northern Wales in the Middle Ages. It was once also a cult centre for the Druids, although the Romans destroyed the sanctuary and killed all the Druids in 61 as a way of crushing the resistance shown by the Celtic population. The island – particularly the pretty Llanddwyn peninsula – continues to be attributed with magic powers, a notion aided by its megalith complexes. The island came to fame as being home to the town with the longest name in Europe: Llanfairpwllgwyngyll—gogerychwyrndrobwllllantysiliogogogoch. The 58-letter mega-word is, however, usually abbreviated to Llanfairpwll or Llanfair PG.

* Beaumaris Castle Towers and walls dot the lush coastal landscape, painting a picturesque scene. After Edward I finally defeated the Welsh revolt, he wanted to ensure his rule was also cemented in Anglesey. The moated castle on the Menai Strait, whose construction began in 1295, was his largest and last. And it was the only one of his castles never to be completed, because Edward needed the money for other conflicts. With its perfect symmetry and ring-shaped outer bailey between the walls, however, it still exemplifies the influential role of English fortress architecture. Edward's intention was no doubt for the nearby town of Llanfaes, northern Wales' centre of trade, to yield to him as well, and for an English port and administrative seat to be established under the castle's protection. The quaint Victorian town today still bears evidence of its former prominence.

Holy Island (opposite), located west of Anglesey, with its South Stack Lighthouse.

The Twr Mawr Lighthouse is located in the western part of the Menai Strait.

The ruins of St Dwynwen's Church on the island of Llanddwyn.

INFO *

ANGLESEY
County town:
Llangefni
Area:
714 sq km
Population:
70,000
Population density:
98 inhabitants/sq km

Discovering Conwy

Conwy Castle is part of the Castles and Town Walls of King Edward in Gwynedd UNESCO World Heritage Site, so it is worth spending some time in this small town near the Snowdonia National Park. The seaside resort of Llandudno and the railway terminus of Betws-y-Coed are also sites of interest to explore.

INFO *

CONWY

County town:
Conwy
Area:
1,130 sq km
Population:
117,000
Population density:
104 inhabitants/sq km

*** Conwy Castle Perched atop a rocky promontory, the mighty castle with its eight towers rises up above the River Conwy. It was Edward I's first and most important fortress in northern Wales. Construction began in 1283 and took just five years to complete under the direction of master builder James of Saint George. The centrepiece of the 'Iron Ring' is nothing more than a show of power, demonstrating the king's right to control Wales. With its two courtyards and royal apartments, however, it still had very comfortable amenities. No less impressive is the city wall built at the same time. It follows on directly from the castle, providing the English with a secure base in enemy territory. Unfortunately, the immense castle ruins today appear jammed between road and railway bridges – a fact compensated by the spectacular circular walk along the well-preserved defensive battlements.

** Llandudno The seaside resort of Llandudno sits on a headland on Wales' 'Golden Coast', almost within sight of Conwy. The prefix 'Llan' in Welsh means 'church', and is often used in connection with saints – and this is also true for Llandudno, the 'church of St Tudno'. The saint is said to have lived in a rock cave here in the 6th century, and founded the church of Cyngreawdr, the Welsh name for the 'Great Orme Head' mountain near Llandudno. Located on the coast between Conwy and Colwyn Bay, the town is considered to be the most renowned – and largest – seaside resort in Wales. Llandudno was a popular summer health resort as early as the

Betws-y-Coed

The typical little Welsh town in the mountains is also known as the 'gateway to Snowdonia'. Considered the centre of Snowdonia National Park and set amongst magical natural landscapes, it is an ideal starting point for excursions into captivating corners of the park. Heading north-east takes you to Swallow Falls. In the early 20th century, the waterfall was used to generate power for Betws-y-Coed, and has been a popular tourist attraction since the 1930s. The landscape south-east of Betws is also thoroughly enchanting, particularly in the mystical Fairy Glen, a magical ravine, and around the equally legendary Conwy Falls. The evergreen forest and lake landscape of Gwydir Forest is another stunning hiking paradise.

19th century – for those who could afford it. To the south of the resort, about 13 kilometres away, extends Bodnant Garden, a magnificent park established in 1874.

Conwy Castle (top), located right by the sea and the first of nine castles to have been built by Edward I in Wales, is today listed as a UNESCO World Heritage Site.

The waterfront of the glamorous seaside resort of Llandudno is lit up beautifully at night.

River Conwy

The River Conwy flows through mystical landscapes as it makes its
way north. It has its source in Llyn Conwy and opens out into
Conwy Bay some 55 kilometres farther along.

Discovering Denbighshire

Two Roman roads once passed through Denbighshire. Several castles were then built here following the region's conquest by Edward I. Hilly moorland alternates with a narrow coastal plain in the north, lively market towns like Llangollen and historic sites such as Bodelwyddan Castle.

** Llangollen This little town in north-eastern Wales is renowned nationally for its International Eisteddfod ('eistedd' being Welsh for 'sit'), which has been held every July since 1947, attracting some 130,000 visitors each time. Musicians, choirs and folkdance groups from all over the world participate in the event, whose patron is Prince Charles, the Prince of Wales. Towering over Llangollen are the picturesque ruins of the 13th-century Dinas Brân castle, which was immortalized by

Llangollen International Musical Eisteddfod Festival

Every July, the quiet town in northern Wales springs to life, with singers and dancers from all over the world seeking to put in top performances at the international music competition. The dance and music festival runs for six days, and was originally established in 1947 by W. S. Gwyn Williams in a bid to create a sense of peace and friendliness between various nations. The vibrant cultural festival has existed ever since, bringing together traditional costumes, folkdances and voices from across the globe. In addition to the competitions, there are also workshops and concerts. The many music stars welcomed by the festival over the years have included Luciano Pavarotti and Montserrat Caballé. Also part of the spectacle is the traditional procession for artists and visitors.

INFO *

DENBIGHSHIRE
County town:
Ruthin
Area:
844 sq km
Population:
95,000
Population density:
114 inhabitants/sq km

William Turner in his painting *The Vale of Llangollen and Dinas Brân*. The bridge over the River Dee, built in the 14th century, is also famous throughout Wales. Travelling down the 73-kilometre-long, often only 2-metre-wide Llangollen Canal, which meanders through a captivating landscape, is a unique experience. The most spectacular point of the navigable canal is the Pontcysyllte aqueduct 36.5 metres above the River Dee, designed by Thomas Telford and opened in 1805.

* Moel Tŷ Uchaf The Moel Tŷ Uchaf hill east of Llandrillo is known for the megalith monument that shares its name. Perched atop the hill is a fully preserved ring of 41 stones measuring 12 metres in diameter, at the centre of which are the remains of a stone cist. The monument is presumed to date back to the Bronze Age. The hill is accessed from Llangollen along a road and an unmade path. Visitors often describe the circle as 'almost perfect', and this can also be said of its loca-

tion – surrounded by lush greenery and a spectacular hilly landscape, the place has a distinctly mystical feel.

The view of Dinas Brân (top) and the picturesque hills at sunset. A close-up of the ruins of Dinas Brân (opposite top).

The train station of the quiet town of Llangollen is located right on the River Dee.

Pontcysyllte Aqueduct

The industrial and later tourist potential offered by waterways was identified early on in Great Britain. And an outstanding example of this is the Pontcysyllte Aqueduct – the largest of its kind in this part of the world, measuring 307 metres in length and some 37 metres in height, and mastering a difficult geographical environment. Soon after the inauguration of the aqueduct conceived by the celebrated

civil engineers Thomas Telford and William Jessop between 1795 and 1805, its design, which features an elegant combination of cast-iron and stone elements, became the blueprint for similar structures all over the world. 'Pontcysyllte' is Welsh for 'the bridge that connects'. Celebrated as a 'stream in the sky', crossing the aqueduct is still a unique experience today. This involves a boat ride down the cast-iron trough holding the water, alongside which runs a towpath where horses once pulled the boats. Visitors particularly enjoy seeing the trough's maintenance valve opened, prompting cascades of water to plunge into the River Dee – this is done once every five years to maintain the aqueduct. Today the Aqueduct and the Canal are listed by UNESCO as a World Heritage Site.

The best travel routes
and city walks

England and Wales enjoy a colourful mixture of nature and culture, which our three routes allow you to explore to the full. In the south of England, the main attractions are the beaches and the coastal resorts, particularly in Cornwall and Devon, and of course the capital, London. Two city walks take you to the most interesting sights in London. The north of England boasts breathtakingly beautiful scenery and many historic sites. Wales, meanwhile, charms its visitors with its very uniqueness.

Scotland

Southern Uplands

Berwick-upon-Tweed

Cornhill-
on-Tweed

815
The Cheviot Hills

Newcastle
upon Tyne

Hexham

Carlisle

N o r t h

S e a

Penrith

Barnard Castle

Whitby

3

Scafell Pike

Lake
District

Scarborough

Gosforth

978

Ripon

Greenodd

The Pennines

Ouse

York

Isle of Man

I r i s h

S e a

Leeds

U N I T E D   K I N G D O M

Anglesey

Carmel Head

Holyhead

Bangor

Conwy

Chester

Caernarfon

Snowdon

1085

Llangollen

Wrexham

Porthmadog

Dolgellau

Welshpool

E n g l a n d

2

Aberystwyth

Severn

Stratford-
upon-Avon

W a l e s

Brecon

811
Black Mtns.

Bourton-
on-the-Water

Oxford

Fishguard

St. David's Head

Carmarthen

Abergavenny

Cotswold Hills

Thames

London

Pembroke

Merthyr Tydfil

Swansea

Newport

Windsor

C e l t i c

Cardiff

Bath

N o r t h   D o w n s

S e a

Bristol Channel

Wells

1

Stonehenge

519

Shaftesbury

S o u t h   D o w n s

Dungeness

Hartland Point

Hastings

East Devon Coast

Portsmouth

Beachy
Head

Tintagel

Swanage

Isle of Wight

Torquay

Bill of
Portland

St. Ives

St. Austell

Land's End

of Scilly

E n g l i s h   C h a n n e l

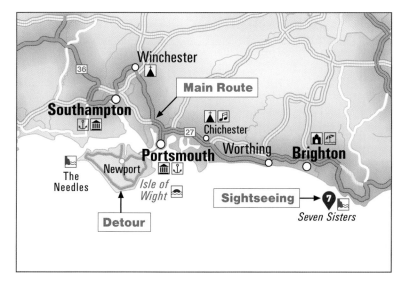

The book's final chapter suggests three routes which will take you through the most magnificent natural scenery and to the most beautiful villages and areas of England and Wales. In addition, there are two walks in central London, with shopping and restaurant tips. The overview map on the left indicates the route of each circuit at a glance. The text accompanying each route introduces the regions and counties through which you will drive as well as their scenic, historic and cultural attractions. The text is complemented by detailed maps, which clearly show the course of each route and the most important stopping points. The main route and any excursions are marked in different colours, and icons (below) symbolize the main attractions that you will encounter along the way. The main must-see destinations are illustrated by beautiful photographs and captions in the margins of each map.

Principal travel routes

🚂 Rail road

Remarkable landscapes and natural monuments

🏔 Mountain landscape
Ravine/canyon
River landscape
Waterfall/rapids
Lake country
National park (landscape)
National park (flora)
National park (fauna)
National park (culture)
Whale watching

Protected area for sea-lions/seals
Coastal landscape
Beach
Island

Remarkable cities, cultural monuments and events

Pre- and early history
Roman antiquity
Places of christian cultural interest
Cultural landscape
Castle/fortress/fort
Palace
Technical/industrial monument
Mine (abandoned)

Remarkable lighthouse
Remarkable bridge
Theater of war/battlefield
Market
Festivals
Museum
Theatre/theater

Sport and leisure sites

Arena/stadium
Horse racing
Sailing
Seaport
Beach resort
Amusement/theme park

The Duddo Five Stones in Northumberland.

Route 1: Magical places in the south of England

Ancient trading routes traverse the south of England, and monumental stone circles bear witness to the earliest settlements. Celts, Romans, Anglo-Saxons and Normans followed these first 'Englishmen' onto the island and transformed its magnificent natural scenery into a cultural landscape of green parks, quaint fishing villages and almighty country estates.

When speaking of the south of England, people usually refer to the region along the southern coastline. For some, the south comprises solely the coastal counties, such as Sussex and Dorset, while others think of the south-east including London, and for others again it only conjures up the south-west with Devon and Cornwall. Some would even say the 'south' reaches far beyond central England. While some areas, such as Greater London with its just under 9 million inhabitants, are densely populated, others, like Dartmoor, seem rather devoid of any human life. 'Steeped in history', that's how the British themselves refer to this region, which is famous for its contrasts: picturesque cliffs and small fishing villages alternate with lively seaside resorts and modern port cities, and green parks merge into windswept

Bath Around 2,000 years ago, the Romans established a bath complex here, which was rediscovered in 1870. Bath was declared a spa town as early as the 18th century.

Stonehenge This world-famous and iconic prehistoric site was erected in the Late Stone Age, between approximately 3,100 and 1,500 BC, and further extended during the Bronze Age.

Blenheim Palace The gigantic stately home dating from 1722 – a Baroque masterpiece – was a gift from Queen Anne to the Duke of Marlborough for his victory in the Battle of Blenheim (1704).

Cotswolds The ancient churches, lush gardens, homely cottages and magnificent manor houses in this part of the country all seem more 'typically English' than in any other part of Britain.

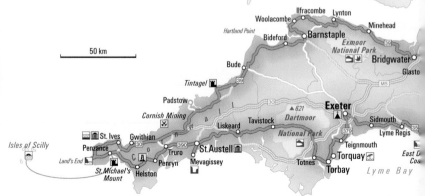

House façades on Marine Parade in the seaside resort of Eastbourne.

The route at a glance:

Length of the route: about 1,200 km | **Time needed:** 2–3 weeks

London → 120 km Hastings → 58 km Brighton → 80 km Portsmouth → 70 km Salisbury → 80 km Weymouth → 100 km Exeter → 37 km Torquay → 110 km St Austell → 86 km Land's End → 200 km Barnstaple → 90 km Bridgwater → 66 km Bath → 137 km Stratford-upon-Avon → 86 km Oxford → 66 km Windsor → 40 km London

moors. While the busy metropolis of London dominates the south-east, the more relaxed south-west is characterized by a holiday atmosphere. The south has always attracted artists and poets. Dickens and Austen, Turner and Constable all lived here or brought the south to life in their work. Numerous nature reserves and gardens invite you to take a longer walk or a casual stroll. It was here on the south coast

that many millennia ago the British islands literally 'broke away' from the mainland. The rising sea levels after the end of the last Ice Age (around 10,000 BC) drowned the land bridge that originally linked the two parts. This geological line of division – a white limestone edge – can still clearly be seen in many areas, for example in Dover and Eastbourne. While the West Country consists predominantly of granite,

the chalk formations are typical of the south-east. Due to its geographical proximity to the continent, the south has always been the entrance gate for settlers, invaders and traders. The nomads of the Old Stone Age arrived on the island around 3,500 BC as cattle breeders and arable farmers. The warm temperatures of the Gulf Stream ensured a mild climate and in some areas a subtropical vegetation. Natural resources such as tin and copper also attracted foreign invaders. Yet since 1066, when William the Conqueror emerged victorious from the Battle of Hastings, Britain has not been conquered by any hostile power. Castles and fortresses bear witness to the vulnerability of the coast, while Britain's castles, cathedrals and venerable universities attest to the historic importance of the south. Along the coast, small fishing communities developed into large port cities and hailed Great Britain's ascent as a maritime power. The British Empire sent its ships to all corners of the globe, and in return exotic goods and people from other countries came to the United Kingdom and changed the lifestyles of the tradition-conscious islanders. During the 19th century, the nobility discovered the pleasures of the coast and went on pilgrimages to elegant seaside resorts like Brighton.

Remains of the Wheal Coates tin mine on the Cornish coast (left).

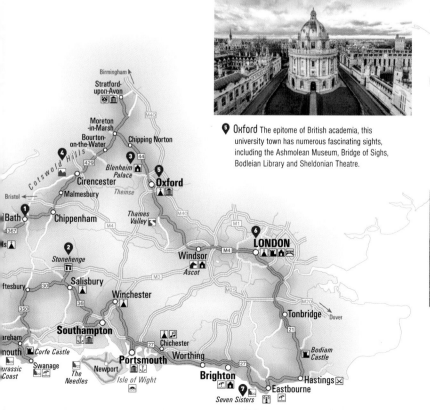

Oxford The epitome of British academia, this university town has numerous fascinating sights, including the Ashmolean Museum, Bridge of Sighs, Bodleian Library and Sheldonian Theatre.

London The capital of the United Kimgdom is both old-fashioned and hyper-modern at the same time. Westminster, the Tower of London, St Paul's Cathedral and the British Museum are absolute must-sees.

Seven Sisters At a height of 163 metres, Beachy Head is Britain's tallest chalk cliff. It is located in the Seven Sisters Country Park, which itself is named after seven clearly discernible chalk cliffs.

The Millennium Bridge, connecting Bankside with the City, is London's most recent bridge. It is open only to pedestrians.

City Walk 1: Historic London

Despite an abundance of modern skyscrapers and new buildings, historical architectural gems can still be found in the heart of this cosmopolitan city. Our walk takes you through the centre and to some well-known and lesser-known buildings.

What to see

The Monument This fluted Doric column topped by a golden urn of gilded fire was erected shortly after the Great Fire of 1666, exactly 61 metres from its starting point in Pudding Lane, to commemorate the catastrophe. The gallery at the top can be reached via a spiral staircase with 311 steps.

St Stephen Walbrook This little church – built from 1672 to1679 to the plans of British architect Christopher Wren – is famous not only for its light and airy beauty but also for its unusual white altar, which was created by the sculptor Henry Moore. A telephone in a glass box symbolizes the Samaritans' telephone helpline, which was inaugurated here in 1953.

Mansion House This Palladian structure was erected in the 18th century and was the official residence of the Mayor of London right from the beginning. It boasts magnificent furnishings, as seemed appropriate for the holder of this office of state. Unfortunately, private visitors are not admitted to the building, except for pre-registered travel groups.

Bank of England The Old Lady of Threadneedle Street, as the Bank of England is often called, has had the state monopoly over money in England and Wales for more than 300 years. The imposing building exudes gravity and power. The bank's own museum relates the history of banking in a fascinating exhibition.

Royal Exchange Trade has been an essential element in the creation of London's wealth since time immemorial. From the 16th century, this was mostly conducted at the Royal Exchange, built in 1566 by Thomas Gresham. Today, financial transactions and trade deals are mostly made in other places within the city but the Exchange – the third structure standing at this site – has stayed true to its original purpose: it is now a luxury shopping centre.

Guildhall Some parts of the Guildhall date from the Middle Ages, probably making it the oldest secular structure in London. The Guildhall was built between 1411 and 1440 by wealthy traders. From the start, the building served as a town hall for the inner district, and today it is still used for cermeonial purposes as well as an administrative building. The Guildhall can be visited.

Barbican Centre A vast performing arts and conference centre built in the east of the City in 1982, the Barbican regularly hosts important concerts and art exhibitions. The complex is also home to the London Symphony Orchestra and BBC Symphony Orchestra, as well as three cinemas.

Museum of London This fascinating museum explains the development of London from prehistoric times to the present with over a million exhibits. Here you can first get an overview of the city's history and then look at individual historical stages in more detail in the themed halls. Interactive stations and guided tours bring the fascinating history of London to life. You can also see the remains of a Roman city wall nearby.

St Paul's Cathedral Sir Christopher Wren's masterpiece rightly deserves a longer visit. It is not only considered to be the most stately church in London, if not England, but also offers a treat for the senses with its lavish yet elegant interior and the magnificent view from the dome. The view from the Golden Gallery, the dome's viewing platform, extends far beyond the Thames and Westminster – a worthwhile climb. Construction of the cathedral began in 1675 and was completed in 1711.

Temple of Mithras The remains of the Mithras Temple, also known as the London Mithraeum, dating from the 3rd century and accidentally discovered during road works in 1954, form one of the oldest parts of London. The Mithras cult, which goes back to a sect in Persia, was particularly popular with Roman soldiers. The excavations are on Queen Victoria Street.

Where to shop

Royal Exchange
A designer handbag from Aspinal of London, a pair of shoes from Church's, a scarf from Hermès, perfume from Jo Malone – this luxury shopping centre really leaves nothing to be desired. For refreshment or as a kind of shock therapy in view of the prices, oysters and champagne are, of course, also available here.
Threadneedle Street
Mon-Fri 10am-6pm
www.theroyalexchange.co.uk

Leadenhall Market Meat and fish were once sold in this Victorian indoor market. Today, restaurants, bars, boutiques and delicatessen shops are hidden behind the wonderfully old-fashioned façades.
Whittington Avenue/Gracechurch Street
Mon-Fri about 10am-6pm
www.leadenhallmarket.co.uk

Petticoat Lane Market Whether you need a new outfit or some household utensils, small decorative items or a gift, you will find them here. There are designer items that purport to be seconds or out of date – but beware: not everything with a recognizable or slightly changed label is actually a branded product! You can also find good, inexpensive clothing here.
Between Middlesex Street and
Goulston Street
Fri-Sun 8am-6pm

Leadenhall Market offers shopping and dining in Victorian surroundings.

Where to eat

1 Lombard Street This Michelin-starred restaurant is located in a listed counter hall. The bar and brasserie are a bit more casual, but the restaurant is extremely classy. The cuisine is European – and, of course, it comes at a price. The bar also serves a selection of tapas from 5pm.
1 Lombard Street
Tel. +44 (0)20 79 29 66 11
Breakfast: Mon-Fri 7.30-10am
Lunch & Dinner: Mon-Fri 11.30am-10pm
www.1lombardstreet.com

Café Below Probably one of the most atmospheric pubs in town, The Place Below is actually 'downstairs', namely in the crypt of Christopher Wren's Church of St Mary-le-Bow. Healthy and, above all, delicious food is served here.
St Mary-le-Bow, Cheapside

Tel. +44 (0)20 73 29 07 89
Breakfast: Mon-Fri 7.30-10am
Lunch: Mon-Fri 11.30am-2.30pm
www.cafebelow.co.uk

Jamies Winebar and Restaurant: London Wall The bar offers delicious cocktails and the modern restaurant serves burgers, sandwiches and snacks.
125 Alban Gate
Mon-Fri 10am-9pm
www.jamies.london

The English Restaurant A genuinely cosy corner café and restaurant, which with its old-fashioned interior stands out pleasantly from the chic and hyper-modern competition in the area.
52 Brushfield Street
Tel. +44 (0)20 72 47 41 10
Mon-Fri 8am-11pm, Sat 9.30am-11pm,
Sun 9.30am-7pm
www.theenglishrestaurant.com

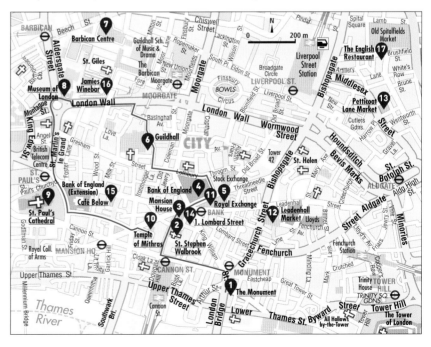

The Elizabeth Tower, widely known as Big Ben, rises up between the Houses of Parliament and Westminster Bridge.

City Walk 2: Royal London

Palaces, parks and the Empire – this walk takes you through royal London and the government district, where you may witness ceremonial appearances by the Queen or her family, and rituals such as the Changing of the Guard.

What to see

❶ Wellington Arch This triumphal arch dating from 1830 stands on a traffic island between Buckingham Palace and Hyde Park. It is an unmistakable landmark also thanks to the Quadriga on top of the arch, which is considered to be the largest bronze statue in Europe. Until 1992 the arch housed a police station; today the tiny rooms serve as a museum.

❷ The Royal Mews The royal stables at Buckingham Palace, designed by John Nash, are now more of a garage than a stable. The Queen's gold state coach, horses and the royal family's entire motorized vehicle fleet are housed there.

❸ Buckingham Palace The official residence of the British monarchs, this is the place where foreign heads of state, the nobility and celebrities are ceremonially received. From July to October, while the Queen is absent, commoners are admitted into the palace, but only to the state apartments.

❹ Clarence House Until her death in 2002, this palace designed by John Nash was the home of the Queen Mum, Queen Elizabeth II's popular mother. Today it is the London residence of Prince Charles and

his wife Camilla , Duchess of Cornwall. In summer there are public tours – but only of the ground floor.

❺ St James's Palace This palace on The Mall is one of the oldest in London. It was originally commissioned by Henry VIII and was the royal residence until 1837. Today the palace comprises several buildings and is still the administrative seat of the royal court and the official residence of Princess Anne, the daughter of Queen Elizabeth II.

❻ Admiralty Arch This three-arched gate from 1912 provides The Mall –the royal road stretching from Trafalgar Square to Buckingham Palace – with a grand entrance. The adjacent buildings house various government offices. The central archway is is reserved for use by royalty and only opened for ceremonial occasions, such as for royal pageants or during state visits.

❼ Banqueting House The Palace of Whitehall was the royal residence since 1530, and in about 1650 it was the largest building in Europe, boasting some 1,500 rooms. It was largely destroyed by a fatal fire in 1698, and the Banqueting House is the only part of the palace that still exists today. The Renaissance style, which was unusual in England at the time, and the wonderful

ceiling paintings by Flemish artist Peter Paul Rubens are unique.

❽ 10 Downing Street The government seat of British prime ministers since 1732, this relatively modest terraced house hardly looks impressive from the outside. However, the simple, yet world-famous façade is deceptive. Behind the black door is hidden a complex made up of what were once three separate houses. It is now home to both offices and private rooms.

❾ Churchill War Rooms In 2002, Winston Churchill was voted the greatest Briton ever in a BBC poll, so it's no wonder that an entire museum is dedicated to this statesman. It was set up in the bunker where the then-prime minister met with his cabinet during World War II. Inside its 21 rooms, history is brought to life. The museum also has a sizable collection of Churchill paraphernalia, including the great man's cigars.

❿ The Palace of Westminster The meeting place of the British government, whose origins date back to the 11th century and which, in its current form, hails from the 19th century, is one of the most famous buildings in London. The main tourist magnet, however, and a symbol of the city, is the clock tower, known as Big Ben.

Westminster Abbey Over 3,300 people are believed to be buried in this truly magnificent Gothic abbey church, including many crowned heads, but also poets, artists, scientists and statesmen. Traditionally, this has also been the coronation church of the English kings since William the Conqueror conquered the English throne by the sword in 1066.

Where to shop

Fortnum & Mason This famously exclusive 'grocery store' is a delicatessen that has been supplying luxury foods and specialities from around the world to the royal family for more than 300 years. It is also famous for its wonderful hampers that the rich and famous like to have delivered to each other as gifts for special occasions.
181 Piccadilly
Mon–Sat 10am–8pm, Sun 11.30am–6pm
www.fortnumandmason.com

Berry Bros & Rudd Fitted with wooden panels, this shop and its vaulted cellar are a true paradise for lovers of fine wines. The best wines in the world, and of course champagne, have been sold here for more than 300 years. The most expensive bottle at just under £900 is a Roederer Cristal Rosé. A bottle of house wine will cost you about £10.
3 St James's Street
Tel. +44 (0)20 73 96 95 57
Mon–Fri 10am–9pm, Sat 10am–5pm
www.bbr.com

Where to eat

Ye Grapes This Victorian pub is a little gem hidden in such an exclusive area – friendly, traditional, more of a village pub than a cosmopolitan bistro. It's a bit tucked away, but its real ales and English dishes are definitely tempting.
16 Shepherd Market, Mayfair
Tel. +44 (0)20 74 93 42 16
Mon–Fri 11am–11pm, Sat 11.30am–11pm,
Sun 12 noon–10.30pm
http://shannon-pubs.com/ye-grapes-1

The Goring This hotel is located in the immediate vicinity of Buckingham Palace, and so tradition here is also infused with nobility. Refined English cuisine is served in the hotel's light and airy restaurant.
15 Beeston Place, Grosvenor Gardens
Tel. +44 (0) 20 7396 9000
Afternoon tea: Sun–Fri 4–4.30pm,
Sat 1–4pm
Cocktail bar: 11am–11pm every day
www.thegoring.com

The Wolseley One of London's great café-restaurants, the Wolseley's classy interior is a testament to European savoir-vivre. The cooking is characterized by its French brasserie-style menu, but the absolute highlight is afternoon tea, which just couldn't be any more stylish.
160 Piccadilly
Tel. +44 (0)20 74 99 69 96
Mon–Fri 7am–11pm, Sat/Sun 8am–11pm
www.thewolseley.com

Mango Tree This elegant Thai restaurant focuses entirely on its exquisite cuisine.
45 Grosvenor Place
Tel. +44 (0)20 78 23 18 88
Mon–Wed 12 noon–3pm, 6–11pm,
Thu–Sat 12 noon–3pm, 6–11.30 pm,
Sun 12 noon–10.30pm
www.mangotree.org.uk

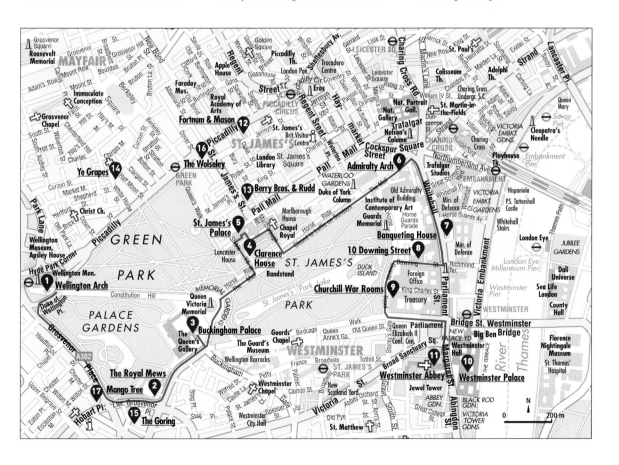

Castlerigg in the Lake District is one of England's largest stone circles.

Route 2: Exploring the north of England

Rolling hills, wide valleys, endless heathland and thickly overgrown moors are characteristic of the north of England. The mystical atmosphere of these landscapes is captured and preserved in several national parks such as the Lake District and the Northumberland National Park. In addition, the northern part of the country is home to cultural treasures such as romantic castles and impressive monastery ruins and, last but not least, lively cities such as York or Durham.

The route at a glance:
Length of the route: about 1,030 km | **Time needed:** about 2 weeks
Leeds → 73 km **Haworth** → 100 km **Windermere** → 150 km **Penrith** → 32 km **Carlisle** → 65 km **Hexham** → 140 km **Berwick-upon-Tweed** → 47 km **Alnwick** → 55 km **Newcastle upon Tyne** → 30 km **Durham** → 100 km **Ripon** → 95 km **Whitby** → 30 km **Scarborough** → 70 km **York** → 44 km **Leeds**

Compared to the landscape in the southern counties of Kent and Sussex, the north of England presents the country in an entirely new light. At lower elevations, various shades of bright green dominate the land, which is criss-crossed by dark and weathered dry-stone walls. The landscape at higher altitudes, however, is rather rougher and more barren in nature. There are few lush pastures for live-stock to be found here; the hills are thickly overgrown with moss, and in summer they are covered with a purple carpet of heather. Small rivers and streams flow through the valleys and are crossed by historic stone bridges.

The roads that lead through the region are adapted to this wilderness. Although they are easy to drive on, they often feature – at least in the two national parks in the heart of

Yorkshire – just one lane, so you need to keep your foot hovering over the brake pedal as visibility before a bend may be strictly limited. It is not uncommon if two vehicles meet that one of them has to reverse to the last passing place in order to let the other one go past. In addition, other important 'road users', who have a right of way on these roads, must not be forgotten: sheep could stand calmly in the middle of the road as you turn a corner. So this area, which can be best explored in car jour-neys and long walks, definitely has a very spe-cial charm.

The region between Leeds and Newcastle is equally rich in art and cultural treasures: mag-nificent palaces and castles still bear witness to the wealth of the aristocracy; imposing ruins of historical monasteries and cathedrals,

which are often impressively integrated into the unique landscape, recall the former influ-ence and wealth of the clergy as well as their eventual decline as a result of Henry VIII's breakaway from the Catholic church. Famous painters such as Thomas Gainsborough, John Constable and J. M. W. Turner have captured these gigantic historical buildings together with the landscapes of the lakes and moun-tains of the Lake District in the west of the country in their paintings. The Yorkshire region was also home to the Brontë sisters, who have created a literary monument to the area through their work .

Hadrian's Wall, also known as the Roman Wall or the Picts' Wall, in the north of England was begun by Emperor Hadrian in about 122. It commemorates the time about 2,000 years ago when the Romans had already conquered an empire of enormous size and were finally pushed back by the Caledonians at precisely this point. As a result, the border area remained the scene of bloody fighting between England and Scotland. Only once Queen Anne had united the two kingdoms did peace return. The wall can be visited north of Newcastle, in Northumberland.

Lake District National Park Romantic lakes, countless mountains, lonely valleys and small villages make England's largest national park one of the most beautiful areas in Great Britain.

Northumberland National Park England's northernmost national park boasts some breathtaking landscapes. When the view is clear, thousands of stars can be seen in the sky at night.

Durham The majestic cathedral on the River Wear is a UNESCO World Heritage Site. It was built in the Romanesque-Norman style and has architectural features from different eras.

Yorkshire Dales National Park Sparsely populated valleys, barren hills and a large area overgrown with heather and ferns characterize this national park. You can explore it on beautiful footpaths and biking trails.

Whitby Abbey The imposing ruins of this former monastery dating from 657 can be seen from afar. They exude a mystical atmosphere and attract many visitors thanks to their spectacular location.

Fountains Abbey The remains of this monastery, a UNESCO World Heritage Site, are among the most beautiful ruins in Europe. In the 12th century, Fountains Abbey was probably the richest monastery in England.

York The cathedral is the largest Gothic church in Great Britain, but York's other churches are equally worth visiting – as are the numerous museums and the 5-kilometre long city wall.

Edinburgh

Berwick-upon-Tweed

Cornhill-on-Tweed
698

Holy Island

Scotland

Bamburgh Castle

2

Northumberland National Park

697

Alnwick

Cragside
Otterburn

Glasgow

Hadrian's Wall

Morpeth

Carlisle
69
Brampton

Hexham

NEWCASTLE
upon Tyne

6

Beamish

3

Keswick
Penrith

Castlerigg Stone Circle

Bishop Auckland

Durham

Egremont

1

Lake District National Park

Barnard Castle
688

66

595

Aysgarth Falls

Richmond

North York Moors National Park

5

Whitby

Greenodd

Levens Hall
Kirkby Lonsdale

4

Yorkshire Dales National Park

Leyburn

1

Rievaulx Abbey

Thirsk

Helmsley

165

65

170

Long Preston

Ripon

Castle Howard

64

Scarborough

6

Fountains Abbey

Skipton
56

Harrogate

Malton

7

Haworth

Harewood

York

64

Kingston upon Hull

50 km

LEEDS

Sheffield

The ruins of Tintern Abbey, a former Cistercian monastery from the 12th century, can be found in the valley of the River Wye.

Route 3: Wales – Nature and culture in the land of the red dragon

The country between England and Ireland, whose coat of arms features a dragon, is characterized by rolling hills, green valleys, quiet lakes and lonely mountains. Attractive beaches and rugged cliffs stretch along its coast. History and culture are steeped in the Celtic heritage and traditions of Wales – and the street signs are generally bilingual, in Welsh and English.

In 1804, the Industrial Revolution began with Richard Trevithick's first steam locomotive in the Taff Valley in Wales, 'the land of the Celts'. After that, the mythical land of King Arthur and the enchanter Merlin was dominated by coal mines, ironworks and the narrow-gauge freight transport trains, known as the Great Little Trains of Wales. By 1890, Cardiff had become the largest coal-shipping port in the world.

Today, a little over three million mostly bilingual people live on around 20,000 square kilometres of land, leaving sufficient space in between for a good 10 million sheep, which graze peacefully in the tranquil and remote landscape. After the collapse of the coal and iron industries in recent decades, agriculture is one of the most important sources of

income for the Welsh economy. Half-wild ponies frolic in the three large national parks of Snowdonia, Pembrokeshire and Brecon Beacons, but nearly 80 per cent of the remaining land area between these parks are used for agriculture. The peaks of the Cambrian Mountains in the Snowdonia National Park rise from sea level to an average height of 800 metres and form an impressive mountain backdrop. The highest mountain in Wales – and in Great Britain outside the Scottish Highlands – is Snowdon (1,085 metres), followed by Canedd Llewellyn (1,062 metres). All three national parks are ideal rambling and climbing regions – despite their low altitude, the conditions are almost alpine. The mountains largely block the way to the rainy Atlantic lows, which results in mild winters and moderate summers, allowing many Mediterranean plant species to flourish in Wales. Prehistoric and Celtic times have bequeathed the country

a variety of stone circles, menhirs and dolmens, from the island of Anglesey to the Preseli Hills, where the famous 'bluestones' were quarried and transported to Stonehenge some 3,000 years ago. Centuries later, the Roman legionnaires arrived, felled the holm oaks and killed the Celtic druids to whom the trees were sacred. They did not leave until 410, after 'importing' Christianity into Wales. Centuries later, this developed into the early medieval saga of King Arthur and Merlin.

From the 11th century onwards, the Norman conquerors began building their castles in Wales – around 400, more than in the rest of Great Britain. Times were warlike right up to the death of the last truly Welsh Prince of Wales in his fight against the English. Following his victory over the Welsh, the English King Edward I built mighty castles in Wales to intimidate the Welsh people. In 1536, Wales was annexed to the Kingdom of England.

The Sunset Falls in the Brecon Beacons.

The route at a glance:
Length of the route: about 900 km | **Time needed:** about 2 weeks
Cardiff → 66 km **Swansea** → 45 km **Camarthen** → 50 km **Pembroke** → 120 km **Aberystwyth** → 125 km **Caernafon** → 35 km **Anglesey** → 28 km **Bangor** → 25 km **Conwy** → 72 km **Chester** → 16 km **Wrexham** → 29 km **Llangollen** → 45 km **Welshpool** → 110 km **Brecon** → 30 km **Merthyr Tydfil** → 30 km **Abergavenny** → 30 km **Newport** → 24 km **Cardiff**

Snowdonia National Park The largest and most spectacular of the three Welsh national parks, it is dominated by the Cambrian Mountains. Although they are only 700–800 metres high on average, they offer alpine conditions for hikers and climbers.

Conwy Castle This castle, built under Edward I, boasts eight well-fortified round towers and 4.50-metre-thick walls. It is located in the town of Conwy, which itself is surrounded by a long town wall with many towers.

Aberystwyth This bustling port and university town at the mouth of the rivers Ystwyth and Rheidol has beautiful beaches with a Victorian promenade and a viewpoint that can be reached by a funicular electric cliff railway.

Cardiff Castle The seemingly medieval castle in fact dates from the late 19th century. A coal baron named Bute had it built in a Victorian Gothic revival style.

50 km

Carmel Head

Holyhead
Anglesey
Menai Bridge
Bangor
Caernarfon
Llandudno
Conwy
Abergele
Holywell
Liverpool
Connah's Quay
Chester
1085
Snowdon
Snowdonia National Park
Lleyn
Porthmadog
Wrexham
Llangollen
Erddig
Dolgellau
Oswestry
Cadair Idris
892
Machynlleth
Welshpool
Aberystwyth
Plynlimon
752
Newtown
Aberaeron
Llangurig
Cardigan
Rhayader
Fishguard
Cilgerran
Pembrokeshire Coast National Park
Pentre Ifan
Builth Wells
Haverfordwest
St.Clears
Carmarthen
Cambrian Mountains
England
Pembroke
Tenby
Cross Hands
Brecon
811
Black Mountains
Brecon Beacons N.P.
Merthyr Tydfil
Abergavenny
Swansea
Birmingham
Port Talbot
Pontypool
Bridgend
Newport
Glamorgan Coast
Cardiff
Bristol
Barry
Penarth

Brecon Beacons National Park Wildly romantic, expansive and lonely landscapes, flocks of sheep and herds of semi-wild ponies characterize this protected area, which is close to the border with England.

Travel Atlas

The maps on the following pages represent England and Wales at a scale of 1:750,000. The geographical details are complemented by a host of useful tourist information – including, for example, the entire road network and icons indicating the type and location of all the most important tourist sights and leisure attractions. UNESCO World Heritage Sites are also marked. An index of place names helps you to find particular sites. Above: The River Thurne traverses the Norfolk Broads.

Explanation of symbols 1:750 000

Motorway / with toll	Railway	E90	European road number
Dual carriageway	Tourist railway	M8 M73	Motorway numbers
Primary route	Car ferry	832 835	Other road numbers
Important main road	Hiking trail		Filling station / restaurant / with motel
Main road	National or nature park		Junction / with number
Secondary road	Restricted area		Not suitable / closed for caravans
Unpaved road	State / provincial border	XI-V 7-12%	Winter closure / slope information
Tourist route	Distances in miles		International / national / regional airport

Significant points of interest

Principal travel routes

- Auto route
- Rail road
- Highspeed train
- Shipping route

Remarkable landscapes and natural monuments

- UNESCO World Natural Heritage
- Mountain landscape
- Rock landscape
- Ravine/canyon
- Extinct volcano
- Active volcano
- Geyser
- Cave
- River landscape
- Waterfall/rapids
- Lake country
- Nature park
- National park (landscape)
- National park (flora)
- National park (fauna)
- Biosphere reserve
- Wildlife reserve
- Whale watching
- Zoo/safari park
- Botanical garden
- Coastal landscape
- Beach
- Island
- Spring
- Underwater reserve

Remarkable cities, cultural monuments and events

- UNESCO World Cultural Heritage
- Remarkable Cities
- Pre- and early history
- Prehistoric rockscape
- Phoenecian culture
- Greek antiquity
- Roman antiquity
- Places of Jewish cultural interest
- Places of Christian cultural interest
- Romanesque church
- Gothic church
- Renaissance church
- Baroque church
- Christian monastery
- Places of Islamic cultural interest
- Cultural landscape
- Historical city scape
- Castle/fortress/fort
- Castle ruin
- Palace
- Technical/industrial monument
- Mine (in service)
- Dam
- Remarkable lighthouse
- Remarkable bridge
- Worth seeing tower
- Windmill
- Striking building
- Tomb/grave
- Monument
- Space telescope

- Market
- Festivals
- Museum
- Open-air museum
- Theatre/theater
- World exhibition
- Olympics

Sport and leisure sites

- Arena/stadium
- Race track
- Golf
- Horse racing
- Skiing
- Sailing
- Diving
- Wind surfing
- Surfing
- Canoeing/rafting
- Seaport
- Deep-sea fishing
- Waterskiing
- Beach resort
- Leisure pool
- Mineral/thermal spa
- Amusement/theme park
- Casino
- Mountain hut
- Aerial tramway
- Lookout point
- Hiking region

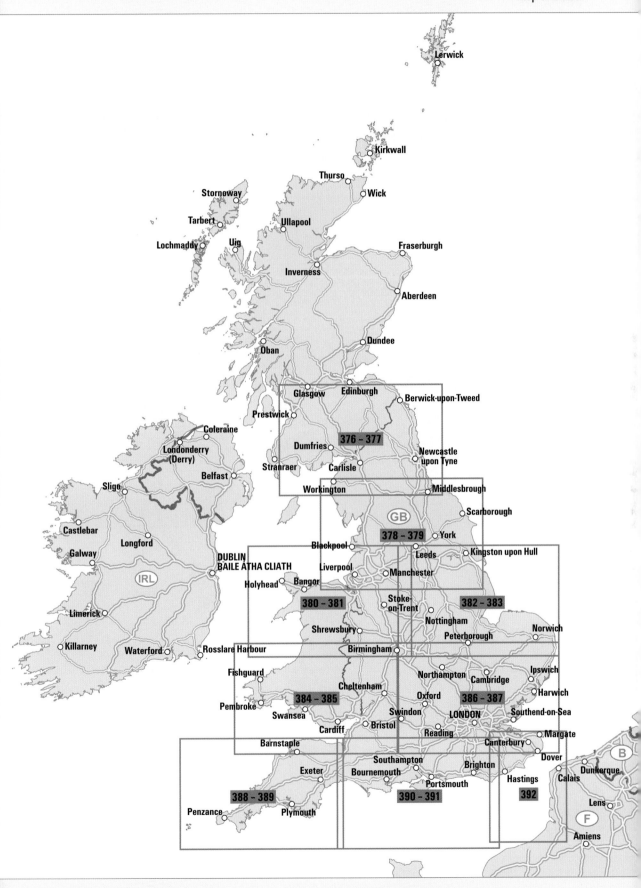

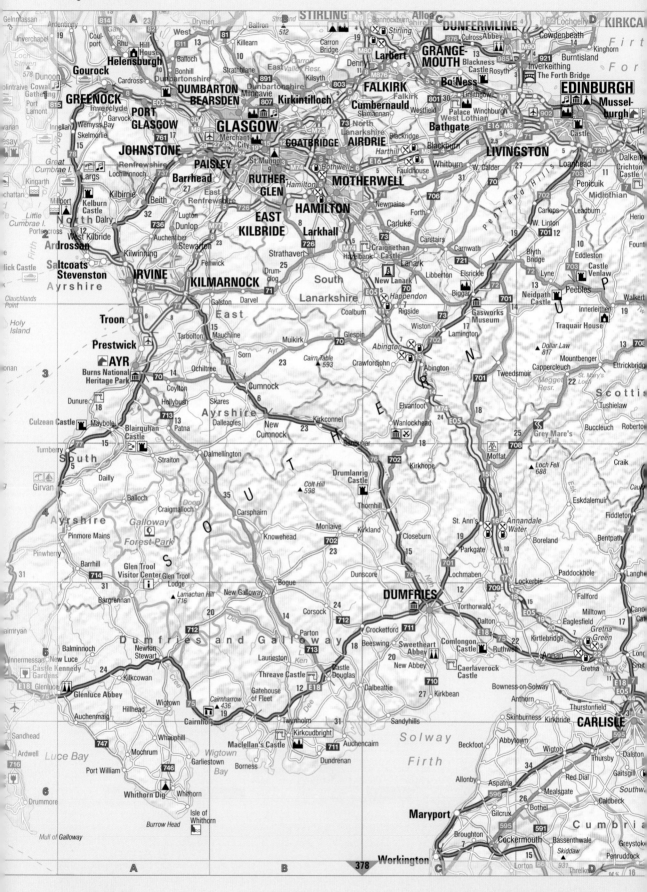

Scale 1:750 000

0   10   20 kilometers

0   10 miles

NORTH

SEA

Fidra Bass Rock
North Berwick Tantallon Castle
198
32
Whitekirk
Orem Ballencrieff Castle
dy
18 Dunbar
Haddington Stenton Spott Barns Ness
East Lothian East Linton
Gifford Garvald Oldhamstocks Cocksburnspath
dy Oldhamstocks
ble Longformacus St. Abb's Head
448 Grantshouse St. Abbs
Lauder 32 Ayton
14 Westruther 1
68 Greenlaw Swinton Berwick-upon-
Gordon Tweed
ashiels Stichill 697 698 Chirnside 15
6089 Duns Ancroft
Abbotsford Earlston Eccles Norham
House Newtown 698 Coldstream Cornhill- Fenwick Holy Island
Melrose St. Boswells Floors Castle on-Tweed Lindisfarne
rose Abbey Dryburgh Kelso 14 Ford 30 Priory and Castle
St. Boswells Abbey 698 Kilham Farne Is.
9 E15 Waterloo Town 697 Belford Bamburgh Bamburgh Castle
kirk Monument Yetholm Wooler Chatton Lucker Seahouses
orders 9 Morebattle Hethpool Newham
12 Jedburgh Oxham Langleeford Wooperton Snook Point
Hawick Denholm Hownam Sourhope North Charlton Dunstanburgh Castle
68 12 Bonchester Camptown 30 Craster
Bridge Upper Eglingham 1 Longhoughton
15 Hindhope Prendwick Powburn Alnwick
s Castle Northumberland Netherton Alnwick Castle Lesbury
E15 Alwinton Edlingham Shilbottle
ghtree The Cheviot Hills National Warton Cragside House 23 Warkworth Amble
Byrness 26 Rochester Thropton Swarland 697
Kielder Elsdon Forestburn 1068 Druridge Bay
ld Castleton 68 Gate Widdrington 21 Cresswell
Kielder Resr. Netherwitton 16
ton Kielder Park Longhorsley Ashington Beacon Point
and Forest Park Northumberland Kirkwhelpington Cambo Morpeth Newbiggin-by-the-Sea
Sighty Crag Bellingham Bedlington 10
518 33 BLYTH
Whygate 15 Belsay 696 12 189
Bewcastle Simonburn Cramlington Seaton Seaton Delaval Hall
Birdoswald Fort Housesteads 7 Hadrian's E15 Delaval
Fort Wall Chollerford Whitley Bay
thington Hadrian's Chesters Fort Stamfordham NEWCASTLE TYNEMOUTH
8 Greenhead Wall 7 Haydon 69 UPON TYNE
Low Row 69 Haltwhistle 30 Bridge 69 Newburn Millennium 1058 SOUTH SHIELDS
ampton E18 S. Tyne E18 Bridge TOLL Tyne and Wear
Midgeholme 686 Hexham 9 Prudhoe 695 184 Boldon
Lambley Whitfield Broomhaugh Whickham GATESHEAD 1018
Ninebanks 14% 13 Rowland's Gill 692 Washington SUNDERLAND
689 Allendale Town Slaley 12% Ebchester Beamish 1231 Houghton-le-Spring
Broadwell Ho 12% 12 17 Museum 532 Washington Seaham
Blanchland Stanley 693 Murton
Alston Edmund- Consett Annfield Chester- M1 182 Shotton 19
Cowshill byers Plain le-Street Hetton- Colliery Easington
Nenthead 18 Ushaw le-Hole 62 Peterlee
Meg and 686 Garrigill Stanhope Esh Winning Moor 181 Wheatley 25 Blackhall
Daughters Cross Fell 689 Tow Law Brandon Durham Hill Wingate
on Melmerby 893 St. John's Crook Bowburn 5 179
Langwathby Chapel Wolsingham Wellington Durham
Penrith Temple Langdon Beck Spennymoor 15 HARTLEPOOL
Sowerby Cow Green Durham 688 18 1 Ferryhill Fishburn Hartlepool
Res. 379 14 Elwick
Middleton Bishop Auckland 60 12
in Teesdale Newbiggin

Scale 1:750 000

0   10   20 kilometers

0   10 miles

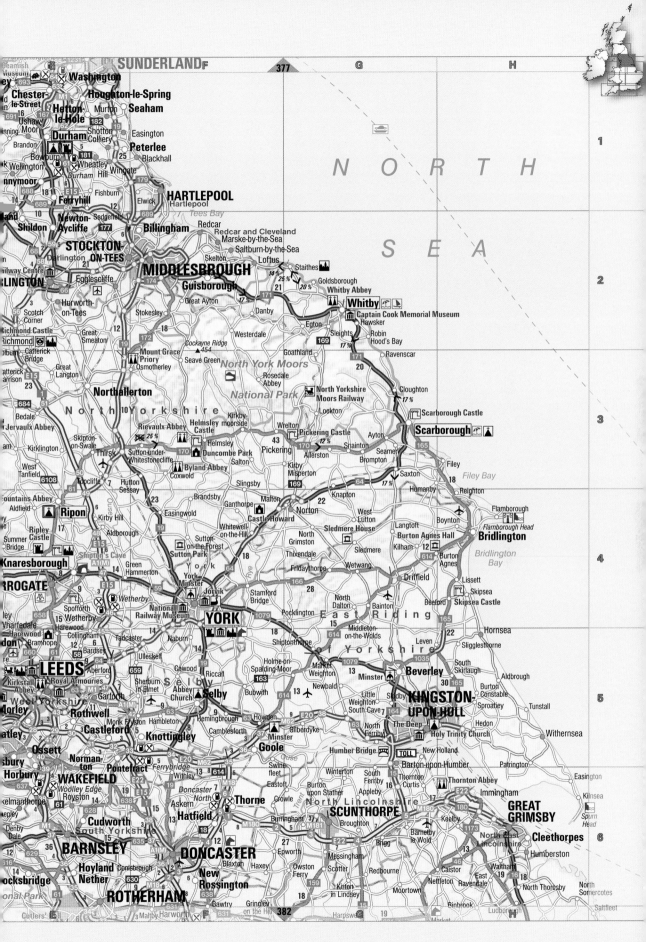

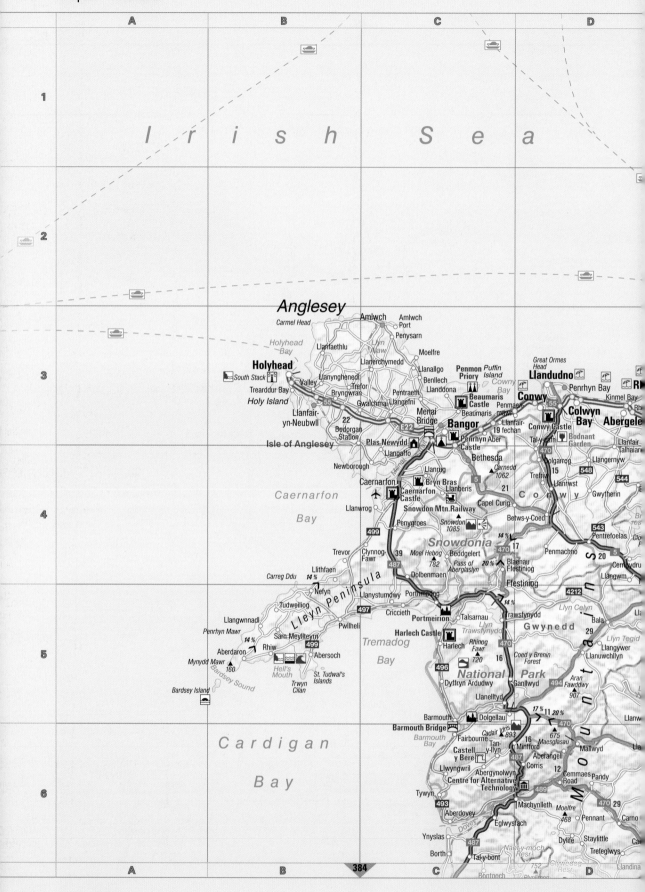

Scale 1:750 000

0   10   20 kilometers

0   10 miles

Scale 1:750 000

0   10   20 kilometers

0   10 miles

1

N O R T H

2

S E A

3

Withernsea

Easington

Kilnsea

Spurn Head

eethorpes

berston

4

horesby

North Somercotes

Saltfleet

outh

Mablethorpe

Withern

Sutton on Sea

Burwell

Maltby le Marsh

Alford

Mumby

Ulceby

Chapel St. Leonards

Willoughby

Ingoldmells

Candlesby

Partney

Spilsby

12

158

Keal

Burgh le Marsh

Skegness

Eastville

Wainfleet All Saints

ey

Friskney

52

48

Wrangle

22

le

tolph's Old Lake

Benington

ston

Freiston

The Wash

5

Brancaster Bay

Holkham Bay

Blakeney Point

Hunstanton

Thornham

Brancaster

Burnham Market

Holkham Hall

Wells next-the-Sea

149

Blakeney

Kelling

W. Runton

Cromer

Overstrand

Docking

N. Creake

Holt

149

Heacham

Lit. Walsingham

Felbrigg Hall

Thorpe Market

Mundesley

Holbeach St. Matthew

Great Snoring

22 **148**

Briston

Little Barningham

Gedney Dove End

Sandringham House

Great Bircham

Barney

Dersingham

Corpusty

Erpingham

Blicking Hall

North Walsham

can's ead

Fakenham

Wood Dalling

149

Castle Rising

Hougton Hall

East Rudham

Guist

Foulsham

Aylsham

23

Honing

Sea Palling

lbeach

N. Wootton

148

1065

Reepham

140

Scottow

de

King's Lynn

148

22

Hillington

Weasenham St. Peter

Brisley

1067

Cawston

Hevingham

Coltishall

Norfolk Broads

Hickling Green

Winterton-on-Sea

Long Sutton

17 **18**

Walpole St. Andrew

Grimston

Litcham

Bawdeswell

Hainford

1151

Horning

Bastwick

149

1101

Wiggenhall St. Mary Magdalen

W. Winch

Castle Acre

Elsing

Wroxham

St.Helen

The Broads

Ormesby St. Margaret

27

E. Winch

47

27

Norfolk

East Dereham

Attlebridge

Wisbech

19

10

42

47

Costessey

Cathedral

NORWICH

Acle

19

Caister-on-Sea

Nelson Museum

11

Marham

Swaffham

Wending

Yaxham

Easton

Norwich Castle

Burgh Castle

Great Yarmouth

Guyhirn

Outwell

1122

Stradsett

Gooderstone

Ashill

Cranworth

Barford

Kimberley

East Poringland

Freethorpe

March

Nordelph

134

32

Oxburgh Hall

1065

Watton

Wymondham

Mulbarton

National Park

Hopton

1101

1122

Stoke Ferry

Thompson

Great Ellingham

Saxlingham Nethergate

146 **16**

Loddon

143

10

Downham Market

Welney

Southery

undford

387

ellinghorpe

387

wellthorpe

Seething

urgh

6

383

C a r d i g a n

Bay

380

I r i s h

S e a

Llwyngwril
Castell
y Bere
Centre for Alternative
Technology
Tywyn
493
Aberdovey
Eglwysfach
Mach
Ynyslas
Borth
Tal-y-bont
487
Nant-y-mo
Resr.

Aberystwyth
Chancery
Llanbadarn
Fawr
44
Lanilar
487
Vale of Rheidol
Railway
Devil's
Bridge
Mynac
Falls

Llanrhystud
Llanon
16
Cross Inn
Bwlchllan
Llanfihangel-
y-Creuddyn
Pontrhydygroes
Pontrhydfendigaid
Ponterwyd
25
Elerch
Bontgoch
Plyn
Traws
5

New Quay
Aberaeron
482
14 %
Mydroilyn
Synod
Inn
Talgarreg
Ystrad
Aeron
Cribyn
Credigion
C a m b r i a
Bryn Brawd
Aberg
Llangybi
484
Lampeter
Llyn
Brianne

Ynys-Lochtyn
Llangrannog
Aberporth
Gwbert
Cardigan
Cardigan
Island
Clegyr
Moylgrove
487
Cemaes Head
Dinas
Head
Trwyn-
y-bwa
Cilgerran
Castle
484
Cenarth
18 14 %
Eglwyswrw
Llechryd
Rhydlewis
486
Horeb
475
Rhydowen
Llanybydder
Dolaucothi
Gold Mines 459
Pumsaint
Crug-
y-bar
Rhandirmwyn
Cynghord
Llandovery
482

22
Ffostrasol
Woolen
Museum
Newcastle
Emlyn
Llangeler
Llandysul
Rhydcymerau
Talley
12
Llangadog
Myde

Strumble Head
Goodwick
Albercastle
St. Nicholas
Fishguard
Newport
Pentre Ifan
Boncath
Moelfre
335
Gwyddgrug
Forest of Brechfa
Brechfa
Llanfynydd
485

Penclegyr
Abereiddy
487
Croes-goch
Trecwn
Mynydd Preseli
478
Llanfyrnach
Trelech
Cwmduad
Newchurch
Pontarsais
Nantgaredig
484
Llandeilo
Carreg Cennen Ca
Dan-y-
Camarthenshire

St. David's Head Carn Llidi
St.David's
Bishop's
Palace
18
Croes-goch
Hayscastle
Wolf's
Castle
Rosebush
Maenclochog
Llys-y-fran
Resr.
Pantymenyn
Cwmbach
15
Carmarthen
Llanarthney
Trapp
Brynamman
Glanaman
Craig-y-
Cwmllynfe
Ammanford

Pembrokeshire Coast
National Park
Camrose
487
Walton E.
Llandissilio
Meidrim
9
Llanddarog
Cross
Hands
E30
474
4067
Seven
Ramsey
Island
Solva
17%
Wiston
40
Whitland
17%
St. Clears
Llangain
Llandyfaelog
476
13
483
48 16
Pontardulais
Felindre
Rhos
Reso

St. Bride's Bay
Pembrokeshire
Newgale
Haverfordwest
22
40
Narberth
Boathouse
Laugharne
Llansteffan
Pontyberem
484
E30
49
476
48
Pont
Abraham
Gurnos
Pontardawe
Aberdulais
Falls
No

Grassbolme
Island
Skomer
Island
Broad Haven
St. Brides
4076
Picton Castle
Martletwy
478
477
Whitland
Pendine
Kidwelly
Trimsaran
Swansea
14
47 46
45
Aberdulais
Falls
Sgiwen
Tonna
Aber

Marloes
Milford
Haven
13
Llangwm
Carew
Castle
23
14%
478
Amroth
Saundersfoot
Pendine Sands
Pendine Sands
Carmarthen
Bay
Burry Port
Llanelli
484
Gorseinon
483
Neath
Port
Cwmafan

Skokholm
Island
Dale
477
Pembroke
Dock
TOLL
Carew
Manorbier
Castle
Monstone Point
Tenby
Whitford Point
Crofty
Llanmadoc
Penrhyn Gwyr
Weobley
Castle
SWANSEA
The Mumbles
5
483
42
Port
Talbot
Maes

St. Ann's
Head
Angle
Rhoscrowther
Pembroke
Manorbier
Caldey Island
Caldey
Abbey
Burry Holms
Llangenith
Rhossili
Gower
Oxwich
Margam
30
38

Castlemartin
Linney Head
Stack Rocks
Bosherston
St. Govan's
Head
Worms Head
Port-Eynon
Port-Eynon
Point
Mumbles
Head
Swansea
Bay
Kenfig
Nottage
Porthcawl
Ogmore-
Tusker Ro
E30
M4
37

C e l t i c   S e a

B r i s t o l

Valley of Rocks
Lynmouth
Combe
Martin
Lynton
25%
39
Ilfracombe
11
Blackmoor
Gate
11 25%
19
Lundy Island
Bull Point
Kentisbury
Woolacombe
West
Down
16
Challacombe

389

Scale 1:750 000

0 ⸺ 10 ⸺ 20 kilometers

0 ⸺ 10 miles

Scale 1:750 000

0   10   20 kilometers

0   10 miles

E | F | 383 Norfolk | G | 1151 | H

Wisbech

NORWICH

Great Yarmouth 1

Lowestoft

CAMBRIDGE

Bury St. Edmunds

IPSWICH 3

Felixstowe
Harwich

Colchester 4

Clacton-on-Sea

Harlow
Chelmsford

Southend-on-Sea 5

NORTH

SEA

Gravesend
Rochester Gillingham

MARGATE

BROADSTAIRS
RAMSGATE 6

MAIDSTONE

CANTERBURY

392

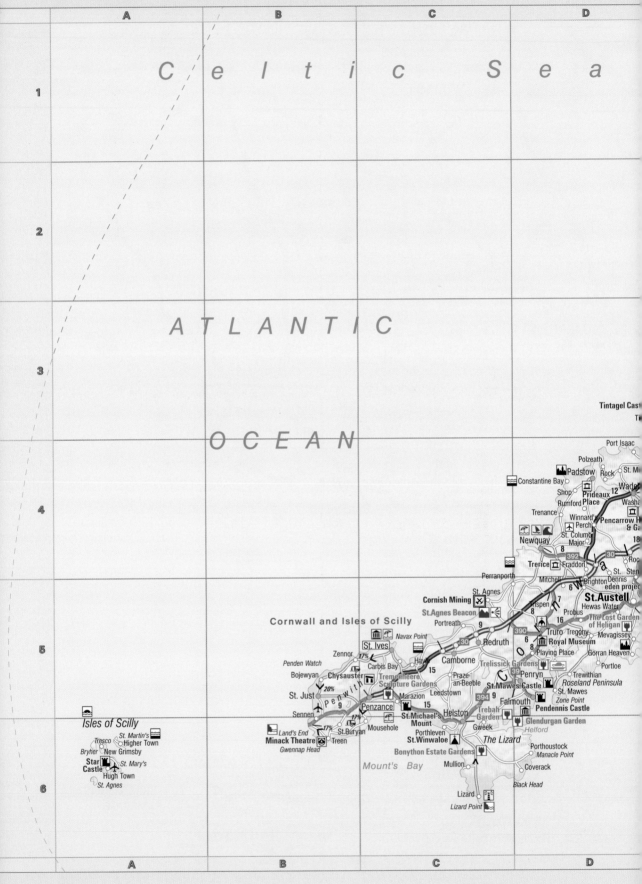

C e l t i c   S e a

A T L A N T I C

O C E A N

Tintagel Cas
Ti

Port Isaac

Polzeath
Padstow Rock   St. Mi
Constantine Bay
Shop   Prideaux   12   Wade
Rumford Place   Washa
Trenance   Winnard's
Newquay   St. Columb   Perch   Pencarrow H
Major   & Ga
8   392   18
Trerice St.   30   Roc
Fraddon   St. Sten
Perranporth   Mitchell   Brighton   Dennis
eden proje
Cornish Mining   St. Agnes   Crispen 7   St.Austell
St.Agnes Beacon   Probus Hewas Water
Portreath   16   The Lost Garden
Cornwall and Isles of Scilly   9   of Heligan
Truro Tregony   Mevagissey
Navax Point   390   Royal Museum
St. Ives   Redruth   Playing Place   Gorran Heaven
Zennor   17%   30   Portloe
Penden Watch   Carbis Bay   Camborne   Praze-   Trewithian
Bojewyan   Chysauster   Hayle   15   an-Beeble Trelissek Gardens Roseland Peninsula
Tremenheere   39   Penryn   St. Mawes
St. Just 20%   Sculpture Gardens   St.Mawes Castle   Zone Point
Marazion Leedstown   9   Pendennis Castle
Penzance   15   Helston 39A Falmouth
Sennen   St.Michael's   Trebah   Glendurgan Garden
17%   Mount Porthleven Garden Helford
17%   St.Buryan Mousehole   St.Winwaloe   Gweek
Land's End   Treen   The Lizard   Porthoustock
Minack Theatre   Bonython Estate Gardens   Manacle Point
Gwennap Head   Coverack
Mount's Bay   Mullion   Black Head

Isles of Scilly
Tresco   St. Martin's
Bryher   Higher Town
New Grimsby   Lizard
Star   Lizard Point
Castle   St. Mary's
Hugh Town
St. Agnes

388 ✚

E   F   G   H

Bristol Channel

Lundy Island

Nash Point
St. Athan Airport
The Vale of Glamorgan
Llantwit Major
Breaksea Point
Rhoose
Barry
Swanbridge
Penarth
Flat Holm
Weston-super-Mare
Steep Holm
Brean
Bleadon
Banwe
Sedgemo
Watchfield
Westha
Puriton
Glaston
13 A

Ilfracombe
Combe Martin
Valley of Rocks
Lynmouth
Lynton
Blackmoor Gate
25%
Minehead
17%
Porlock
Watchet
Kilve
Stockland Bristol
Cannington
M5
39

Bull Point
Woolacombe
West Down
11
Kentisbury Ford
Challacombe
11
25%
19
25%
Dunster
Dunster Castle
7
Williton
Holford
17
39

Baggy Point
Croyde
16
12
Barnstaple
Arlington Court
16%
Simonsbath
Timberscombe
Wheddon Cross
Crowcombe
Elworthy
Bridgwater
M5

Barnstaple or Bideford Bay
Braunton
Long Bridge
361
39
Landkey
361
Charles
North Molton
Exmoor
Exford
National Park
Wimbleball Lake
Wiveliscombe
Bishop's Lydeard
North Petherton
39
7

Yelland
9
South Molton
396
Tarr Steps
28
Dulverton
Upton
Westonzoyla
Othery
West Lyng
Langport
Long S

Hartland Point
Clovelly
Westward Ho!
Northam
7
Umberleigh
Alswear
Meshaw
Oldways End
361
Waterrow
Milverton
Taunton
Hestercombe
Thornfalcon

Hartland
Stoke
Fairy Cross
14%
Bideford
9
Great Torrington
Little Torrington
RHS Rosemoor Garden
Chulmleigh
41
Chawleigh
Witheridge
Nomansland
Cove
Oakford
Knightshayes Court
38
Corfe
Culmstock
Hemyock
Taunton Deane
358
Mart
South Petherton
303

South Hole
Meddon
13
Bradworthy
Stibb Cross
13
Dolton
Tiverton
Tiverton
8
Dunkeswell
Marsh
Broadway
Montacu
Ilminster

Morwenstow
Kilkhampton
39
388
20
Chilsworthy
386
Meeth
377
Winkleigh
Lapford
Stockleigh Pomeroy
Cullompton
16
Bickleigh
Cullompton
M5
11
Yarcombe
8
30
Forde Abbey
Chard
18
Dri
Broadwindsor

Bude
Stratton
10
Holsworthy
Devon
Highampton
Hatherleigh
North Tawton
Exbourne
Copplestone
Crediton
396
Clyst Hydon
373
Honiton
30
Axminster
Kilmington
13
Birdsmo
Gate

idemouth Bay
14
Wainhouse Corner
Whitstone
14
Halwill
Ashwater
Henfort
11
14%
Okehampton
14
Tedburn St. Mary
26
EXETER
Royal Albert Mem. Museum
Exeter Cathedral
Newton Poppleford
Ottery St. Mary
Sidford
Colyton
17%
Seaton
14%
14%
Lyme Regis
Col
Harbour
West

oscastle
Davidstow
15
395
Launceston
30
Lifton
Lewdown
386
Whiddon Down
Castle Drogo
Crockernwell
17%
Dunsford
20%
730
730
4
Exeter
10
Kenn
Newton
Bicton Gardens
Sidmouth
Beer
Jurassic (East Devon Co

Bodmin Moor
22
Camelford
Fivelanes
Treburley
388
Milton Abbot
386
Mary Tavy
Lydford Gorge
Dartmoor
Moretonhampstead
17%
Haytor
Bovey Tracey
19
380
Starcross
Powderham Castle
Budleigh Salterton
Exmouth
Lyme Bay

Colliford Reservoir
The Hurlers
Coad's Green
10
Bray Shop
Gunnislake
Tavistock
17%
Two Bridges
Widecombe-in-the-Moor
25%
Ponsworthy
25%
Ashburton
Newton Abbot
Kingsteignton
Teignmouth
Dawlish

Pensilva
12
Kellybray
Callington
386
Horrabridge
Cotehele House
13
Princetown
National Park
Yelverton
Buckland Abbey
Buckfastleigh
Ipplepen
8
Kingskerswell
TORQUAY
Kents Cavern
TORBAY

Liskeard
38
6
Lanhydrock House & Gardens
Saltash
TOLL
Royal Citadel
Plympton
18
Ivybridge
Dartmoor Wildlife Park
11
Totnes
Greenway
Paignton Zoo
5
Paignton
Berry Head
Brixham

ostwithiel
Trerulefoot
6
Torpoint
4
Saltram House
Yealmpton
9
Modbury
9
Brownston
Halwell
Kingswear
Kingsbridge
15
Dartmouth
17%
Berry Head

owey
14%
Looe
Polperro
Cawsand
Rame Head
PLYMOUTH
Heybrook Bay
Noss Mayo
379
Churchstow
Churchstow
East Portlemouth
379
Torcross
Start Point

Bigbury-on-Sea
Burgh Island
Hope
Salcombe
Prawle Point

English Channel
La Manche

Scale 1:750 000

0   10   20 kilometers

0   10 miles

NORTH SEA

English Channel

La Manche

Strait of Dover

Pas de Calais

Côte d'Opale

Scale 1:750 000

0   10   20 kilometers

0   10 miles

A

Abbas Combe 390 B2
Abberley 385 G2
Abbey Dore 385 F3
Abbots Bromley 381 H5
Abbots Leigh 385 G6
Abbots Ripton 386 D2
Abbotsbury 390 A4
Abbytown 376 D6
Aber 380 C3
Aberaeron 384 C2
Aberaman 385 E4
Aberangell 380 D6
Abercarn 385 F5
Abercraf 384 D4
Aberdare 385 E4
Aberdaron 380 B5
Aberdovey 380 C6
Abereiddy 384 A3
Aberford 379 E5
Abergavenny 385 F4
Abergele 380 D3
Abergwesyn 384 D3
Abergwynfi 384 D5
Abergynolwyn 380 C6
Aberlady 377 E1
Abermule 381 E6
Abersoch 380 B5
Abertillery 385 F4
Aberystwyth 384 D1
Abingdon 386 B5
Abington 376 C3
Abington 387 E3
Abridge 387 E5
Accrington 378 C5
Acle 383 H6
Acre 378 C5
Adderley 381 F5
Adlington 381 G3
Airdrie 376 C1
Albercastle 384 A3
Albrighton 381 F5
Albrighton 381 G6
Alcester 386 A2
Alconbury 386 D2
Aldborough 379 E4
Aldbourne 386 A6
Aldbrough 379 H5
Aldeburgh 387 H3
Alderbury 390 C2
Alderley Edge 381 G3
Aldershot 391 F1
Aldfield 379 E4
Aldford 381 F4
Aldsworth 386 A4
Aldwincle 386 C2
Alford 383 E4
Alfreton 382 B4
Allendale Town 377 F6
Allenheads 377 F6
Allerston 379 G3
Allhallows 387 F6
Allington 385 H6
Allonby 376 C6
Alnwick 377 G3
Alpheton 387 F3
Alston 377 E6
Alswear 389 G2
Althorne 387 F5
Alton 381 H5
Alton 391 E2
Alveston 385 G5
Alwinton 377 F4
Amble 377 G4
Ambleside 378 B2
Amersham 386 C5
Amesbury 390 C2
Amlwch 380 C3
Amlwch Port 380 C3
Ammanford 384 D4
Ampthill 386 D3
Amroth 384 B4
Anchor 385 F1
Ancroft 377 F2
Andover 390 D1
Andoversford 385 H4
Angle 384 A4
Annan 376 D5
Annfield Plain 377 G6
Anthorn 376 D5
Appleby 382 C2
Appleby Magna 381 H6
Appleby-in-
   Westmorland 378 C2
Appledore 392 B3
Appletreewick 378 D4
Ardleigh 387 G4
Ardrossan 376 A2
Arlingham 385 G4
Arncott 386 B4
Arnesby 386 B1

Arnold 382 B5
Arnside 378 B3
Arundel 391 F3
Ascot 386 C6
Asfordby 382 C6
Ash 387 E6
Ashbourne 381 H4
Ashburton 389 G4
Ashbury 386 A5
Ashby-de-la-Zouch
   382 A6
Ashdon 387 E3
Ashford 392 B2
Ashford-in-the-Water
   381 H4
Ashill 383 F6
Ashington 377 G4
Ashington 391 F3
Ashkirk 377 E3
Ashley 387 F3
Ashmore 390 C2
Ashperton 385 G3
Ashton Keynes 385 H5
Ashton-in-Makerfield
   381 F2
Ashton-under-Lyne
   381 G3
Ashwater 389 F3
Ashwell 382 C6
Ashwell 386 D3
Ashwellthorpe 387 G1
Askern 382 B2
Askerswell 390 A3
Askett 386 C4
Aspatria 376 C6
Aston 382 B3
Aston 386 A5
Ateham 385 F2
Atherstone 381 H6
Attleborough 387 G1
Attlebridge 383 G6
Auchencairn 376 B6
Auchenmaig 376 A5
Auchentiber 376 A2
Audlem 381 F5
Avebury 385 H6
Avening 385 H5
Axford 391 E2
Axminster 389 H3
Aylesbury 386 C4
Aylesham 392 B2
Aylsham 383 G5
Aylton 385 G3
Ayr 376 A3
Aysgarth 378 D3
Ayton 377 F2
Ayton 379 G3

B

Bacton 387 G2
Bacup 378 D5
Badby 386 B2
Badminton 385 G5
Bagley 381 F5
Bainbridge 378 D3
Bainton 379 G4
Bakewell 381 H4
Bala 380 D5
Balcombe 391 G2
Baldock 386 D4
Balloch 376 A1
Balloch 376 A4
Balminnoch 376 A5
Balsam 387 E3
Bamburgh 377 G3
Bamford 381 H3
Bampton 389 G2
Banbury 386 B3
Bangor 380 C3
Bangor-is-y-Coed
   381 F4
Banstead 386 D6
Banwell 385 F6
Bar Hill 387 E2
Barber Booth 381 H3
Bardney 382 D4
Bardsea 378 B3
Bardsey 379 E5
Barford 383 G6
Barford Saint Martin
   390 C2
Bargoed 385 E5
Bargrennan 376 A5
Barking 387 E5
Barkston 382 C5
Barkway 387 E3
Barlow 382 A3
Barmouth 380 C5
Barnard Castle 378 D2
Barnes 386 D6
Barnetby le Wold
   382 D2

Barney 383 G5
Barnoldswick 378 D4
Barnsley 382 B2
Barnsley 385 H4
Barnstaple 389 F2
Barrhead 376 B2
Barrhill 376 A4
Barrowby 382 C5
Barrow-in-Furness
   378 B4
Barrow-upon-Soar
   382 B6
Barry 385 E6
Barton 381 H6
Barton Mills 387 F2
Barton-upon-Humber
   379 G5
Baschurch 381 F5
Basildon 387 F5
Basingstoke 386 B6
Baslow 381 H4
Bassenthwaite 376 D6
Bassingham 382 C4
Baston 382 D6
Bastwick 383 H6
Bath 385 G6
Bathgate 376 C1
Batley 379 F5
Battle 391 H3
Baumber 382 D4
Bawdeswell 383 G6
Bawdsey 387 H3
Bawtry 382 B3
Beaconsfield 386 C5
Beaminster 390 A3
Beare Green 391 G2
Bearsden 376 B1
Beaulieu 390 D3
Beaumaris 380 C3
Bebington 381 E3
Beccles 387 H2
Beck Side 378 B3
Beckfoot 376 C6
Beckingham 382 C3
Beckington 385 G6
Bedale 379 E3
Beddau 385 E5
Beddgelert 380 C4
Beddwas 385 E5
Bedford 386 D3
Bedlington 377 G5
Bedworth 386 A1
Beeford 379 H4
Beer 389 H3
Beeston 382 B5
Beeswing 376 C5
Beith 376 A2
Belbroughton 385 H2
Belford 377 G3
Bellingham 377 F5
Belmont 378 C6
Belper 382 B4
Belsay 377 F5
Belvoir 382 C5
Bembridge 391 E4
Benefield 386 C1
Benington 383 E5
Benllech 380 C3
Benson 386 B5
Bentpath 376 D4
Benwick 387 E1
Bere Regis 390 B3
Berkeley 385 G5
Berkhamsted 386 C4
Berkswell 386 A2
Berriew 381 E6
Berwick-upon-Tweed
   377 F2
Bethersden 392 A2
Bethesda 380 C4
Bettws Cedewain
   381 E6
Betws-y-coed 380 D4
Beulah 385 E3
Beverley 379 G5
Bewcastle 377 E5
Bexhill 391 H3
Bibury 385 H4
Bicester 386 B4
Bickleigh 389 G3
Bickley Moss 381 F4
Biddenden 392 A2
Biddestone 385 H6
Biddulph 381 G4
Bideford 389 F2
Bigbury-on-Sea 389 F5
Biggar 376 C2
Biggleswade 386 D3
Bignor 391 F3
Billericay 387 F5
Billesdon 382 C6
Billingborough 382 D5
Billingham 379 F2

Billinghay 382 D4
Billingshurst 391 F2
Binbrook 382 D3
Bingham 382 C5
Bingley 378 D5
Birdlip 385 H4
Birdsmoor Gate 390 A3
Birkenhead 381 E3
Birmingham 386 A1
Bishop Auckland
   379 E1
Bishop's Castle 385 F1
Bishop's Lydeard
   389 H2
Bishop's Stortford
   387 E4
Bishop's Waltham
   391 E3
Bisley 385 H4
Bitton 385 G6
Black Notley 387 F4
Blackburn 376 C1
Blackburn 378 C5
Blackhall 377 H6
Blackmoor Gate 389 F1
Blackpool 378 B5
Blackridge 376 C1
Blackwater 391 E1
Blackwood 385 E5
Blaenau Ffestiniog
   380 C4
Blaenavon 385 F4
Blaengarw 385 E5
Blagdon 385 F6
Blaina 385 F4
Blakeney 383 G5
Blakeney 385 G4
Blakesley 386 B3
Blanchland 377 F6
Blandford Forum
   390 C3
Blaxton 382 C3
Bleadon 385 F6
Bletchingdon 386 B4
Bletsoe 386 D3
Blewbury 386 B5
Blockley 386 A3
Bloxham 386 B3
Blyth 377 G5
Blyth Bridge 376 D2
Bo'ness 376 C1
Bodfari 381 E4
Bodmin 389 E4
Bodorgan Station
   380 B3
Bognor Regis 391 F3
Bogue 376 B4
Bojewyan 388 B5
Boldon 377 G5
Bolnhurst 386 D3
Bolsover 382 B4
Bolton 381 G2
Bolton Abbey 378 D4
Bolton-le-Sand 378 B4
Boncath 384 B3
Bonchester Bridge
   377 E3
Bonhill 376 A1
Bontgoch Elerch
   384 D1
Bonvilston 385 E5
Bootle 378 A3
Bordon 391 E2
Borehamwood 386 D5
Boreland 376 D4
Borness 376 B6
Borth 380 C6
Bosbury 385 G3
Boscastle 389 E3
Bosherston 384 B5
Bosley 381 G4
Boston 383 E5
Botesdale 387 G2
Bothel 376 D6
Botley 391 E3
Bottesford 382 C5
Bourn 386 D3
Bourne 382 D6
Bournemouth 390 C3
Bourton-on-the-Water
   386 A4
Bovey Tracey 389 G4
Bovingdon 386 C5
Bowburn 377 G6
Bowes 378 D2
Bowness-on-Solway
   376 D5
Box 385 G6
Boxford 386 B6
Boynton 379 H4
Bracebridge Heath
   382 D4
Brackley 386 B3

Bracknell 386 C6
Bradfield 386 B6
Bradford 378 D5
Bradford-on-Avon
   385 G6
Bradwell-on-Sea
   387 G5
Bradworthy 389 E2
Brailes 386 A3
Braintree 387 F4
Bramhope 379 E5
Brampton 377 E5
Brampton 387 H2
Brancaster 383 F5
Brandon 377 G6
Brandon 387 F2
Brandsby 379 F4
Brant Broughton
   382 C4
Bratton 385 H6
Braughing 387 E4
Braunton 389 F2
Bray Shop 389 E4
Brean 385 F6
Brechfa 384 C3
Brecon 385 E3
Bredenbury 385 G2
Bredgar 387 F6
Bredon 385 H3
Bredwardine 385 F3
Brentwood 387 E5
Brenzett 392 B3
Bretford 386 B2
Bretforton 385 H3
Bridgend 385 E5
Bridgnorth 381 G6
Bridgwater 389 H2
Bridlington 379 H4
Bridport 390 A3
Brigg 382 D2
BrigHouse 378 D5
Brightlingsea 387 G4
Brighton 388 D5
Brighton 391 G3
Brimfield 385 G2
BrinkWorth 385 H5
Brisley 383 F6
Bristol 385 G6
Briston 383 G5
Brixham 389 G5
Brize Norton 386 A4
Broad Chalke 390 C2
Broad Haven 384 A4
Broad Hinton 386 A5
Broad Oak 392 A3
Broadstairs 387 H6
Broadwas 385 G3
Broadway 385 H3
Broadway 390 A2
Broadwell Ho 377 F6
Broadwey 390 B4
Broadwindsor 390 A3
Brockenhurst 390 D3
Brome 387 G2
Bromley 387 E6
Brompton 379 G3
Bromsgrove 385 H2
Bromyard 385 G3
Brook 390 D3
Brookhouse 378 C4
Broomfield 387 F4
Broomhaugh 377 F5
Brough 378 C2
Broughton 376 C6
Broughton 378 B5
Broughton 381 E4
Broughton 382 C2
Broughton 390 D2
Broughton Astley
   386 B1
Broughton Poggs
   386 A4
BroughtonIn-Furness
   378 B3
Brown Candover
   391 E2
Brownhills 381 H6
Brownston 389 G5
Broxton 381 F4
Bruton 390 B2
Brynamman 384 D4
Bryncethin 385 E5
Bryngwran 380 B3
Bryngwyn 385 F3
BrynHenllan 384 B3
Brynmawr 385 F4
Bubwith 379 F5
Buccleuch 376 D3
Buckden 378 D3
Buckden 386 D2
Buckfastleigh 389 G4
Buckingham 386 B3
Buckland 386 A5
Bucklay 381 E4

Buckminster 382 C5
Bucknell 385 F2
Bucks Green 391 F2
Budby 382 B4
Bude 389 E3
Budleigh Salterton
   389 H4
Builth Wells 385 E3
Bungay 387 H2
Buntingford 387 E4
Bures 387 F4
Burford 386 A4
Burgess Hill 391 G3
Burgh le Marsh 383 F4
Burgh Saint Peter
   387 H1
Burley In Wharfedale
   379 E4
Burlton 381 F5
Burnham Market
   383 F5
Burnham-on-Crouch
   387 F5
Burnham-on-Sea
   385 F6
Burnley 378 D5
Burntisland 376 D1
Burringham 382 C2
Burry Port 384 C4
Burscough 378 B6
Burton Agnes 379 H4
Burton Constable
   379 H5
Burton Latimer 386 C2
Burton upon Stather
   382 C2
Burton-in-Kendal
   378 C3
Burton-upon-Trent
   381 H5
Burwash 391 H2
Burwell 383 E3
Burwell 387 E2
Bury 381 G2
Bury Saint Edmunds
   387 F2
Bushey 386 D5
Butley 387 H3
Buttington 381 E6
Buxton 381 H3
Bwlch 385 E4
Bwlchllan 384 D2
Bwlch-y-ffridd 381 E6
Bwlch-y-Sarnau 385 E2
Byford 385 F3
Bylchau 380 D4
Byrness 377 E4

C

Caerleon 385 F5
Caernarfon 380 C4
Caerphilly 385 E5
Caersws 380 D6
Caister-on-Sea 383 H6
Caistor 382 D3
Caldbeck 376 D6
Callington 389 E4
Calne 385 H6
Calver 381 H3
Calvering 387 E4
Camber 392 B3
Camblesforth 379 F5
Cambo 377 F4
Camborne 388 C5
Cambridge 387 E3
Camelford 389 E4
Camptown 377 E3
Camrose 384 B4
Candlesby 383 E4
Canewdon 387 F5
Cannington 389 H2
Cannock 381 G6
Canonbie 376 D5
Canterbury 387 G6
Canvey Island 387 F5
Capel Curig 380 C4
Capel Saint Mary
   387 G3
Cappercleuch 376 D3
Carbis Bay 388 C5
Cardiff 385 E5
Cardigan 384 B3
Cardross 376 A1
Carew 384 B4
Cark 378 B3
Carlisle 376 D5
Carlops 376 D2
Carlton 382 B6
Carlton 386 C3
Carlton-on-Trent
   382 C4
Carluke 376 C2

Carmarthen 384 C4
Carnforth 378 B4
Carno 380 D6
Carnwath 376 C2
Carron Bridge 376 B1
Carsphairn 376 B4
Carstairs 376 C2
Carterton 386 A4
Cartmel 378 B3
Cashmore 390 C3
Castle Acre 383 F6
Castle Ashby 386 C2
Castle Bytham 382 C6
Castle Cary 390 B2
Castle Combe 385 H5
Castle Douglas 376 B5
Castleford 379 E5
Castlemartin 384 A4
Castleton 381 H3
Castleton 385 F5
Caterham 386 D6
Catlowdy 376 D5
Catterick Bridge 379 E3
Catterick Garrison
   379 E3
Cawood 379 E5
Cawsand 389 F5
Cawston 383 G6
Caxton 386 D3
Caynham 385 G2
Caythorpe 382 C5
Cellarhead 381 G4
Cemmaes Road 380 D6
Cenarth 384 C3
Cerne Abbas 390 B3
Cerrigydrudion 380 D4
Chale 390 D4
Challacombe 389 G1
Challock 392 B2
Chancery 384 D2
Chandler's Ford 390 D2
Chapel Saint Leonards
   383 E4
Chapel-en-le Frith
   381 H3
Chard 390 A3
Charing 392 B2
Charlbury 386 A4
Charles 389 G2
Charlton Kings 385 H4
Charney Bassett
   386 A5
Chartridge 386 C5
Chastleton 386 A4
Chatham 387 F6
Chatteris 387 E2
Chatton 377 F3
Chawleigh 389 G3
Cheadle 381 G3
Cheadle 381 H5
Checkendon 386 B5
Cheddar 385 F6
Cheddleton 381 G4
Chedworth 385 H4
Chelford 381 G3
Chelmsford 387 F4
Chelsworth 387 G3
Cheltenham 385 H4
Chenies 386 C5
Chepstow 385 G5
Cheriton 391 E2
Chertsey 386 C6
Chesham 386 C5
Cheshunt 387 E5
Chester 381 F4
Chesterfield 382 A4
Chester-le-Street
   377 G6
Chew Magna 385 G6
Chicheley 386 C3
Chichester 391 F3
Chiddingfold 391 F2
ChiddingStone 391 H2
Chigwell 387 E5
Chilcompton 385 G6
Childrey 386 A5
Chilham 392 B2
Chilmark 390 C2
Chilsworthy 389 E3
Chinnor 386 C5
Chippenham 385 H6
Chipping 378 C5
Chipping Campden
   386 A3
Chipping Norton
   386 A4
Chipping Ongar 387 E5
Chirbury 381 E6
Chirnside 377 F2
Cholderton 390 D2
Cholesbury 386 C4
Chorley 378 C5
Christchurch 390 C3
Chulmleigh 389 G2

Index

Picture Credits · Imprint

A = Alamy; C = Corbis; G = Getty; M = Mauritius Images

Covers: front cover: shutterstock/ Alexey Fedorenko (View of Castle Combe, Wiltshire), back cover: G/Backyard Production (Llangollen); G/Chris Hepburn (York Minster); G/David Townsend (Broadstairs, Kent); spine: Zielske (Westminster Abbey)

P. 002-003 G/Ed Norton; P. 004-005 Look/Robert Harding; P. 006-007 G/Joe Daniel Price; P. 008-009 M/Alamy; P. 012-013 G/FotoVoyager; P. 014-015 G/Grant Symon; P. 016 G/Andrzej Sowa; P. 016 G/David Townsend; P. 017 G/Chris Clor; P. 017 M/Alamy; P. 017 M/Steve Vidler; P. 018 M/Alamy; P. 019 M/Egon Bömsch; P. 019 M/Martin Dr.Schulte-Kellinghaus; P. 019 M/Martin Dr.Schulte-Kellinghaus; P. 019 M/Jaime Abecasis; P. 020 M/Alamy; P. 020 M/United Archives; P. 021 M/H.-D. Falkenstein; P. 022 M/Alamy; P. 023 M/Jevgenija Pigozne; P. 022-023 G/Valery Egorov; P. 023 G/Sarah Dawson; P. 024 Look/Heinz Wohner; P. 024-025 Look/Heinz Wohner; P. 026 Look/age; P. 026 G/Patricia Hamilton; P. 027 M/Alamy; P. 027 Look/age; P. 027 M/Alamy; P. 026-027 Look/Robert Harding; P. 028-029 G/Nigelfrench; P. 029 M/Alamy; P. 029 G/Paul Mansfield; P. 029 C/John Doornkamp; P. 030 M/Alamy; P. 030 M/Slawek Staszczuk; P. 030 M/Alamy; P. 030 G/Alex Robinson; P. 031 M/Alamy; P. 030-031 H. & D. Zielske; P. 032-033 Look/age; P. 034-035 M/Alamy; P. 034 M/Mark Goble; P. 035 G/Clive Nichols; P. 035 M/Alamy; P. 035 G/Clive Nichols; P. 036 M/Alamy; P. 036 M/Alamy; P. 036 M/Alamy; P. 037 G/Rob Ball; P. 037 M/Alamy; P. 038 M/Steve Bardens; P. 038 M/Alamy; P. 039 M/Alamy; P. 040 G/Simon West; P. 041 G/Simon West; P. 041 G/Tom Shaw; P. 042 M/Alamy; P. 042-043 G/Slawek Staszczuk; P. 043 M/Alamy; P. 043 G/John Freeman; P. 043 M/Slawek Staszczuk; P. 043 G/John Freeman; P. 044 M/Science Source; P. 045 M/Alamy; P. 045 M/Alamy; P. 046 G/Adam Burton; P. 046-047 G/Andreas Jones; P. 046 M/Linda McKie; P. 047 G/Ivan Vdovin; P. 047 G/John Freeman; P. 048 M/United Archives; P. 049 M/United Archives; P. 050 G/Keven Osborne; P. 050-051 M/Alamy; P. 050-051 G/Daniela White Images; P. 051 M/Peter Noyce; P. 051 G/Pearl Bucknall; P. 052-053 C/Alan Crowhurst; P. 054 M/Alamy; P. 055 C/Angelo Hornak; P. 055 C/Steven Vidler; P. 055 Look/Superstock; P. 055 G/Banana Pancake; P. 056-057 G/Tony Eveling; P. 056 G/Manfred Gottschalk; P. 057 M/Alamy; P. 058 G/Joe Daniel Price; P. 059 M/Alamy; P. 059 G/Joe Daniel Price; P. 059 M/Alamy; P. 060 M/United Archives; P. 061 C/Michael Freeman; P. 062 G/Stephen Dorey; P. 062 M/Roger Rozencwajg; P. 062-063 M/Alamy; P. 063 M/United Archives; P. 064-065 G/Guy Edwardes; P. 066-067 G/Joe Daniel Price; P. 066 G/Joe Daniel Price; P. 067 G/Rosane Miller; P. 067 M/Alamy ; P. 068-069 G/Joe Daniel Price; P. 070-071 G/Julian Elliott; P. 071 M/Alamy; P. 071 M/Alamy; P. 071 Look/age; P. 072 M/Alamy; P. 072 M/Chris Warren; P. 073 M/Loop RF; P. 073 G/Meleah Reardon; P. 074 M/Alamy; P. 074 Look/The Travel Library; P. 074 G/Carolyn Eaton; P. 076 C/Franz-Marc Frei; P. 076 G/Joe Daniel Price; P. 076-077 C/Franz-Marc Frei; P. 077 Look/age; P. 078 G/Joe Daniel Price; P. 078 G/Stephen Spraggon; P. 079 G/Andrew Holt; P. 079 G/Franz-Marc Frei; P. 080 G/Matt Cardy; P. 080 C/Adam Burton; P. 080 C/Adam Burton; P. 081 G/Tony Howell; P. 082 G/Thomas Faull; P. 082 G/Southern Lightscapes; P. 083 M/Alamy; P. 082-083 M/Alamy; P. 084-085 G/Chris Hepburn; P. 084 G/James Osmond; P. 085 M/Alamy; P. 085 G/Heritage Images; P. 085 G/Josie Elias; P. 086 G/Julian Elliott; P. 087 M/Alamy; P. 087 M/Kerry Dunstone; P. 087 M/Alamy; P. 088 C/Walter Bird; P. 088-089 G/Bettmann; P. 090 G/Rachel Dewis; P. 090 Peter Round; P. 090 M/Alamy; P. 090 Look/age; P. 091 M/Alamy; P. 091 M/Adam Burton; P. 092-093 M/Alamy/UK City Alamy; P. 094 M/Andy Fox; P. 094-095 Look/Franz Marc Frei; P. 095 M/United Archives; P. 095 G/De Agostini Picture Library; P. 096 G/Mrtom-uk; P. 096 Look/Robert Harding; P. 097 G/Maurizio Grasso; P. 096-097 G/Joe Daniel Price; P. 098-099 G/Peter Unger; P. 099 G/Hugh Hastings ; P. 099 M/Alamy; P. 100-101 M/Ross Hoddinott; P. 100 M/Steve Vidler; P. 101 G/Milangonda; P. 102-103 M/Alamy; P. 104-105 G/Valery Egorov; P. 104 G/Tony Howell; P. 104 Look/Robert Harding; P. 105 M/Alamy; P. 106 M/Alamy ; P. 106 M/Alamy ; P. 107 M/Alamy ; P. 107 M/Natasha Breen ; P. 108 Look/Robert Harding; P. 108-109 C/Adam Burton; P. 109 G/Ian Cook; P. 110-111 G/Clive Nichols; P. 111 G/Clive Nichols; P. 111 G/Clive Nichols; P. 111 Look/Design Pics; P. 112 Look/Robert Harding; P. 112 G/Allard Schager; P. 112-113 G/Guy Edwardes; P. 113 G/Clive Nichols; P. 114-115 G/Vladimir Zakharov; P. 116 G/Maremagnum; P. 116-117 C/Alan Copson; P. 117 G/Laurie Noble; P. 117 C/Massimo Borchi; P. 122 G/Gonzalo Azumendi; P. 122-123 C/Rudy Sulgan; P. 123 G/Peter Adams; P. 124 C/Rudy Sulgan; P. 124 G/P. Vannini; P. 124-125 M/United Archives; P. 125 H. & D. Zielske; P. 125 C/Rupert Horrox; P. 126 C/Rudy Sulgan; P. 126-127 M/Alamy; P. 127 C/Pool Photograph; P. 128-129 C/Alan Copson; P. 128 Look/age; P. 128 M/Alamy; P. 129 G/Sergio Amiti; P. 129 H. & D. Zielske; P. 130-131 G/Neil Mockford; P. 131 G/Samir Hussein; P. 131 G/Max Mumby; P. 132 M/Ralf Poller; P. 132 H. & D. Zielske; P. 132-133 G/Julian Elliott; P. 133 G/Roger Cracknell; P. 134 H. & D. Zielske; P. 134 G/Pawel Libera; P. 135 M/Alamy; P. 135 C/Dennis Gilbert; P. 136 H. & D. Zielske; P. 137 G/Pawel Libera; P. 136-137 G/Doug McKinlay; P. 138-139 G/Alphotographic; P. 140 G/David Hyde ; P. 140-141 M/Alamy; P. 141 M/Alamy; P. 142-143 G/Neil Brown; P. 142 M/Alamy; P. 142 M/Alamy; P. 143 G/John Tarlton; P. 143 G/Barcroft Media; P. 144 M/Alamy; P. 144 M/Alamy; P. 145 M/Alamy; P. 145 M/Alamy; P. 144-145 G/Rod Edwards; P. 146 G/Adrian Bysiak; P. 146 G/Graham Custance; P. 147 M/Alamy; P. 147 G/Bill Allsopp; P. 147 G/Ivan Vdovin; P. 148-149 G/Alan Copson; P. 148 G/Alan Copson; P. 149 M/Alamy; P. 149 G/Alan Copson; P. 150 G/Ivan Vdovin; P. 150-151 G/David Clapp; P. 151 G/David Clapp; P. 151 G/Matty Langley; P. 152 M/United Archives; P. 152-153 M/Alamy; P. 153 G/Tony Marshall; P. 153 M/United Archives; P. 153 M/Alamy; P. 154-155 G/De Agostini Picture Library; P. 155 G/Heritage Images; P. 155 G/Photo Josse; P. 156 M/Alamy; P. 156 M/Chris Herring; P. 156 M/Rick Bowden; P. 157 M/John Warburton-Lee; P. 157 M/John Warburton-Lee; P. 156-157 G/Visinheski; P. 158-159 G/Steven Docwra; P. 158 G/Bill Allsopp; P. 158 G/Alan Copson; P. 159 G/Rod Edwards; P. 160-161 G/UIG; P. 162 G/Olaf Protze; P. 162 G/Sion Touhig; P. 162-163 G/SAKhan Photography; P. 164 G/WPA Pool ; P. 165 G/Tim Graham; P. 166 G/Bernard Cahier; P. 166 G/Rolls Press; P. 166 G/Bettmann; P. 166 M/Alamy; P. 166-167 G/Octane; P. 168 M/Alamy; P. 168 M/Alamy; P. 168-169 G/Peteholyoak; P. 169 M/Alamy; P. 170 M/Alamy; P. 170 M/Bill Allsopp; P. 171 M/Bill Allsopp; P. 171 M/Alamy; P. 171 M/Alamy; P. 172-173 M/Alamy; P. 172 M/Alamy; P. 172 M/Alamy; P. 173 M/Bill Allsopp; P. 173 Look/age; P. 174 M/Alamy; P. 174 M/Alamy; P. 175 M/United Archives; P. 175 M/United Archives; P. 175 M/Louise A Heusinkveld; P. 175 M/Alamy; P. 175 M/United Archives; P. 176 M/Alamy; P. 176 G/Inaki Relanzon; P. 176 M/Richard Bowden; P. 177 M/Alamy; P. 176-177 M/Alamy; P. 178 M/John Warburton-Lee; P. 178 Look/age; P. 179 M/Linda McKie; P. 179 M/Alamy; P. 180 M/Alamy; P. 181 M/Alamy; P. 181 M/Alamy; P. 182-183 M/Alamy; P. 182 M/Alamy; P. 183 G/Ivan Vdovin; P. 183 G/Christopher Furlong; P. 184-185 G/Joe Daniel Price; P. 185 M/Alex Hyde; P. 185 M/Alamy; P. 185 Look/The Travel Library; P. 186-187 G/John Finney; P. 188-189 G/Joe Daniel Price; P. 190 G/Sergio Mendoza Hochmann; P. 190-191 G/Kodachrome25; P. 191 G/Andy McGowan; P. 191 M/Stuart Black; P. 192 G/Fine Art Images; P. 192-193 C/Robbie Jack; P. 194 M/Alamy; P. 194-195 G/Lee Beel; P. 195 M/Alamy; P. 195 M/Alamy; P. 195 G/Heritage Images; P. 195 G/Alan Cookson; P. 196-197 M/Alamy; P. 196 M/Chris Warren; P. 197 M/Alamy; P. 197 M/Charles Bowman; P. 198 G/Charles Bowman; P. 198 G/Charles Bowman; P. 199 M/IOB; P. 199 G/Jane Sweeney; P. 199 G/Chris Hepburn; P. 200-201 M/Steve Vidler; P. 200 M/Alamy; P. 201 G/Olaf Protze; P. 201 M/Steve Vidler; P. 201 M/Jenny Lilly; P. 201 M/Alamy; P. 202 M/Alamy; P. 203 M/Alamy; P. 203 M/Alamy; P. 203 M/United Archives; P. 204 M/Alamy; P. 204 Look/Robert Harding; P. 205 G/Aubrey Stoll; P. 204-205 G/David Dean ; P. 206 M/Alamy; P. 206 M/Alamy; P. 207 Look/age; P. 207 M/Alamy; P. 207 M/Alamy; P. 208 G/James Osmond; P. 208 M/Alamy; P. 208-209 M/Alamy; P. 209 M/Alamy; P. 210-211 G/Southern Lightscapes; P. 212 M/Alamy; P. 212-213 G/Bill Allsopp; P. 213 M/David Cheshire; P. 214 M/Alamy; P. 214-215 G/Lpettet; P. 215 M/Alamy; P. 216 M/Alamy; P. 216-217 M/United Archives; P. 216 Look/age; P. 216 Look/Robert Harding; P. 217 M/Alamy; P. 217 M/Alamy; P. 217 M/United Archives; P. 217 M/Alamy; P. 218-219 G/C. Bevilacqua; P. 219 G/Science & Society Picture Library; P. 220 M/Alamy; P. 220 Look/Robert Harding; P. 220-221 Look/Robert Harding; P. 221 M/Alamy; P. 222-223 G/Peplow; P. 222 M/Alamy; P. 223 M/Ron Evans; P. 223 G/Peter Packer; P. 223 M/Alamy; P. 224-225 Look/Robert Harding; P. 226 G/Joe Daniel Price; P. 226 G/Frank Fell; P. 227 G/View Pictures; P. 227 M/Mark Sykes; P. 226-227 G/Joe Daniel Price; P. 228 M/Alamy; P. 228-229 M/Alamy; P. 229 G/Craig Roberts; P. 229 G/Heritage Images; P. 229 G/Heritage Images; P. 230 M/Alamy; P. 230 M/Alamy; P. 231 M/Alamy; P. 232 M/Alamy; P. 232-233 M/Alamy; P. 233 M/Mark Sykes; P. 233 M/Alamy; P. 234-235 G/Kelvinjay; P. 235 M/Steve Vidler; P. 235 M/Steve Vidler; P. 235 M/Alamy; P. 236-237 M/Alamy; P. 237 M/United Archives; P. 237 G/Clayborough photography; P. 237 M/United Archives; P. 237 M/Alamy; P. 238 M/David Noton; P. 238 Look/Robert Harding; P. 239 G/Terry Roberts; P. 238-239 Look/Robert Harding; P. 240 M/Alamy; P. 241 M/Alamy; P. 242-243 M/Paul Williams; P. 242 G/Panoramic Images; P. 243 M/Alamy; P. 243 M/United Archives; P. 244 Look/Robert Harding; P. 244-245 M/Alamy; P. 245 G/Maremagnum; P. 245 M/Alamy; P. 246 G/Chris Hepburn; P. 246 G/Sammy Vision; P. 246 G/Allan Baxter; P. 247 M/Alamy; P. 247 Look/Design Pics; P. 247 G/Mark Sykes; P. 248 G/Heritage Images; P. 248 H. & D. Zielske; P. 249 M/Alamy; P. 249 G/Joe Cornish; P. 250 M/Paul Williams; P. 250-251 G/Joe Daniel Price; P. 250 M/Alamy; P. 251 M/Alamy; P. 252-253 M/Alamy; P. 252 M/Alamy; P. 253 M/Alamy; P. 253 G/Allan Baxter; P. 254-255 G/Alex West; P. 256 G/Ed Rhodes; P. 256 M/Alamy; P. 257 M/Alamy; P. 257 M/Roy Shakespeare; P. 257 G/Joe Daniel Price; P. 258-259 G/George Standen; P. 260 G/Mark Sykes; P. 260 G/Ed Rhodes; P. 260 M/Alamy; P. 262 G/Joe Daniel Price; P. 262 G/Joe Daniel Price; P. 263 M/Alamy; P. 263 G/Joe Daniel Price; P. 263 M/Alamy; P. 264-265 M/Alamy; P. 266 C/Paul McMullin; P. 266 Look/age; P. 267 G/David Clapp; P. 266-267 C/Richard Klune; P. 268-269 G/John Pratt; P. 270 G/Mark Sykes; P. 270 M/Alamy; P. 271 Look/Design Pics; P. 271 M/Alamy; P. 271 M/Alamy; P. 272 M/Alamy; P. 272-273 M/Alamy; P. 273 M/Alamy; P. 273 M/Alamy; P. 274 G/Daniel Kay; P. 274-275 G/FotoVoyager; P. 275 M/Alamy; P. 276-277 G/John Finney; P. 278 G/Hulton Archive; P. 278 M/Alamy; P. 279 M/Alamy; P. 280 Look/age; P. 280-281 G/Chris2766; P. 280 M/Alamy; P. 281 M/Alamy; P. 282-283 M/Alamy; P. 283 M/Alamy; P. 283 M/Alamy; P. 284 G/Linden Adams; P. 284-285 G/Jan Treger; P. 285 G/Tr3gi; P. 285 G/Iridiumphotographics; P. 286-287 G/Adam Burton; P. 288 M/Alamy; P. 288 M/Alamy; P. 289 G/Dave Porter; P. 289 G/Nick Webley; P. 290-291 G/Golfer2015; P. 292 M/Jason Friend; P. 293 M/Alamy; P. 293 M/age; P. 293 M/Alamy; P. 293 G/Mark Sykes; P. 294 Look/Design Pics; P. 294 M/Alamy; P. 295 M/Alamy; P. 294-295 G/Jonny Maxfield; P. 296 G/Alphotographic; P. 296 G/Alphotographic; P. 296-297 G/Daverhead; P. 297 M/Alamy; P. 298 M/Alamy; P. 299 M/Alamy; P. 298-299 M/Alamy; P. 300-301 G/Joe Daniel Price; P. 302 M/Alamy; P. 302 Look/Hauke Dressler; P. 302-303 G/John Short; P. 303 M/John Short; P. 304 M/Alamy; P. 304-305 G/Blackbeck; P. 305 M/Funkystock; P. 306-307 M/Alamy; P. 308 G/UIG; P. 308 M/Alamy; P. 309 G/Michael Roberts; P. 310-311 M/Alamy; P. 310-311 G/Angel Villalba; P. 312 G/Massimo Borchi; P. 312 M/Alamy; P. 312-313 Look/age; P. 313 M/Alamy; P. 313 G/Maremagnum; P. 314-315 M/Alamy/Keith Morris; P. 315 M/Steve Vidler; P. 315 M/Marco Faggi; P. 315 M/Alamy/Keith Morris; P. 316 G/Billy Stock; P. 317 M/Alamy; P. 316-317 M/Alamy; P. 318 G/Tony C French; P. 318-319 M/Alamy; P. 319 M/Alamy; P. 320 G/Andrew Ray; P. 321 M/Alamy; P. 320-321 Look/age; P. 322 G/Michael Roberts; P. 323 Look/Thomas Stankiewicz; P. 323 G/Joff Lee; P. 323 M/Alamy; P. 324-325 G/; P. 324 G/Bob Davis; P. 324 G/Paul Fram; P. 325 G/UIG; P. 325 M/Chris Warren; P. 326-327 M/Alamy; P. 328 Look/Robert Harding; P. 328 M/Alamy; P. 328 G/Adam Burton; P. 329 G/Tracy Williams; P. 329 G/Joe Daniel Price; P. 330-331 G/Joe Daniel Price; P. 332 M/Alamy; P. 333 M/Chris Warren; P. 332-333 G/Joe Daniel Price; P. 334 M/Alamy; P. 334 M/Alamy; P. 335 Look/age; P. 336-337 M/Alamy; P. 337 M/Alamy; P. 337 G/Nick Servian; P. 337 M/Alamy; P. 338-339 G/James Ennis; P. 338 C/Adam Burton; P. 338 M/Alamy; P. 339 G/Alan Novelli; P. 340-341 G/lloyd-horgan; P. 342-343 G/Guy Edwardes; P. 342 M/R. Ian Lloyd; P. 343 M/Alamy; P. 344-345 M/Alamy; P. 346-347 G/Heritage Images; P. 347 M/Alamy; P. 348 M/Alamy; P. 348 G/Joe Daniel Price; P. 348 M/Alamy; P. 349 M/Alamy; P. 350 G/Joe Daniel Price; P. 350-351 M/Alamy; P. 351 M/Alamy; P. 352-353 Look/Robert Harding; P. 354 G/Adina Tovy; P. 354 G/Joe Daniel Price; P. 354-355 G/Backyard Production; P. 355 G/Alan Copson; P. 356-357 G/Sebastian Wasek; P. 358-359 Look/Robert Harding; P. 361 M/Jim Gibson; P. 362 G/Joe Daniel Price; P. 362 M/Alamy; P. 362 G/Adam Burton; P. 362 G/Meleah Reardon; P. 362 C/Franz-Marc Frei; P. 363 G/Joe Daniel Price; P. 363 C/David Osborn; P. 363 C/John Doornkamp; P. 363 Look/Franz Marc Frei; P. 364 G/Eurasia Press; P. 365 H. & D. Zielske; P. 366 C/Julian Calverley; P. 368 Look/The Travel Library; P. 369 G/Joe Daniel Price; P. 369 G/John Finney; P. 369 M/age; P. 369 M/Paul Williams; P. 369 M/David Noton; P. 369 G/Tim Daniels; P. 369 M/Alamy; P. 370 G/Pawel Libera; P. 370 G/Vbaines photography; P. 371 Look/Robert Harding; P. 371 G/Joe Daniel Price; P. 371 G/Joe Daniel Price; P. 371 G/Britain on View; P. 371 G/James Ennis; P. 372-373 M/Bill Allsopp.

MONACO BOOKS is an imprint of Kunth Verlag GmbH & Co KG
© Kunth Verlag GmbH & Co KG, Munich - Mairdumont, Ostfildern
For distribution please contact:
Monaco Books
c/o Kunth Verlag GmbH & Co. KG, München
St.-Cajetan-Straße 41
81669 München
Tel. +49.89.45 80 20-0
Fax +49.89.45 80 20-21
www.kunth-verlag.de
info@kunth-verlag.de
www.monacobooks.com

FSC
www.fsc.org
MIX
Aus verantwortungsvollen Quellen
FSC® C127233

Printed in EU
ISBN 978-3-96965-031-8
Text: Christa Pöppelmann, Reinhard Pietsch, Claudia Lensch, Annika Voigt
Translation: Sylvia Goulding, Emily Plank; Editor: Mike Goulding; Proofreader: Julie Brooke.

All rights reserved. Reproductions, storage in data-processing systems, reproduction by electronic, photomechanical or similar means should only be made with the express permission of the copyright holder. All facts have been researched to the best of our knowledge and belief, with the greatest possible care. However, the editorial team and the publisher cannot guarantee the absolute correctness and completeness of the information. The publisher is always grateful for any hints and suggestions for improvement.